KENT COUNTY, DELAWARE LAND RECORDS

VOLUME 10
1772-1775

Irma Harper

HERITAGE BOOKS
2008

HERITAGE BOOKS
AN IMPRINT OF HERITAGE BOOKS, INC.

Books, CDs, and more—Worldwide

For our listing of thousands of titles see our website
at
www.HeritageBooks.com

Published 2008 by
HERITAGE BOOKS, INC.
Publishing Division
100 Railroad Avenue #104
Westminster, Maryland 21157

Copyright © 1999 Irma Harperr

Other books by the author:

Heirs and Legatees of Caroline County, Maryland
MARYLAND EASTERN SHORE NEWSPAPER ABSTRACTS, *Volume 5: Northern Counties, 1825-1829*
MARYLAND EASTERN SHORE NEWSPAPER ABSTRACTS, *Volume 7: Northern Counties, 1830-1834*
Kent County, Delaware, Land Records. Volume 9: 1768-1772
Kent County, Delaware Land Records, Volume 10: 1772-1775

All rights reserved. No part of this book may be reproduced or transmitted in any form or by any means, electronic or mechanical, including photocopying, recording or by any information storage and retrieval system without written permission from the author, except for the inclusion of brief quotations in a review.

International Standard Book Number: 978-1-58549-014-1

Table of Contents

Introduction .... v.

Deed Book Volume "V" 1

Index 141

INTRODUCTION[1]

Few records of the Swedish Colony (1638-1655) have survived. From 1655 to 1664 and from 1673 to 1674, the Dutch West India Company and the City of Amsterdam were proprietors of the land which became Delaware (ignoring claims by the Calverts of Maryland). The surviving records are held by the Archives of New York at Albany.

The Duke of York was proprietor from 1664 to 1673 and from 1674 to 1682. These land records are also held at Albany. *Original Land Titles in Delaware*, commonly known as *The Duke of York Record, 1646-1679*, was printed by order of the General Assembly of the State of Delaware (1899), reprinted by Family Line Publications in 1989.

Kent County, originally a part of Whorekill District (created in 1664), became an independent territory under the name of St. Jones County in 1680. In circa 1682, simultaneous with the transfer of government from the Duke of York, the name was changed to Kent County.

Subsequent to 1674, settlers (principally from Maryland) began to take up land in this area. On 13 April 1676, patents were issued to persons residing within the limits of Kent County, as follows:

> William Stevens, *Yorke*, 600 acres.
> William Ford, Ducke Creeke, 800 acres.
> William Sharpe, Ducke Creeke, 500 acres.
> John Morgan, Ducke Creeke, 300 acres.
> William Simpson, *Simpson's Choice*, 400 acres.
> John Briggs, *Aberdeane*, 400 acres.
> Peter Baucom, 200 acres.
> Thomas Philip, Jones' Creek, 600 acres.
> Robert Francis, Jones' Creek, 400 acres.
> Francis Neal, Jones Creek, 400 acres.
> John Stevens, *Content*, Duck Creek, 1200 acres.
> John Stevens, *London*, Little Creek, 1300 acres.

---

[1] Most of the information was obtained from J. Thomas Scharf, *History of Delaware, 1607-1888* (1888). Philadelphia: Richards, 2 vols. Reprinted by Family Line Publications, 1990.

Later the following patents were granted:

5 March 1678
> John Kiphaven and Peter Hanson, *Hopewell*, 413 acres, on north side of Murder Creek.

23 February 1678
> John Briggs, *Poplar Ridge*, 260 acres, above Jones' Creek adjoining Poplar Neck.

11 March 1678
> Robert Hart, Jr., *Pritchard's*, 600 acres, on north side of Misspan Creek.
> Orphan's Lot, 600 acres near *Pritchard's*.
> Cornelius Verhoofe, *New Sevenhaven*, 1218 acres, on north side of Misspan Creek, by Indian Bridge and Beaver Creek.

12 March 1678
> John Briggs and Mrs. Mary Phillips, *Kingston Upon Hull*, 450 acres, "where they now dwell," on the north side of Jones' Creek; a portion of it was formerly taken by George Whale in June 1671.

10 September 1679
> Peter Groenendike, *New Sevenhaven*, 400 acres, on north side of Murderkill Creek.

14 February 1680
> Thomas Garvin, *Garvin's*, 300 acres, on St. Jones' Creek, adjoining John Brinkloe.
> Thomas Clifford, 400 acres on St. Jones' Creek.

10 May 1680
> William Sherritt, *Sherritt's Choyce*, 116 acres, on south side of Duck Creek.

F. Edward Wright
Westminster, Maryland
1999

ABBREVIATIONS USED

a - acre
ackn - acknowledge(d)
adj - adjoining
adminr - administrator(s)
afsd - aforesaid
amt/o - amount of
atty - attorney(s)
br - branch
co - county
cr - creek
dau(s) - daughter(s)
decd - deceased
DEL - Delaware
e - east
esqr - esquire
gent - gentleman

junr - junior
MD - Maryland
mi - mile(s)
n - north
NJ - New Jersey
PA - Pennsylvania
Phila - Philadelphia
pt/o - part of
purch - purchase or purchased
s - south
senr - senior
Suss - Sussex
tr(s) - tract(s)
w/o - wife of
w - west

KENT COUNTY, DELAWARE DEEDS, VOLUME "V"

1. 5 Jan 1769 Indenture between Mary Lurtey of Talbot County, Maryland (she being one of daus of Elizabeth Stevens by her husband, William Stevens, both decd, and said Elizabeth being one of daus of John Edmondson of Talbot County, also decd and John Reed of Philadelphia, merchant. Consideration of one hundred pounds she now conveys her right, title and interest to lands in counties of Newcastle, Kent and Sussex on Delaware. Wit: Elizabeth Lurtey, Peter Maxwell. French Battell apptd atty. Ackn 5 Jan 1769 (V:p1)

2. 13 Aug 1772 Indenture between Allan Palmatree and Lettice, his wife of Duck Creek Hund, Kent on Delaware, yeoman and John Palmatree, his bro, farmer of same place. Robert Palmatree, father to John and Allan was seized of tract part of greater tract called Robert's Chance situate in Duck Creek Hund. Description mentions . . . running along John Hawkin's land . . . land now possessed by Benjamin Truax . . . containing one hundred twenty five acres. Robert by will devised to three sons, John, Allan and Robert tract of land with right to sell and now for sum of forty pounds, Allan and Lettice Palmatree convey the land. Wit: John Draughten, John Joy. Ackn 20 Aug 1772 (V:p1)

3. 30 May 1772 Indenture between Charles Ridgely, Esq town of Dover, Kent on Delaware, admin of goods and chattels of James Rash left un-admin by Reynatur Forcum, extr of Rash's will, and Thomas Nixon of Dover, merchant. James Rash and certain John Rash on 21 Nov 1768 entered in alienation writing to each other and bonded the land they then possessed to each other in order to swap plantations. James Rash made will devising estate in equal parts to Joseph Rash and Hannah Forcum, wife of Reynatur Forcum, extr who conveyed the tract to John Rash and whereas John Rash by his deed on 15 Feb 1769 (Book S, folio 107) quickly after James decease conveyed land according to will to heirs, Joseph Rash and Hannah Forcum, said tract contains one hundred acres of land called Betty's Folly, part of Barn's Chance (?) orig granted to Lewis Johnson. James Rash was indebted to various persons and Reynatur Forcum died before paying estate's debts and court ordered land to be sold, falling to Thomas Nixon for sum of one hundred fifty two pounds one shilling. Charles Ridgely now conveys the land. Wit: Saml. McCall, John Hillyard. Ackn 13 Aug 1772 (V:p1)

4. 20 Aug 1772 Indenture between John Grier of Kent on Delaware, farmer and Mary his wife and Francis Edmondson same co, yeoman. Consideration of one hundred sixty eight pounds ten shillings convey land purchased at vendue being property of Ezekiel Thompson called Bare Gardin. Beginning at cor of John Clothier's land . . . to tract called Bald Eagle . . . stake of Preston Burry's purchase

from Ezekiel Thompson . . . containing one hundred sixty acres. Wit: Richard McNatt, John Reed, Junr. Mary Grier privately examined gave consent. Ackn 11 Aug 1772 (V:p2)

5. 27 Jun 1772 Indenture between Samuel Morris of Duck Creek Hund, Kent on Delaware, miller or otherwise called bolter and Jacob Jones of same place, gent. Samuel Morris is seized of two tracts of land adj each other in Duck Creek Hund situate between main branch of Duck Creek and Green's Branch. Beginning at cor of Jacob Jones's other land . . . to Samuel Morris' mill pond . . . road leading from head of Chester River in Maryland to town of Salisbury on Duck Creek . . . with James Hiatt's lott . . . containing fifty five acres and eighteen square perches. Consideration of three hundred three pounds two shillings four pence. Wit: Tho. Brown, Hester Brown. Ackn 12 Aug 1772 (V:p2)

6. 14 Nov 1769 Indenture between James Spence of Kent on Delaware and Betty his wife and John Leadenham same place. Consideration of twenty pounds conveys part of tract located on branch of Nanticose(Nanticoke) River in forrest of Mispillion Hund suveyed by William Killing on 6 Feb 1752 containing thirty six acres. Wit: Zachariah Nicols, Richard McNatt, Francis Jester. Ackn 12 Aug 1772 (V:3)

7. 13 May 1772 Indenture between Vincent Loockerman of town of Dover, Kent on Delaware, merchant and Samuel Magaw same place, minister of the Gospel. Consideration of four hundred twenty four pounds two shillings six pence conveys parcel of land in Murtherkill Hund on west side of mansion plantation belonging to Charles Ridgely. Beginning at a cor stone . . . passing by plantation of William Wallace, decd and is also a cor of tract Denbigh lately purchased by Charles Ridgely from Loockerman . . . tract called Skipton . . . cor of land purchased by Ridgely from Benjamin Chew Esq . . . containing ninety four and a quarter acres. Wit: John Banning, Wm. Rodney. Ackn 15 Aug 1772 (V:p3)

8. 28 Aug 1772 Indenture between Solomon Seamans the younger of Little Creek Hund, Kent on Delaware and Solomon Semans the elder of Kent County, Maryland, yeoman. In division of real est of Richbell Mott of Little Creek Hund among his heirs on 30 Aug 1764 part of a tract called York was allotted to Elizabeth one of Mott's daus. Beginning on the line of Timothy Jenkin's land . . . land of Abraham Vanoy . . . by land of Richard Mott, an heir . . . containing sixty six acres. Elizabeth Mott married Solomon Seamans the younger and who on 5 Feb 1771 by alienation bond to Seamans the elder for conveyance of the land but before deed could be passed, Elizabeth Seamans died and Seamans the younger petitioned the court for authority to make the conveyance for consideration of five

hundred pounds paid by Seaman the elder. Wit: Garret Sipple, Geo. Painter. Ackn 8 Aug 1772. (V:p4)

9. 18 June 1772 Indenture between John Willcocks of city of Philadelphia, physician, son and heir of Robert Willcocks town of Dover, decd and Vincent Loockerman of town of Dover, Kent on Delaware, shop keeper. Consideration of ten pounds conveys lott in Dover marked No. 8 laid out for one hundred forty three perches and one tenth part of a perch. Wit: John Bell, Junr, John Willson. Ackn 25 Aug 1772 (V:p4)

10. 14 May 1772 Indenture between James Scotten, seniour(sic), famer of Little Creek Hund, Kent on Delaware and James Scotten, juniour(sic) same place, carpenter. For natural good will and affection toward his son, James Scotton, junior, James Scotten, senior conveys one moiety or half part of tract called James's Park laid out for two hundred acres of land. Richard Smyth of Kent Co appt atty. Wit: James Smyth, John Scotten. 27 Aug 1772 (V:p5)

11. 10 Aug 1772 Indenure between William Abbot, Sylvester Abbot, Catharine Abbot, Thomas Wyatt and Sarah his wife, all of Kent on Delaware and Solomon Townsend same place, yeoman. Consideration of fifty pounds conveys tract in Mispillion Hund called Abbot's Gift surveyed 8th day 10th mo 1739 for Sylvester Abbot, decd, grandfather of above named Abbots and Sarah Wyatt. Beginning . . . point of marsh called Robinson's Arm . . . laid off for one hundred sixty one and one quarter acres. John Banning, David Hilford apptd attys. Wit: Daniel Cavender, Walter Mileham. Ackn 25 Aug 1772 (V:p5)

12. 27 Aug 1772 Indenture between George Fleming of Kent on Delaware, yeoman and Margaret his wife and William Tharp, Junr of same place, yeoman. Anthony Rawlings of Kent co, decd, by deed made 10th 11th mo 1741 granted to William Eagle two hundred acres of land in Mispillion Hund on north side of Brown's Branch, called Rawling's Lott. Eagle by will devised the land to two sons, William and Solomon Eagle who with his wife, Lydia, by deed 12th 8th mo 1763 to George Fleming a certain part supposed to contain one hundred fifty acres (which by late survey is found to contain one hundred seventy nine acres) (Book Q, folio 151). Consideration of two hundred twenty five pounds conveys tract as found by late survey. Margaret Fleming privately examined gave consent. Wit: John Clarke, Zadock Crapper. Ackn 27 Aug 1772 (V:p6)

13. 27 Aug 1772 Indenture between George Fleming of Kent on Delaware, yeoman and Robert Fleming same place, yeoman. Survey made 23 Nov 1739 for tract of land in Mispillion Hund containing two hundred seven acres for William

Fleming called Taylor's Hall. Description mentions land of Robert Knox. Fleming by will 27 Feb 1765 devised to son, George, one hundred acres, who for consideration of seventy five pounds conveys the same to Robert Fleming. Wit: Zadock Crapper, John Clarke. Ackn 27 Aug 1772 (V:p6)

14. 24 Aug 1772 Indenture between Joseph Mason of Kent on Delaware, yeoman and extr of will of William Manlove same co, decd and Nathan Adams same co, merchant. Joseph Mason was empowered by court to sell tract called The Improvement belonging to Manlove to pay estate debts. Tract was sold at public vendue to Anthony Rawlings for sum of four hundred fifteen pounds nine pence who died before puchase money was paid or conveyance made. Nathan Adams married admx of Anthony Rawlings whose est was insufficient to pay purchase money so Adams agreed to take the land at the afsd value. Beginning at cor of lott of John Anderson . . . landing place on Mispillion Creek called the New Wharf . . . to a division made in the tract hereby granted and part sold by London Company to Craige & Hunter of Philadelphia . . . lott belonging to Mary Kelly . . . laid off for two hundred twenty seven scres and sixty seven perches. Wit: Tho. Bowman, Junr, David Hilford. Ackn 27 Aug 1772 (V:p7)

15. 24 Aug 1772 Indenture between James White of Kent on Delaware, yeoman and Nathan Adams same place, merchant. William Manlove, decd, by deed of 11th 5 mo 1758 (Book P, folio 71) granted to James White a lott of land situate in Mispillion Hund on Mispillion Creek above Nathan Adams' wharf, part of tract called The Improvement. Beginning at a place called Millstone Landing . . . cor of land of heirs of Anthony Rawlings, decd, formerly belonging to Levin Adams . . . laid off for one quarter acre. Consideration of nine pounds. Wit: Thomas Bowman, Junr, Joseph Mason. Ackn 27 Aug 1772 (V:p8)

16. 25 Aug 1772 Indenture between William Pegg of Kent on Delaware, yeoman and Rachel, his wife and Patrick Hugg same place, shoemaker. Consideration of thirty nine pounds five shillings six pence three farthings conveys tract in Mispillion Hund. Description mentions land sold by Pegg to Charles Kimmy . . . land sold by Pegg to Elizabeth Brown . . . line of James Garden's land . . . laid off for forty seven acres thirty perches. Rachel Pegg privately examined gave consent. Wit: Elizabeth Brown, Elener Marin. Ackn 26 Aug 1772 (V:p8)

17. 24 Aug 1772 Indenture between Alexander Huston of Kent on Delaware and Ann his wife and Robert Bostick same co, husbandman. Consideration of sum of two hundred twenty pounds ten shillings conveys all that portion of land late in possession of William Watson being also part of tract called Katon situate in Brown's Neck in Mispillion Hund surveyed to William Watson on 10 Mar 1763

which Alexander Huston bought of Watson. Beginning at a white oak standing by the mill pond, a cor of land belonging to heirs of George Morgan, decd . . . cor of John Arnett's land . . . laid out by platt made by Samuel McCall for one hundred forty seven acres. Ann Huston privately examined gave consent. Wit: Jonathan Sipple, Elijah Sipple. Ackn 24 Aug 1772 (V:p9)

18. 10 Apr 1772 Indenture between Ezekiel Cowgill of Little Creek Hund, Kent on Delaware, yeoman and Thomas Irons same place, Esqr. Consideration of four hundred thirty three pounds fifteen shillings conveys all parcels of land in Little Creek Neck adj land of Thomas Irons and known by name of Willingbrook, is also part of est of Clayton Levick, decd, recently purchased by Cowgill at public auction from Henry Stevens, admin. who sold the land to pay debts and for the bringing up of the smaller children. Beginning at a stone in line of Willingbrook and London . . . branch near to Schoolhouse Lott . . . laid off for fifty two acres and one hundred fifteen square perches. Wit: Robert McGermant, Joshua Deweese. Ackn 26 Aug 1772 (V:p9)

19. 12 May 1772 Indenture betwee Thomas Irons of Little Creek Neck & Hund, Kent on Delaware, Esq and Ezekiel Cowgill same place, yeoman. Consideration of seven pounds conveys a parcel in Little Creek Neck, part of tract called London. Description mentions deeds made by Mary Richardson to Joshua Clayon and John Levick . . . laid off for one hundred forty two square perches of land. Wit: Robert McGermant, Joshua Deweese. Ackn 26 Aug 1772 (V:p10)

20. 26 Aug 1772 Indenture between William Thomas of Kent on Delaware, yeoman and Thomas Beadwell same co, farmer. Consideration of one hundred pounds conveys the plantation whereon Beadwell now dwells in Murtherkill Hund containing one hundred acres. Wit: Richard Lockwood, Nathl. Chambers. Ackn 26 Aug 1772 (V:p10)

21. 27 Aug 1772 Indenture between Moses Ratledge of Murtherkill Hund, Kent on Delaware, and Anne his wife and Jonathan Finsthwait of Mispillion Hund. A division of real estate of John McNatt on 6 Apr 1746 among his heirs resulted in tract called Pleasant between William McNatt, oldest son; Elizabeth McNatt; and one third was laid off to Elizabeth, senior as widow during her natural life with reversion to William who then was vested in two thirds. Beginning at cor of land of Jonathan Finsthwait conveyed to him by his father . . . prong of Brown's Branch . . . being ninety one acres. William McNatt died leaving only dau: now Anne Ratledge, and John Clarke married Elizabeth entitled to one third. Consideration of twenty nine pounds Tract is guaranteed agst claims of Moses Ratledge and wife, Anne, and agst claims of Abraham Wyncoop. Wit: Saml. McCall, John Smalley.

Anne Ratledge privately examined gave consent. Ackn 27 Aug 1772 (V:p11)

22. 25 Aug 1772 Indenture between James Caldwell, high sheriff of Kent on Delaware and William Kirkley of Murtherkill Hund, yeoman. By writ of attachment on 18 June 1771, sheriff attached about one ninth part of two hundred acres of land of Elijah Bedwell, Kent Co, yeoman, to answer to Thomas Wallace in a plea of trespass. Land belonged to James Bedwell, father of Elijah, situtate in forrest of Murtherkill Hund on south side of Isaac Web's Branch . . . tract sometime called Wedmore, orig called Tanten Burrow and surveyed for William Rodney 10 May 1685 by warrant on 14 Feb 1681 for 500 acres, James Bedwell's part begins at cor hickory sapling . . . cor of tract belonging to Stephen Lewis . . . cor in land of Thomas Wallace . . . cor for lands of James Howel and Caleb Webb . . . containing in the whole two hundred three and one quarter acres confirmed by survey made by Mark McCall by order of Samuel McCall, surveyor, excepting three acres sold by Bedwell to Robert Hodgson now property of Thomas Hale. Sheriff executed attachment order and sold the land to William Kirkley for sum of twenty eight pounds for twenty two and one quarter acres (or one ninth part). Wit: Saml. McCall, John Smally. Ackn 26 Aug 1772 (V:p11)

23. 20 Apr 1772 Indenture between Benjamin Chew, Charles Ridgely and Benjamin Wyncoop, extrs of John Vining of Kent on Delaware and Joseph Rogers of same co, yeoman. Vining was seized of land in Murtherkill Hund called the Reserve and by will 13 Nov 1770 directed that all his properties in Pennsylvania, lower counties of Delaware, province of East and West New Jersey and elsewhere be sold for best prices that could be obtained. Consideration of one thousand six hundred fifty four pounds ten shillings convey plantation and tract of land part of the Reserve. Beginning at cor of said tract and another tract called Break Nock which stands nr branch below Thomas Hanson's mill house . . . laid out for five hundred fifty one and one half acres. Wit: Caesar Rodney, Miers Fisher. Ackn 26 Aug 1772 (V:p11)

24. 26 Aug 1772 Indenture between Thomas Moor of Mutherkill Hund, Kent on Delaware, yeoman (who is son of Joseph Moor, late decd) and John White of same place, yeoman. A survey was made for Joseph Moor in forrest of Murtherkill Hund adj lands of John Oldfield and William White. Joseph Moor entered in an alienation bond to William White on 21 Nov 1751 for conveyance of part of tract in presence of Peter and Catherine Lowber but Moor and White both since decd. John White had the bond proven in court by Peter Lowber and Thomas Moor, only heir desires to establish title to John White. Consideration of fifty shillings paid by William White to Joseph Moor and further consideration of five shillings paid at time of these presents Thomas Moor conveys small parcel of land laid out for four

acres and one hundred thirty two square perches. Description mentions land of William Harris and Robert Meredith. Wit: Mark McCall, Geo. Painter. Ackn 26 Aug 1772 (V:p13)

25. 1 August 1771 I, Jonathan Manlove of Kent on Delaware in consideration of sum of three hundred pounds paid by Matthew Manlove of same place, yeoman, have bargained and sold one negro boy, Pompey; another named George and one named Doller, with three yoke of oxen, twenty cows and calves, sixty head of dry cattle young and old; one negro wench, Poll; one negro man, Frank; one negro girl, Jude; another named Grace; one named Nan and another named Moll; one negro lad named George; two featherbeds and furniture, one desk, two tables, one chest, three mairs and colts; seven head of horses, forty head of sheep and twenty head of hogs with all my household furniture and farming utensils now remaining in my possession and confirm the sale by placing the negro boy, Pompey, in his possession this day. Wit: Samuel Meridith, Nathan Manlove. (V:p13)

26. 4 Nov 1772 Indenture between James Howel of Carolina by his atty in fact, Joseph Howel, and Joseph Howel for himself and David Howel and Thomas Howel, all three of Murtherkill Hund, Kent on Delaware, yeoman and George Blackiston, Kent County, province of Maryland, gent. By warrant granted 1 Aug 1716, survey made 19th Sept following to John Thompson of Murtherkill Hund on two hundred acres of land, patent granted 17 Aug 1737 (Book A, vol 8, page 243, etc.). Thompson conveyed same in 1749 to James Howel who by obligation 20 Mar 1739 purchased a piece of land from John Glenn adj the patent and afterwards found to be the greatest part in an ancient tract called Howel's Lot orig surveyed for James Wells which became property of Philip Kearney of Perth Amboy and James Howel, the elder on 14 Dec 1749 purchased part of Howel's Lot and including a great part of former purchase from Glenn. James Howel, the elder on 8 Oct 1753 by will devised to his eldest son, James Howel (now in Carolina) a certain part as described and all residue to be to other three sons: Joseph, David and Thomas jointly. John and Richard Glover in 1683 obtained survey of twelve hund acres which is now found to include all said lands except what is in Howel's Lot and even part of that except eight acres eight perches which is within the patent to Thompson but not in Glover's survey being part of orig for William Rodney called Tantan Courrow adj Glover's survey called Hazard. French Battell and James Stevens of town of Dover now have title of Hazard and by deed even date have conveyed to George Blackiston all of the lands within Hazard who now will have ancient titles to all the lands. Joseph, David and Thomas Howel will convey to Blackiston their right, title and interest to inherited lands through their father, decd, or the death of their bro, James Howel, in Carolina. For consideration of eleven hundred forty three pounds fifteen shillings, Joseph, David and Thomas Howel

convey tract by survey made by Mark McCall on 15th & 16th Oct last past situate in Murtherkill Hund on Isaac Webb Branch on a prong called School House Branch. Mentions land called Tantan Courrow . . . agreeable to patent of John Thompson and also land called Wedman . . . land in possession of Bryan Seeney . . . land of Robert Bohanan . . . land now of William Henry . . . land of Thomas Lewis . . . land of William Wallace . . . containing in the whole four hundred fifty seven and a half acres. Wit: James Cheffins, George McCall. Ackn 12 Nov 1772 (V:p13)

27. 12 Nov 1772 Indenture between John & Philemon Dickinson of one part and Isaac Carty of other part. Consideration of five hundred fifty pounds conveys parcel of land in Duck Creek Hund, Kent on Delaware, bounded by lands of James Gardner, Isaac Carty and lands contracted for by Joseph Wood of the Dickinsons, containing one hundred forty five acres seven perches being part of tract called The Partnership and formerly allotted by division to David Finney, Esq. reserving out of granted premises one acre for use of Baptist Congregation to be laid off in most convenient manner including old burial ground. Wit: Saml. McCall, Joseph Pryor. Ackn 17 Nov 1772 (V:p15)

28. 4 Nov 1772 Indenture between French Battel town of Dover, Kent on Delaware, inn keeper and James Stevens same place, gent of one part and George Blackiston of Kent County, Maryland of other part. Survey was made for John and Richard Glover 15th 11th mo 1683 by warrant granted 21st 10th mo 1680 for twelve hundred acres in forrest of Murtherkill Hund on head branches of a sprout of Dover River called Isaac Webb's Branch and on west prong known as School House Branch. John Glover deceased wihout division and the land called Hazard became property of bro, Richard, who died leaving one son, John Glover, who died leaving only child, Mary, who before age twenty one married William Manson who died before her. In her widowhood, she conveyed all the tract to French Battell and James Stevens. John Thompson had a survey made on a part of Hazard during minority of John Glover, Junr and afterwards conveyed same to James Howel, who by will devised all lands to sons: James, Joseph, David and Thomas Howel, they now have sold same to George Blackiston and procured Battell and Stevens to release the land which belonged to their father. Consideration of fifty pounds paid by the Howels, Battell and Stevens release their claim. Beginning ... and to ....land of William Kirkley called Wedmore orig surveyed by William Rodney by name of Tantan Courrow . . . to stake in lane by road where John Thompson crosses the line . . . land held by Bryan Seeney . . . land of late Robert Bohannon, decd . . . containing three hundred ninety acres of land. Wit: Saml. McCall, James Chiffins. Ackn 13 Nov 1772 (V:p15)

29. 11 Nov 1772 Indenture between John Baynard and Mary, his wife of Kent on Delaware and Henry Carter of Queen Anne's County (Maryland). Consideration of eighty two pounds sixteen shillings conveys parcel of land in forrest of Murtherkill Hund containing one hundred thirty eight acres and allowance surveyed for Baynard on 26 Oct 1748. Beginning at cor tree of John Dill's . . . John Loftis' land. Wit: Joseph Campbell, John Reed, Junr. Mary Baynard privately examined gave consent. Ackn 11 Nov 1772 (V:p16)

30. 5 Dec 1771 George the third by the Grace of God of Great Britain, France and Ireland, King, Defender of the Faith and so forth . . . TO: James Hamilton, Joseph Turner, William Logan, Richard Peters, Lynford Lardner, Benjamin Chew, Thomas Cadwalader, James Tilghman, Andrew Allen, Edward Shippen, Junior, and William Hicks, Esquires, Members of the Proprietary and Governors Council and to Charles Ridgely, Andrew Caldwell, James Sykes, William Rhodes, John Clarke, Jacob Stout, Fenwick Fisher, Thomas Tilton, Warner Mifflin, James Boyer, Thomas Hanson, Jonathan Emmerson, Samuel Chew, John Chew, Richard Smith, Richard Lockwood and Zadock Crapper of Kent on Delaware . . . GREETINGS. Reposing special trust and confidence in your loyalty, integrity and ability, know that we have assigned you jointly and severally our justices our peace in the county afsd. Witness: Richard Penn, Esq by virtue of commission from Thomas and John Penn, Esq. A True Copy. (V:p16)

31. 5 Oct 1772 Appointment: To John Cook of Kent on Delaware . . . know that reposing special trust and confidence in your loyalty, integrity and ability, we appoint you to be Sheriff of said county. Witness: Richard Penn Esq. by virtue of commission from Thomas and John Penn, Esqrs. A True Copy. (V:p16)

32. 5 Oct 1772 To all judges, justices, magistrates and other officers, freemen and all other person in Kent on Delaware, by a certain commission bearing even date, we have granted unto John Cook Esq the office of Sheriff of said co we do therefore by these presents require and command you, that you be aiding and assiting in all things that to the said office may in any wise belong lawfully . . . Witness: Richard Penn, Esqr by virtue of of a commission from Thomas and John Penn, Esqrs. A True Copy. (V:p16)

33. 5 Oct 1772 Appointment: To Caleb Furby of Kent on Delaware . . . know that reposing special trust and confidence in your loyalty, integrity and ability, we have appointed you to be coroner of said county. Witness: Richard Penn Esqr by virtue of commission from Thomas and John Penn, Esqrs. A True Copy. (V:p17)

34. 12 Nov 1772 Indenture between Solomon Seamans of Kent County, Province

of Maryland, yeoman and Rachel, his wife and Govey Emmerson of Kent on Delaware, yeoman. By division and partition of Richbell Mott's lands, decd, in Little Creek Hund among his children and by order of court 10 May 1764, there was assigned to Elizabeth Mott, his dau, part of tract called York. Beginning in line of Timothy Jenkins . . . land of Abraham Vannoy . . . containing sixty six acres. Elizabeth married with Solomon Seamans, the younger, son of Solomon Seamans of these presents who by bond on 5 Feb 1771 became bound to Solomon (Elder) for sum of one thousand pounds for making over the land. Elizabeth died before conveyance was made and Solomon, the younger, as admin conveyed the land on 28 Aug 1772. Consideration of five hundred pounds now Solomon (Elder) and his wife, Rachel convey the sixty six acres. BE IT REMEMBERED THAT SOLOMON SEAMANS DON'T WARRANT THE SCHOOL HOUSE LOTT. Wit: Fras. Gardner, John Patten. Rachel Seamans privately examined gave consent. Ackn 12 Nov 1772 (V:p17)

35. 9 Oct 1772 Indenture between Edward Tilghman of city of Philadelphia but now of city of London, gent by John Chew of Kent on Delaware, his atty and Samuel Hanson of Kent co, gent. Edward Tilghman by letter of attorney on 18 Apr 1772 saying that he was seized of a parcel of land being sixty one and a half acres part of larger tract called White Oak Survey by division of real est of Samuel Chew, Esq had been allotted to Elizabeth, mother of Edward, who by order of orphan's court had the tract valued to him. Edward Tilghman of Queen Anne's Co, Maryland, father of afsd Edward, and John Chew, atty for afsd Edward, to sell the woodland to best advantage. For consideration of one hundred eighty one pounds fourteen shillings, John Chew, atty, conveys the land. Beginning at cor of Samuel Hanson's land . . . land of Thomas Hanson . . . land of Charles Hillyard . . . laid out for forty five acres and sixty eight square perches. Wit: Timothy Caldwell, Reuben Gildert, Junior. Ackn 11 Nov 1772 (V:p18)

36. 9 Nov 1772 Indenture between Elijah Morris of Kent on Delaware, yeoman and Mary, his wife and Matthias Mastin same place, yeoman. A survey made for Moses Jones of said co on 5 Apr 1746 by warrant of 31 May 1745 for tract in forrest of Mispillion Hund containing two hundred acres. Jones by deed 8 Aug 1748 conveyed the land to John Chadwick and was taken into execution by sheriff to satisfy John Vining and Andrew Caldwell, trustees of General Loan Office and was sold at auction on 28 Aug 1770 to Elijah Morris. Consideration of twenty one pounds convey forty eight acres and forty nine perches of land beginning at cor of Long Green. Wit: William Mastin, Hezekiah Mastin. Ackn 12 Nov 1772 (V:p19)

37. 10 Nov 1772 Indenture between John Beauchamp of Murtherkill Hund, Kent on Delaware, yeoman and Isaac Beauchamp same place, blacksmith. Marcey Beauchamp, father of John and Isaac, was seized with tract of land part of larger

tract called Great Geneva situate in hund and co afsd and being so seized by deed made over a part to son, John Beauchamp, on eastern side next to the Great Road leading from Dover to Lewis Town (over the draw bridge) commonly called the lower Kings Road. Marcey Beauchamp remained seized of remaining part of the mansion tract of land and plantation not included in aforegoing deed. He devised to son, John, residue of dwelling place subject to lifetime of Grace Beauchamp, his widow, subject that John should make over three acres whereon the smith shop of Isaac Beauchamp did and still stands. John to fulfill his devise and the sum of five shillings conveys the land beginning cor of land of David Anderson, etc. Wit: Wm Jordan, Jno. Smithers. Ackn 11 Nov 1772 (V:p20)

38. 1 Aug 1772 Indenture between Nimrod Maxwell of Murtherkill Hund, Kent on Delaware, yeoman and Benjamin Coombe same place, yeoman. Consideration of three pounds six shillings four pence conveys parcel of land situate in the Duke of York's Manner called The Cave surveyed for John French. Beginning at cor of Simon Hirons . . . land called the Flying Jibb . . . containing one acre and seventeen square perches. Wit: Mark McCall, Thomas Edmondson. Ackn 11 Nov 1772 (V:p21)

39. 1 Aug 1772 Indenture between Benjamin Coombe of forrest of Murtherkill Hund, Kent on Delaware, yeoman and Nimrod Maxwell same place yeoman. Consideration of eleven pounds seventeen shillings four pence conveys a parcel of land called the Flying Jibb which Coombe lately purchased from William Sipple, orig surveyed for Armwell Howard. Beginning at cor of Joseph Campbell's land and also land of Nimrod Maxwell . . . land belonging to Maxwell orig surveyed for Simon Hirons. . . laid off for seven acres and one hundred forty six square perches. Wit: Mark McCall, Thomas Edmondson. Ackn 11 Nov 1772 (V:p21)

40. 12 Nov 1772 Indenture between James McMullan of Kent on Delaware, gent and William Gray same co, merchant. A warrant issued on 15 May 1743 and a survey was made on 19 July following for Richard Downham and Ann, his wife, of one hunded forty one acres with allowance of six acres situate in forrest of Murtherkill on south side of Hudson's Branch adj where William Trippet's mill pond was and upper Kings Road running through the tract. Downham and his wife conveyed on 13 Feb 1754 the land to William Cardeen, or guardian, (Book O, folio 221) who with his wife, Elizabeth, conveyed the land on 10 Feb 1755 to James McMullan. Consideration of one hundred thirty pounds conveys one hundred forty one acres. Description mentions land of William Scantlin . . . line of Burberry's Berry . . . line of land formerly of Joseph Campble. Excepting one quarter acre excepted by Richard Downham and Elizabeth, his wife, for a burying ground. Wit: Alexr. Reynolds, Archd. McSparran. Ackn 12 Nov 1772 (V:p22)

41. 11 Nov 1772 Indenture between Authur Alston of forrest of Appoquinomink Hund of Newcastle on Delaware, yeoman and Martha Alston of Little Creek Hund, Kent on Delaware, widow, both of one part and Thomas Keeth said co, yeoman. Thomas Alston late of Kent Co devised a tract to be divided between his two sons, Authur and Randle, late husband to said Martha Alston. No division being made, Randle devised his part of land to be sold by Martha, sole extx. Consideration of two hundred twenty seven pounds convey the land. Beginning at cor of William Coursey's land and land late of Nicholas Powel . . . cor of James Lewis's land . . . cor of Daniel Durhams land . . . near a tract called Chester . . . containing two hundred ten acres. Wit: Elijah Chance, John Rees. Ackn 11 Nov 1772 (V:p22)

42. 11 Nov 1772 Indenture between George Lambdin and Elizabeth, his wife of Kent on Delaware and Henry Carter of Queen Anne's Co,(Maryland). In consideration of seventy five pounds conveys parcel of land in forrest of Murtherkill containing one hundred five and a half acres surveyed for George Lambdin on 12 Oct 1770. Beginning at marked oak by William Dill's improvement . . . line of John Baynard's land . . . oak of John Dill's and John Baynards . . . cor of Charles Cottenham's land. Wit: Joseph Campbell, John Reed, Junr. Elizabeth Lambdin privately examined gave consent. Ackn 11 Nov 1772. (V:p23)

43. 11 Nov 1772 Indenture between Thomas Collings of Kent on Delaware, Duck Creek Hund and Mary, his wife and John Tucker same co, yeoman. Consideration of four hundred ninety six pounds twelve shillings convey land in Mispillion Hund on west main branch of Murtherkill Creek being part of Barren Point alias Dury's Purchase and called by some of late Thousand Acre Tract purchased by Collings of Hannah Dury of Island of Barbados by her atty William Morris. Description of part being granted mentions Ivy Branch, Fork Branch, Manlove's Branch . . . lot now possessed by Thomas Ogle . . . Ogle's Mill Dam . . . containing three hundred eighty two acres. Wit: Thos. Tilton, Elizabeth Nielsos(?). Mrs. Mary Collings privately examined gave consent. Ackn 11 Nov 1772 (V:p23)

44. 11 Nov 1772 Indenture between John Tucker of Kent on Delaware, yeoman and Margaret his wife and Lucy Hall, relict of William Hall, John Hall, William Hall and Lucy Powel, wife of James Powel in Maryland, children of William Hall, decd. John Tucker contracted with Caleb Davis of afsd co for sale of one hundred acres of land in Mispillion Hund and part of tract purchased from Thomas Collins; also part of large tract called Barren Point alias by some The Thousand Acre tract. Tucker entered into bond on 12th 1st mo 1771 and before conveyance was made, Davis contracted for sale of the land to William Hall, decd. Now Tucker and his wife, Margaret, for sum of one hundred fifty pounds convey the afsd mentioned

land. Description mentions a post in orig lines of Barren Point and land called Clayton. Wit: John Crompton, Richard Reynalds. Ackn 11 Nov 1772 (V:p23)

45. 23 Oct 1772 Quit Claim: John Tumlin of Kent on Delaware, shop joynor, for divers good causes and considerations, quit claim unto Susannah Piper of Newcastle Co, widow, all right, title and claim to parcel of land allotted to Susannah by division ret'd to court including one half of widow's thirds with eleven acres and sixty perches eastward of division line of my mother's thirds which eleven acres sixty perches is in exchange of same amount to westward of King's Road, adj William Rhoads and heirs of Ebenezer Clampit. Description mentions Spring Branch . . . cor of Edward Gibbs's twenty acres bought from John Tumlin . . . included the eleven acres sixty perches containing one hundred forty two acres. Wit: John Jones, John McKee. Ackn 12 Nov 1772 (V:p24)

46. 23 Oct 1772 Quit Claim: Susannah Piper of Newcastle on Delaware one of heirs and reps of John Tumlin late of Kent Co decd for divers good causes and considerations, have remised, released and forever quit claimed unto John Tumlin of Kent Co, all right, estate, title, etc. had to that divident allotted to John Tumlin by order of court including a part of her mother's thirds also eleven acres sixty perches to westward of King's Road adj William Rhoads and heirs of Ebenezer Clampit. . . containing one hundred thirty one acres and one other piece of land in exchange for piece of land of equal quantity contained within the circumscription . . . containing eleven acres sixty perches. Wit: John Jones, John McKee. Ackn 12 Nov 1772 (V:p24)

47. 30 Apr 1767 Indenture between James Green of Duck Creek Hund, Kent on Delaware, farmer and Thomas Ross same hund and co, yeoman. Consideration (not given) conveys a lot of ground at the cross roads beginning at cor of land laid off for Samuel Ball . . . cor of William Jordan's lot . . . laid off for one fourth acre of land. Free and clear of all and all manner of charge and incumbrance . . . agst himself and his heirs and the heirs of his father, Thomas Green. Nicholas Vandyke appt atty. Wit: William Cahoon, Junr, Richard Wild. Ackn 12 Nov 1772 (V:p25)

48. 21 Feb 1770 Indenture between Thomas Ross of Duck Creek Hund, Kent on Delaware, yeoman and Robert Wilds same place, inn holder. Consideration of thirty pounds conveys a lot of ground near the cross roads (see previous deed for description). Nicholas Vandyke apptd atty. Wit: Hamilton Ballantine, Jno. Russel. Ackn 12 Nov 1772. (V:p25)

49. 31 Oct 1772 Indenture between James Wallace of city and co of Philadelphia, merchant, and Elizabeth, his wife and Thomas Tilton of Kent on Delaware, Esq.

Consideration of one hundred nine pounds conveys all undivided part or shares in parcel of land in Duck Neck containing one hundred fifty acres part of tract called Whitewell's Chance late in possession of John Tilton the elder late of Kent Co decd, conveyed by Richard Hoff and Rachel, his wife, late wife of Joseph Tilton, decd, eldest son of John Tilton, to James Wallace by deed on 6 Aug 1765. Caesar Rodney and Jacob Stout apptd attys. Wit: Theos. Gardner, Peter Footman, Thos. McKean. Ackn 2 Nov 1772 in Philadelphia before Issac Jones, Esq. Ackn 12 Nov 1772 (V:p26)

50. 31 Mar 1770 Bond of Conveyance: William Molleston of Kent on Delaware is firmly bound to Jonathan Molleston of same place, yeoman, in full sum of six hundred pounds. Condition that William Molleston is to make over a tract of land in afsd co known by name of Betty's Purchase to Jonathan Molleston. Wit: John Browne, Nathaniel Luff. Ackn 11 Nov 1772 (V:p27)

51. 11 July 1769 Indenture between Mary Manson of Kent on Delaware, widow, only heir to John and Richard Glover of same co, decd, and French Battell and James Stevens of same co as tenants in common but not joint tenants. . Consideration of one hundred pounds conveys tract of land of twelve hundred acres called Hazard surveyed 1st 11th mo 1683 to John and Richard Glover. Wit: John Irons, Junrr, John Martin. Ackn 12 Nov 1772 (V:p27)

52. 3 Nov 1772 Indenture between Robert Wild of Newcastle Co formerly of the Crossroads in Duck Creek Hund, Kent on Delaware, tavern keeper and Thomas Skillington of last said place, tavern keeper, in same place where Robert Wild lived. Thomas Green late of said hund was seized of parcel of land called Graves End on both sides of road leading from Salisbury Town (also called Duck Creek Town) to Dover and devised the land to sons, James and Thomas Green. Division was made on 26th & 27th Oct 1767 by Mark McCall and James Green has sold lots off to sundry persons and also by deed 30 Apr 1767 conveyed a lot to Thomas Ross. Beginning at cor of Samuel Ball's lot . . . William Jordan's lot . . . containing one quarter of an acre. Thomas Ross on 21 Feb 1770 sold lot to Robert Wild. Consideration of fifty pounds paid by Thomas Skillington. Nicholas Vandyke apptd atty. Wit: John Russel, William Rees. Ackn 12 Nov 1772 (V:p27)

53. 13 Mar 1772 Indenture between Joseph Shawn of Duck Creek Hund, Kent on Delaware, planter, and Elizabeth, his wife and Mary Green same place, widow. Consideration of three hundred pounds conveys two parcels of land part of tract called Graves End. First begins at cor of Samuel Ball's lot and of Allen McLane's land . . . cor of Thomas Skillington's land . . . in line of Thomas Green's land . . . cor of Enoch Potter's land at Millstone Landing (called Enoch's Lane) . . . to

William Reese's lot . . . to William Jordan's lot . . . containing twenty eight acres. Other lot begins at cor of Thomas Skillington's and Samuel Ball's lot . . . line of Fenwick Fisher, Esq . . . Squire Fisher . . . containing six acres. Wit: Sarah Pugh, Junr, Lydia Hussey, Thomas Brown. Ackn 11 Nov 1772 (V:p28)

54. 13 Oct 1772 Indenture between Jonathan Cottingham of Kent on Delaware and Lydia his wife of same place and John Spalden of Queen Anne's County (Maryland). Consideration of three hundred twenty two pounds convey all land that Jonathan bought of his brother, Charles, containing one hundred acres, part of land surveyed for James Thiselwood in forrest of Mispillion Hund and likewise parcel of land called Herring's Choice laid off for Joseph Tumblin containing one hundred ten acres, and likewise a tract called Cottingham's Outlet containing two hundred twenty acres surveyed for Jonathan Cottingham . . . containing in the whole four hundred thirty acres. Wit: Henry Wells, Joseph Campbell, Junr."Lady Cottinham" privately examined gave consent. Ackn 12 Nov 1772 (V:p29)

55. 8 Jun 1772 Indenture between William Killen of Mispillion Hund, Kent on Delaware and Henry Killen of Murtherkill Hund, yeoman. Consideration of fifteen pounds eleven shillings ten pence conveys his part of tract of land which father, Robert Killen, decd, purchased of Philamon Dickison of city of Philadelphia. Beginning at a marked oak by a branch, then with Seames Carbines land . . . by Masculine Clark's land . . . by John Housman's land . . . in Randal Blackshare's line . . . by John Jones' land . . . by Stephen Stanton's . . . laid out for three hundred twelve acres. Richard Delaner and Nimrod Maxfield apptd attys. Wit: Mark Killen, Nathan Fleming. Ackn 11 Nov 1772 (V:p31)

56. 6 Oct 1772 Indenture between John Hill of Kent on Delaware (son of Arthur Hill of Dorchester Co, Maryland, decd) and John Thompson of Kent Co. Consideration of twenty seven pounds nine shillings six pence conveys fifty five acres and one hundred fifty three perches of land situate in forrest of Mispillion Hund, part of tract laid out for Arthur Hill on 30th 10th mo 1739 pursuant to warrant dated 27th same mo, in the whole one hundred twenty acres devised to John by his father. John Banning and David Hilford apptd attys. Wit: Wm. Anderson, Francis Jester. Ackn 11 Nov 1772 (V:p32)

57. 2 Nov 1772 Indenture between Mary Wynkoop, Phebe Vining and Benjamin Wynkoop surviving extrs of will of Abraham Wynkoop, Esq, decd, and Jonathan Collins of Kent on Delaware. A tract of land in forrest of Mispillion Hund on Roger's Branch granted to Thomas Davison by warrant on 22 June 1747 and suveyed 20 Nov 1750 who sold same to Abraham Wynkoop. Beginning at cor of whole tract and other lands surveyed for Davison . . . part sold by Benjamin

Wynkoop to Robert Davis . . . containing one hundred seven acres. Consideration of eleven pounds nineteen shillings. Caesar Rodney or John Cook apptd attys. Wit: Smith Fearset, William Cullen. Ackn 11 Nov 1772 (V:p32)

58. 2 Nov 1772 Indenture between Mary Wynkoop, Phebe Vining and Benjamin Wynkoop surviving extrs of Abraham Wynkoop, Esq, decd and Jonathan Collins, Yeoman of Kent on Delaware. Two parcels of land in forest of Mispillion Hund, Kent Co containing two hundred seventy eight and three quarter acres granted to Thomas Davison by two warrants of 2 June 1746 and on 16 Mar 1749, surveyed on 15 & 16 Oct 1750 by William Killen, depty surveyor. Davison sold the land to Abraham Wynkoop beginning at cor of land late of John Dyer by Rogers Branch . . . by Simon Bealey's land . . . cor of land late of John Johnson . . . of John Turner's land . . . in Abram Smith's line . . . land surveyed for Alexander Hamilton . . . laid out for qty afsd. Consideration of thirty one pounds one shilling. Caesar Rodney and John Cook apptd attys. Wit: Smith Farset, William Cullen. Ackn 11 Nov 1772 (V:p33)

59. 10 Nov 1772 Indenture between Robert Smith of Kent on Delaware, yeoman and William Hudson same place, yeoman. Consideration of fifty pounds conveys parcel of land in Mispillion Hund adj lands of John Simpson and William Biggs, contiguous to where New Landing Road crosses the Beaver Dam Road. Beginning at an oak standing nr house of sd Simpson . . . containing ten acres of land. Zadock Crapper and William Killen appd attys. Wit: Zadock Crapper, John Killen. Ackn 11 Nov 1772 (V:p34)

60. 12 Feb 1772 Indenture between Jonathan Manlove of Kent on Delaware, yeoman and Miers Fisher of City of Philadelphia. Manlove by writing obligatory stands bound to Fisher in sum of two hundred forty pounds conditioned for payment of one hundred twenty pounds on 12 Feb next. For securety of the debt and sum of five shillings conveys his dwelling plantation in Kent Co bounded by lands of John Clark, Nathaniel Hunn and Thomas Bowman, said land devised by Matthew Manlove, father, to son, Jonathan, and also part purchased by Jonathan from Thomas Nixon. Wit: Thomas Rodney, Caesar Rodney. George Read Esq to act as atty. Wit (to the power of atty, Richard Tilghman, Matthew Manlove) Ackn 12 Nov 1772 (V:p34)
(A receipt fastened in the ledger). " Miers Fisher , mortager in foregoing mortgage do hereby ackn to have received from Matthew Manlove, heir of Jonathan Manlove, mortagor, by hands of Andrew Barrat, Esq, one hundred fifty three pounds seventeen shillings with an abatement of thirty six pounds as a former payment . . . . empower Andrew Barrat to ackn satisfaction on record of said mortgage and judgment obtained . . . 2 Apr 1802. (signed) Miers Fisher."

61. 7 Nov 1772 Indenture between Samuel Magaw of Kent on Delaware and Sarah, his wife and James Sykes same co afsd. Consideration of five shillings sterling money of Great Britain conveys tract known by name of Skipton in orig warant orig laid out for Thomas Clifforth and possessed by Samuel Magaw of three hundred acres. Wit: John Chew, John Pryor. Sarah Magaw privately examined gave consent. Ackn 10 Nov 1772 (V:p35)

62. 17 Nov 1772 Indenture between John Dickinson of city and co of Philadelphia, Esq and Philemon Dickinson of Hunterdon Co in West New Jersey. gent, of one part and Levi Dungan, Daniel Davis, David Miles, Enoch Jones and Samuel Griffin, all of Kent on Delaware, yeoman, of oher part. A messuage or tenement commonly called the Welsh Meeting House and lot of land where it stands situate in forest of Duck Creek Hund, Kent co, for many years past have and now are used and occupied by many of the Inhabitants of said hund and others of neighborhood as a house for divine public worship and burying ground. Beginning at a cor in line of John Pattison's land . . . to land late of John and Philemon Dickinson . . . containing one acre, part of tract called Partnership. Consideration of five shillings. To and for the use, benefit and behoof of the inhabitants of Duck Creek Hund and neighborhood for the time being, being Protestants, of the Annabaptist Denomination as a place of public worship and as to the land . . . use and behoof all the said inhabitants being Protestants of every denomination as a burial ground. Wit: F. Battell, Will. Killen. Ackn 17 Nov 1772 (V:p36)

63. 26 Nov 1772 Indenture between Thomas Kelly of Kent on Delaware, yeoman and Rebekah, his wife, and Archibald McSparrant same place, yeoman. James Lacey same co, decd, father of Rebekah, devised parcel of land in Mispillion Hund to her and Joseph Mason and Mary, his wife, by deed 26 Nov 1772 granted to Rebekah all above parcel of land. Beginning at a cor of Henry Reynold's land called Home Tract, now belonging to said McSparran . . . running with lines of Fairfield . . . laid out for eighty acres . . . supposed to be in tract Fairfield but by late suvey found to be part in Fairfield and residue within tract called Wheatfield. Consideration of one hundred pounds. Defended against claims . . . the Proprietaries quit rents as afsd and legal claims of Mary Lacey, widow, under said testament only excepted. Wit: Zadock Crapper, Thos. Bowman, Junr. Rebekah Kelly privately examined gave consent. Ackn 26 Nov 1772 (V:p36)

64. 23 Nov 1772 Indenture between Jehu Davis of Kent on Delaware, taylor and Rhoda, his wife and Archibald McSparran, same place, yeoman. Consideration of two pounds five shillings convey a parcel of cripple on small branch falling in to Clark's Brook . . . part of land purchased by Davis of John Cox. Beginning by an old dam made by James Lacey, decd . . . laid off for two acres thirty five perches.

Wit William Rhodes, Isaac Mason, Junr. Rhoda Davis privately examined gave consent. Ackn 26 Nov 1772 (V:p37)

65. 23 Nov 1772 Indenture between Joseph Mason of Kent on Delaware, yeoman and Mary, his wife and Rebekah Kelly, wife of Thomas Kelly, same co, yeoman. Joseph Mason by deed 9 May 1759 granted to James Lacey, decd, a parcel of land in Mispillion Hund, part of Fairfield. Beginning at cor of Henry Reynold's land called Home Tract . . . laid out for eighty acres. Lacey by will on 10 Oct 1764 devised same to dau, Rebekah Kelly and by recent survey by Pennsylvania Land Company, London, it has been discovered part of above land lies within tract called Wheatfield. Mason purchased Wheatfield from the Company on 1st November 1771 and now for consideration of thirty pounds paid by James Lacey conveys above described parcel of land. Wit: John Tucker, John Funhas. Mary Mason privately examined gave consent. Ackn 26 Nov 1772 (V:p37)

66. 26 Nov 1772 Indenture between Jonathan Collings of Kent on Delaware, planter and James Benn of Dorchester Co (Maryland), yeoman. Consideration of twenty pounds conveys part of tract in Mispillion Hund on northeast fork of Nanticoke River surveyed by William Killen 20 Sept 1750 unto Thomas Davison, decd who by deed granted same to Abraham Wynkoop whose extrs sold the tract to Collings. Beginning at cor white oak of this tract and others of Davison . . . part conveyed by Benjamin Wynkoop to Robert Davis . . . on north side of Roger's Branch . . . containing one hundred seven acres. Wit: John Cook, Saml. McCall. Ackn 26 Nov 1772 (V:p38)

67. 26 Nov 1772 Indenture between James Powell of Queen Anne's Co (Maryland) yeoman and Lucy, his wife and William Hall of Kent on Delaware, yeoman. William Hall, decd, father of Lucy Powell and William Hall, contracted for purchase of one hundred acres from Caleb Davis which Davis purchased from John Tucker who by conditions in said bond granted title to land to heirs of William Hall. Description mentions Fork Branch . . . land called Barren Point alias Thousand Acre Tract . . . containing one hundred acres . . . consideration of twenty pounds paid. Wit: George McCall, James Craige. Lucy Powell privately examined gave consent. Ackn 26 Nov 1772 (V:p39)

68. 9 Nov 1772 Indenture between John Furchase of Kent on Delaware, house carpenter and Frances, his wife and Thomas Kelly said co, planter. Consideration of one hundred pounds conveys a part of tract called Furchase's Outlet situate in Kent Co and Mispillion Neck. Beginning at cor of land surveyed for Daniel Durham now possessed by Winlock Hall . . . to land called Anghton . . . conaining one hundred twelve acres. Wit: John Clark, Ann Clarke. Frances Furchase

privately examined gave consent. Ackn 26 Nov 1772 (V:p40)

69. 27 Nov 1772 Indenture between Peter Lowber of Kent on Delaware, yeoman and Catharine, his wife, late wife of Isaac Killam, decd, and one of the daus of John Fullerton, the elder, late of said co, yeoman and Elizabeth Warren of same co, widow and relict of Benjamin Warren, decd. Peter Lowber and Catharine, his wife, in her right are seized with three full and equal eight parts and one half of an eighth part into two parcels of land in Mispillion Hund yet to be divided, laid out for one hundred acres, part of tract called Whitewell's Delight. Also other parcel lying between Dover River and Mill Creek laid out for three hundred acres called Mill Neck, reserving one hundred acres devised by Stephen Simons by will to his dau, Mary. Consideration of two hundred eighty six pounds fourteen shillings convey their share afsd . . . late estate of John Fullerton (except as before excepted) who died intestate leaving John Fullerton, the younger; Mary Fullerton, Thomas Fullerton; the said Elizabeth Warren, William Fullerton, the said Catharine Killam, and Ann Fullerton now wife of Alexander Huston. John, the younger, Thomas, Mary and William Fullerton died intestate without issue. Wit: Richd. Smith, Samuel Chew. Catharine Lowber privately examined gave consent. Ackn 27 Nov 1772. (V:p40)

70. 26 Nov 1772 Indenture between Jordan Robinson of Kent on Delaware, house carpenter and David Rees same co, yeoman. Consideration of sixty pounds conveys two small parcels of land in forest of Little Creek Hund. Beginning at a cor of land now or late belonging to James Lewis . . . line of Robert Reddick late decd . . . containing twenty three acres . . . heretofore on 29 May 1760 granted by John Rees, decd, late father of David Rees, and Hester, his wife, to Jordan Robinson. The other parcel (description mentions land of Moses Ham . . . land late of Moses Barnett . . .) laid out for sixteen and a half acres to Robert Reddick on 24 Nov 1755 and devised one third to his wife, Catharine Reddick for life, with reversion to son, John Reddick, who conveyed the same in 25 Aug 1762 to Jordan Robinson. Wit: Will Killen, John Wood. Ackn 26 Nov 1772 (V:p41)

71. 10 Nov 1772 Indenture between Finwick Fisher of Kent on Delaware, Esq. and Mary, his wife and Heny Farson same co, farmer. Consideration of seventy five pounds convey two lots of ground nr crossroads in Duck Creek Hund. Beginning nr corner stone of Henry Farson's lot called The Tanyard Lott . . . in line of Robert Holliday's land . . . co of Lott No. 7 . . . line of Nancy Wilson's lott . . . including in the bounds two lotts, No. 8 & No. 9 containing two acres six perches. Wit: Thos. Brown, Andrew Jamison. Ackn 15 Dec 1772 (V:p42)

72. 29 Feb 1772 Indenture between Isaac Cox of Dover Hund, Kent on Delaware,

carriage maker and Susannah, his wife and Garret Sipple and Powell Cox both of Murtherkill Hund, gents. Isaac Cox lately purchased a grist mill and ten acres of land from William Rhodes, Esq on south side of Bishop's Branch, part of tract called Bishop's Choice laid out for Benoni Bishop. As by writing obligatory from William Rhodes to Isaac Cox who is now about to convey same by deed of mortgage. Consideration of five hundred two pounds convey the land as surety for full payment of the indebtedness. Wit: Thos. Hanson, John Patten. Susannah Cox privately examined gave consent. Ackn 17 Dec 1772. (V:p42)

73. 4 Nov 1772 Indenue between Edward Tilghman late of Philadelphia, gent, by John Chew of Kent on Delaware Esq, his atty and Charles Hillyard of same co, gent. Edward Tilghman was seized of parcel of woodland of sixty one and one half of an acre in Jone's Hund part of tract called the White Oak Survey which in division of real est of Samuel Chew, decd, was allotted to Elizabeth Tilghman, mother of Edward and by order of court was valued to Edward Tilghman, her only son. Edward Tilghman of Queen Anne's Co (Maryland and his father and John Chew were by him apptd attys to convey the said land. Edward Tilghman party to these presents by his atty, John Chew, in consideration of seventy five pounds seven shillings convey woodland beginning at cor of Charles Hillyard's land. . . cor of Thomas Hanson's land . . . to cor of Samuel Hanson's land . . . laid out for eighteen acres and one hundred thirty four square perches. Wit: William Killen, William Berry. Ackn 16 Dec 1772 (V:p43)

74. 16 Dec 1772 Indenture between Owen Irons of Dover Hund, Kent on Delaware, yeoman and Penelope, his wife and Titus Irons of Forest of Murtherkill Hund, son of Owen and Penelope. Consideration of twenty five pounds conveys a parcel of land in the forest part of a tract surveyed for Penelope as Penelope Freeman on 14 Feb 1743 by warrant 22 April that year. Beginning at cor of land of Joshua Meredith and land of Richard Smith . . . laid off for one hundred fifty acres. Wit: Saml. McCall, Sarah McCall. Penelope Irons privately examined gave consent. Ackn 16 Dec 1772 (V:p44)

75. 11 Nov 1772 Indenture between Samuel Smith late of Duck Creek Hund, Kent on Delaware now of Murtherkill Hund, cart wright and Tamsey, his wife and Robert Rees of Duck Creek Hund, yeoman. Consideration of four hundred fifty pounds convey parcel in last named hund devised to Samuel Smith by his father for one hundred fifty acres but on accurate survey is found to be two hundred seven acres and one hundred eight square perches. Beginning at cor of other land possessed by Robert Rees fomerly of James Steel . . . land of heirs of Daniel Smith, decd . . . land of heirs of Isaac Hazel, decd . . . laid out according to survey. Wit: John Cook, William Rees, John Smith. Mark McCall apptd atty. Tamsey

Smith privately examined gave consent. Ackn 16 Dec 1772. (V:p44)

76. 24 Nov 1772 Indenture between Andrew Doz of city of Philadelphia, merchant and James King of MIspillion Hund, Kent on Delaware, black smith. Consideration of two hundred two pounds conveys parcel of land formerly surveyed for George Cullin called Angleton. Begins on Cullin Branch . . . to line of tract called Middletown . . . land now possessed by Anne King, widow of Isaac King, Senr. . . . to Caleb Luff's part of the land called The Increase . . . formerly surveyed for Baptist Newcomb. . . containing one hundred thirty acres. Samuel McCall apptd atty. Wit: Waitman Sipple, Thomas Peterkin Ackn 15 Dec 1772 (V:p45)

77. 10 Nov 1772 Indenture between Anne King, relict and widow of Isaac King, Senr late of Mispillion Hund, Kent on Delaware and Andrew Doz, city of Philadelphia, merchant. Cornelius Dewese and Esther his wife by deed 11 Feb 1746 (Liber N, folio 122) conveyed to Isaac King a parcel of land containing two hundred ninety one acres part of a larger tract surveyed for George Cullin known as Angleton. King by will dated 15 June 1749 devised one half to his wife, Anne, and the other half to his son, Isaac King, Junr, who died intestate. Andrew Doz hath since become seized in all the estate by deed from James Caldwell, sheriff, 27 Nov 1771 (Book T, folio 183). No division was made between Anne and Isaac, Junr. and by survey made by Mark McCall on 30 and 31 July last past, it was found to contain three hundred seventeen acres and eighty nine square perches then divided each piece containing one hundred fifty eight acres and one hundred twenty square perches. Consideration of five shillings, Anne King and Andrew Doz confirm the division line. Begins at cor of land purchased by Isaac King from Govey Trippet, part of Angleton . . . line in tract called Richmore . . . laid out as surveyed. Wit: Phillip Barratt, Wm. Betts. Ackn 15 Dec 1772 (V:p45)

78. 10 Nov 1772 Indernture between Andrew Doz of city of Philadelphia, merchant and Anne King, widow and relict of Isaac King decd of Mispillion Hund, Kent on Delaware. Cornelius Deweese and Esther his wife by deed 11 Feb 1746 granted to Isaac King two hundred ninety one acres of land part of tract surveyed for George Cullin called Angleton, said deed (Liber N folio 122). Isaac King devised the land one half to his wife, Anne King, and the other half to his son, Isaac King, Junr. who died intestate. Andrew Doz became seized of all of the estate by deed from James Caldwell, sheriff. No partition was made between Anne and Isaac King, Junr during his lifetime. By a recent survey made by Mark McCall, surveyor, it was found the tract contained three hundred seventeen acres and eighty nine square perches divided equally between Anne and Isaac, Junr, making each part one hundred fifty eight acres and one hundred twenty square perches. Andrew Doz for consideration of releasement and confirmation of the dividend and sum of five

shillings hereby grants to Anne King all that dividend or moiety or half part. Begins nr the beginning corner of land from Corneilius Deweese to Isaac King . . . also part of Angleton purchased by King from Govey Trippet . . . land called Middletown . . . line in tract called Richmore . . . laid out as surveyed. Wit: Waitman Sipple, Thomas Peterkin. Samuel McCall apptd atty. Ackn 16 Dec 1772 (V:p46)

79. 15 Dec `1772 Indenture between Sarah Hart, relict and widow of John Hart late of Dover Hund alias St. Jone's, Kent on Delaware and Caesar Rodney of town of Dover. Paul Brunett was seized of a parcel of land in Dover Hund & Neck situate on Hog Pen Branch, part of a tract called Great Pipe Elm surveyed for William Winsmore and after decease of Paul Brunett land became property of John Lewey-Colly by inheritance who sold same to Robert Fitzgarrald who by deed 13 Aug 1747 (Book N, folio 158) granted part to John Hart. Laid off for five acres and John Hart died intestate leaving Sarah, his widow and sundry children. Five freeholders were chosen to view the land for partition and Charles Marim, John Nickerson, Joshua Gordon, David Pleasonton and George Stevens viewed the property and said it could not be divided. Sarah, widow, accepted the land as valued she having purchased dividend of the oldest son. Consideration of twenty five pounds now releases the said land to Caesar Rodney. Wit: Ezek. Cowgill, Simon W. Willson. Ackn 17 Dec 1772 (V:p46)

80. 15 Dec 1772 Petition of William Atkinson sheweth that Jonathan Morgan and others obtained judgements and executions against John Newman, late of Kent on Delaware, school master, and James Caldwell did take in execution all right, title and claim of Newman to parcel of land in forrest of Murherkill Hund which was sold to your petitioner as highest bidder for sum of thirty pounds six pence and James Caldwell has not conveyed the premises. Petitioner prays the court to authorize John Cook, present sheriff to execute a deed. Being read to the court, is considered and granted the court orders John Cook to convey the land. Test: Samuel Chew. (V:p47)

81. 15 Dec 1772 Indenture between John Cook, high sheriff of Kent on Delaware and William Atkinson of same co, farmer. Jonathan Morgan lately in court of Common Pleas recovered a debt agst John Newman, planter, late of Kent Co but now of Dorchester Co (Maryland) school teacher of twenty six pounds three shillings four pence and forty one shillings six pence in damages. James Caldwell by virtue of a writ seized in execution a parcel of land in forrest of Murtherkill Hund belonging to John Newman and sold same at public vendue to William Atkinson, he being highest bidder, for sum of thirty pounds. Said tract contains two hundred acres surveyed and laid out for William Willson beginning at cor of

Samuel Willson's land . . . cor of Andrew Caldwell's land . . . containing one hundred twenty nine acres and fifty one square perches. Other part residue thereof being one other tract adj laid out for William Scandlin by warrant 4 Dec 1749 begins at cor of first parcel . . . to cor of William Trippet's land . . . cor of Elizabeth Frazier's land . . . laid out for seventy one aces, in the whole two hundred acres and fifty one perches of land. Wit: Thos. Skillington, Geo. Painter. Ackn 15 Dec 1772 (V:p47)

82. 12 Feb 1773 Indenture between William Wallace of Kent on Delaware, planter and Charles Ridgely same co, physician. Consideration of six hundred thirty six pounds ten shillings conveys tract of land known as Skypton but formerly sold by Richard Johns to William Wallace late of said co, decd, father of afsd William Wallace by name of Sciptop as by deed on 15 Feb 1753 recorded in Murderkill Hund. Begins in orchard of John Clayton, decd . . . along line of Mark Bardons . . . line of James Armitage . . . laid out for two hundred twelve acres. Also that other part or tract called Greenwich beginning at a stump orig tree of Greenwich and also beginning of tract called Long Reach . . . cor marked hickory of Matthew Manlove's land . . . laid out for twelve acres and ninety perches. Wit: John Hillyard, Thomas Parke. Ackn 12 Feb 1773 (V:p48)

83. 10 Feb 1773 Indenture between James Reed and Ann, his wife, of Kent on Delaware, cordwinder and George Saxton same co, farmer. Consideration of fifty pounds conveys parcel of land in Murtherkill Hund situate on Hudson's Branch adj a tract called Guilfords and patented to Samuel Mann of Kent Co who devised to his niece, Margaret Hudson who married afsd James Reed and having male issue who survived her, the afsd Reed became seized in his own right. Beginning at cor of land of William Meredith and Pratt . . . laid out for eight acres and twenty two perches of land. Wit: Thomas Freeman, Moses Stuart. Ann Reed privately examined gave consent. Ackn 10 Feb 1773 (V:p49)

84. 9 Feb 1773 Indenture between Thomas Keith of Little Creek Hund, Kent on Delaware, yeoman and John Barber same co, yeoman. By warrant 18 Sept 1735 granted to Thomas Lucas, survey was made for tract called Canterbury said to contain two hundred thirty six acres and allowance situate in fork of Saint Jone's alias fork of Dover Hund on north side of middle branch of Dover River. Beginning at cor of Jonathan Clark's land. Lucas by deed 5 Sept 1738 granted same to Hugh Durborow then of sd co who by deed 23 Jan 1753 granted the land to his son, Daniel, who by deed 24 Feb 1768 (Book R, fol 256) conveyed a part to Thomas Keith. Description mentions Jonathan Clark's land . . . land of James Lewis . . . heretofore belonging to Robert Willson . . . tree of William Hanzer's land . . . land of Charles Ridgely, Esq . . . containing one hundred fifty acres. Consideration

of one hundred fifty pounds. Wit: Saml. McCall, George McCall. Ackn 10 Feb 1773. (V:p49)

85. 10 Feb 1773 Indenture between Michael Offley of Apoquimamink Hund and Co Newcastle, farmer and Samuel Morris same place, yeoman. Consideration of seventeen pounds conveys piece of meadow ground in Duck Ceek Hund part of Gravesend lying between the mill race and Green's Branch. Description mentions land of late Rowland Parry . . . containing abou four acres of land. Wit: William Cahoon, Junr, Wm. Jordan. Ackn 11 Feb 1773 (V:p50)

86. 10 Feb 1773 Indenture between Isaac Cox of Dover Hund, Kent on Delaware, chaise maker and Susannah, his wife and Francis Edmiston of Murtherkill Hund, yeoman. Isaac Cox is seized with part of tract called Bishop's Choice and also part of St. Collum both surveyed for Benoni Bishop. Beginning on Doctor's Branch at a cor of land of Robert Beauchamp . . . containing one hundred seventy two acres of land. Cox sold the land at thirty shillings per acre according to a true survey made. Wit: Thos. Hanson, William Wells. Susannah Cox privately examined gave consent. Ackn 11 Feb 1773. (V:p50)

87. 10 Feb 1773 Indenture between Moses Ratlidge of Murtherkill Hund, Kent on Delaware, yeoman and Anne his wie and George Gullet of forrest of Mispillion Hund, yeoman. Isaac Merrit formerly of Mispillion Hund died intestate leaving issue five daughters, one who married William McNatt, she died leaving one dau, Anne, wife of Moses Ratlidge. By warrant granted to Merrit on 8 Aug 1740, a survey was made for the heirs on 17 May 1768 called Merrit's Adventure of four hundred forty nine and a half acres and allowance in forrest of Mispillion Hund. George Gullet by deed 7 Jan last past purchased one third part undivided from Absalom Hudson and Rachel, his wife, and Charles Kimmey and Mary, his wife. Also signed were Moses Ratlidge and Anne, his wife who now grant to George Gullet their unidivided one fifth part for consideration of thirty pounds. Wit: Saml. McCall, George McCall. Anne Ratlidge privately examined gave consent. Ackn 10 Feb 1773 (V:p51)

88. 26th day 11th mo 1768. Receipt Then received of James Anderson full satisfaction of said Anderson for a tract or parcel of land called John's Purchase formerly bought in partnership between one Abraham Bright and William Anderson and James Anderson and all oher accounts being at the same time only a note of hand for six pounds excepted - I say received by me. (signed) Abraham Bright. Testes: Benjamin Chipman, Henry Clampitt. A true copy test. (V:p51)

89. 10 Feb 1773 Indenture between John Gordon and Hannah his wife of Kent on

Delaware and John Wear of said co. Consideration of fifty two pounds ten shillings conveys fifteen acres of land by will of Griffith Gordon late this co, decd, was bequeathed to his dau, Elizabeth Gordon now wife of Benjamin Coombe who conveyed same to Thomas Buckmaster on 16 Aug 1766 (Book R, folio 111) who conveyed same to John Gordon (Book S, folio 119), part of larger tract called Lisburn. Description mentions land of Robert Fitzjarrel late decd. Wit: John Chew, Joseph Berry. Hannah Gordon privately examined gave consent. Ackn 11 Feb 1773 (V:p51)

90. 9 Jan 1773 Indenture between Jonathan Sipple of Mispillion Hund, Kent on Delaware and Ruth, his wife, and Elijah Sipple of one part and Philip Barret of same co, gent. Consideration of three hundred forty nine pounds conveys part of tract called Ousby orig surveyed for Thomas Heathard. Part of real est of Waitman Sipple, Junr, decd, who was father to Jonathan and Elijah. Beginning at cor formerly conveyed by Waitman Sipple to Barret and Miriam, his wife, and is also cor of one hundred acres of land lately laid off to Captain William Hazelton and Miriam his wife . . . to a point of land called the Boat Yard where boats and shallops are wont to be built . . . to part divided off to Hannah Whitacre, one of daus of Thomas Heathard and about this cor some depositions have lately been taken . . . part of Ousby sold by Thomas Heathard to Edmund Needham and Anna, his wife . . . then became property of Richard Shirley, Ezekiel Needham, John Hall, John Redman and from his heirs to Benjamin Warren called one hundred five acres . . . in last line passed by Whitaker and of land sold by John Edmunds to Benjamin Warren Senr. formerly of Samuel Brooks . . . to land now of Waitman Sipple, bro to Jonathan and Elijah . . . containing one hundred seventy four and a half acres. Wit: William Rhodes, John Sipple. Ruth Sipple privately examined gave consent. Ackn 10 Feb 1773 (V:p52)

91. 13 Aug 1772 Indenture between Thomas Green of Duck Creek Hund, Kent on Delaware, yeoman and Mary, his wife and William Jordan same place, house carpenter. Consideration of four hundred two pounds convey parcel of land part of tract called Gravesend. Beginning at run of Green's Branch . . . division line between Thomas and James Green . . . to cor of Finwick Fisher's land . . . containing one hundred eighty seven acres and thirty three perches. Wit: John Dorrach, Mary Vanwinkle. Ackn 10 Feb 1773 (V:p53)

92. 24 Oct 1772 Indenture between Edward Moore of Kent on Delaware, farmer and Daniel Cox said co, yeoman. William Clark by warrant on 28 June 1740 by virtue of a survey was made by George Stevenson, surveyor, and Clark contracted with William Watson for the tract receiving consideration for same. Watson died before deed was made but devised the land to his son, Francis Watson, a minor and

William Clark conveyed the land to the minor by deed 13 Aug 1747 (Book N, folio 165) and Francis Watson conveyed same to John Chicken on 10 Mar 1760 (Book P, folio 224). A private bargain has subsisted between John Chicken and Matthew Crosier in partnership respecting the tract and Crosier entered into obligation to Edward Moore for conveyance of the land and Crosier has procured John Chicken to join in making the conveyance. Consideration of two hundred forty pounds, Moore conveys parcel in forrest of Mispillion Hund beginning on road from Tappahannah to Forest Landing . . . part sold by John Chicken to Richard Mannering . . . cor of Archibald Kearsey's land . . . of Joshua Meredith's land . . . laid out for two hundred seventeen acres. Henry Elbert apptd atty. Wit: N. S. Wright, Amos Hinesley. Ackn 10 Feb 1773 (V:p54)

93. 9 Feb 1773 Indenture between Thomas Hatfield of Kent on Delaware, yeoman and Sarah, his wife and George Lamdin same place, yeoman. A survey was made for Jonathan Cottonham on 22nd 6th mo 1747 for a parcel of land in the forrest of Murtherkill Hund called Cotonborough containing one hundred sixty nine acres and the usual allowance. Consideration of seventy six pounds ten shillings paid to Thomas Hatfield and his wife, Sarah, they convey one hundred five and a half acres of said tract. Wit: Jas. Caldwell, John Reed, Junr. Sarah Hatfield privately examined gave consent. Ackn 10 Feb 1773 (V:p55)

94. 7 Jan 1773 Indenture between Absalom Hudson and Rachel, his wife; Charles Kimmey and Mary, his wife; and Moses Ratlidge and Anne, his wife of one part and George Gullet of forrest of Misspillion Hund, Kent on Delaware, yeoman. Isaac Marritt or Meritt fomerly of forrest of Mispillion Hund obtained a survey to be made by Hugh Durborow, surveyor, on 25 May 1727 for a parcel of land in afsd hund called Marrit's Adventure said to contain three hundred twenty acres of land. As no warrant was granted, Marrit obtained a warrant afterwards on 8 Aug 1740 and survey was made by William Killen but did not include all lands in orig survey. Isaac Marrit died intestate leaving issue five daus: Elizabeth who married William McNatt and died leaving one dau, Anne wife of Moses Ratlidge. Another dau, Rachel is married to Absalom Hudson; also a third dau, Mary married Charles Kimmey; a fourth dau, Sarah, is now wife of Daniel Bensten who dwells on said land. Fifth dau, named Anne is now wife of Jacob Wooters and Absalom Hudson hath also a settlement on said tract and John Hubbard as tenant thereon and Jacob Wooters hath also a settlement thereon. At request of Daniel Bensten, a copy of warant on 2d Mar 1768 was directed to Samuel McCall, surveyor, who found four hundred forty nine and a half acres and allowance. Beginning on prong of old Marshy Hope Branch called Little Branch which runs between land of John Gullet and whereon Daniel Bensten dwells . . . to place whereon Allen Howard formerly lived . . . heirs are about to convey one third of the whole. Consideration of one

hundred forty nine pounds sixteen shillings is paid. Samuel McCall and Mark McCall apptd attys. Wit: George McCall, Sarah McCall, Junr. Mary Kimmey, Rachel Hudson and Anne Ratlidge privately examined gave consent. Ackn 10 Feb 1773. (V:p55)

95. 10 Feb 1773 Indenture between Thomas Calloway of Kent on Delaware, husbandman, Richard Brinckle said co, husbandman and Pheebe his wife, admx and Joseph Marrit said co, yeoman, admr of goods and chattles of James Calloway lately decd at time of his death who died intestate of one part and Benjamin Wynkoop of city of Philadelphia, merchant. Thomas Calloway is seized of three hundred seventy acres of land adj lands of John McKinney, Richard Underwood, John Chadwick and Peter Galloway in upper part of Mispillion Hund. by his bond or obligation dated 9 Aug 1769 to James Calloway in penal sum of five hundred pounds condition of making over the afsd tract of land with covenants agst the claim of dower or thirds of Elizabeth Calloway, mother of said Thomas and of the widow of one John McNatt then decd and agst the heirs of John McNatt. James Calloway died intestate before deed was passed, his personal estate found to be insufficient to pay debts. The admx and admr petitioned the court for permission to sell sufficient land to pay the debts and it was so ordered, said land sold at public vendue to Benjamin Wynkoop. Consideration of five shillings to Thomas Calloway and eighty pounds to Richard Brinckle and Pheebe, his wife, and to Joseph Marrit, now convey that part of McKnatt's Range . . . containing ninety acres . . . also all parcel of land adj (excepting hereinafter excepted) of three hundred ninety seven acres and allowance surveyed and laid out for John McKnatt on 15 Sept 1750 by virtue of warrant on 2 June 1746. Excepting nevertheless part of the last mentioned tract conveyed by John McKnatt in his life time to Philip Riccards containing one hundred acres and allowance of six percent. Wit: John Carter, Suchak Carter, Richard McNatt, Ezekiel Anderson. Ackn 10 Feb 1773 (V:p57)

96. 12 Sept 1771 Indenture between Eliazar Badger of Kent on Delaware, taylor and Edmund Badger of city of Philadelphia, cordwainer, two children of Edmund Badger late of town of Dover, decd and Samuel Hanson, Thomas Hanson, Ezekiel Cowill, John Cowgill, Samuel Hanson, Junr. and Henry Cowgill, gents, all members of society of people called Quakers belonging to that place and are members of a meeting held in Little Creek Neck known as Little Creek Meeting House. Edmund Badger, the father, on 14 Dec 1763 devised to the society of Quakers, those of the Little Creek Meeting, as guardians to same half acre of ground on which to build a meeting house. On north end of lott adj North St and High St . . . to lot belonging to Thomas Skillington . . . leaving the residue to son, Edmund Badger, Junr. who along with Eleazar Badger now convey the land according to wishes of their father's will. Saml. McCall, Mark McCall apptd attys.

Wit: Henry Bell, John Bell, Richard Swetman. Ackn 10 Feb 1773 (V:p58)

97. A Map and Certificate of Robert Porter's land called Porter's Lodge containing four hundred acres of land (on St. Jones's Creek) Adj lands of Wm. Berres, John Walker, John Glover and Thos. Cliford. Surveyed 8 Nov 1680 (signed) Richd. Noble by order of Ephr. Herman, surveyor of St. Jone's and Newcastle Counties. (V:p59)

98. 9 Dec 1772 Indenture between John Fothergill of London, doctor in Physick, Daniel Zackary of London, gent, Devereux Bowly of London, watchmaker, Jacob Hagan, Silvanus Grove, and William Heron of London, merchants, surviving trustees of proprietorship known as Pennsylvania Land Company of London by their attys, Jacob Cooper, Samuel Shoemaker and Joshua Howell of Philadelphia, merchants and Michael Offley of Appoquinomink Hund, Newcastle on Delaware, yeoman. By indenture of lease and release on 17th & 18th Feb 1762 made between John Whitehead of Bristol, haberdasher, eldest son and heir of George Whitehead of Bristol, merchant (who survived William Donn, Abraham Lloyd, Charles Harford, Edward Lloyd, Caleb Lloyd, Richyate Coole, Benjamin Coole and Richard Stafford, merchants and John Scandrett, grocer, all of Bristol, decd) of one part and John Fothergill, Daniel Zackary, Thomas How, Devereux Bowly, Luke Hinds, Richard How, Jacob Hagan, Silvanus Grove and William Heron, officers in trust to sell and dispose of lands in Pennsylvania and Maryland belonging to Bristol Naval Stores Company copartnership vested in John Whitehead as heir of George Whitehead. Roger Pugh of Kent on Delaware purchased the company's advertised land at public auction, he being highest bidder and died devising the land to his son, William Pugh. By sundry conveyances is now vested in Michael Offley who for consideration of one hundred seven pounds two shillings eleven pence paid to the attys by him receives tract in Duck Creek Hund beginning cor of Matthew Griffin's land . . . by land of Roger Pugh, decd . . . containing ninety five acres being part of the Manner of Frieth. Also a piece of land (description mentions) Green's Creek . . . mill house . . . land of Rowland Parry, decd . . . containing four acres. William Killen apptd atty. Wit: Peter Thomson, Samuel Morris. Ackn 11 Feb 1773 (V:p59)

99. 9 Nov 1772 Indenture between Mary Sykes of Dover Hund, Kent on Delaware, spinster and James Sykes, father of said Mary, Esq. and French Battell of Dover. Mary Sykes for barring all estates tail for settling of tracts of land and sum of five shillings and French Battell in good and common recovery sells to James Sykes a moiety or half part of two tracts know by name of Great and Small Tynhead Corte on main branch of Little Creek. Beginning . . . along line of John Nickerson's land . . . along tract called Edenton. . . tract called Little Pipe Elm. . . containing seven

hundred acres. One full moiety or parcel of a tract of four hundred acres in Dover Hund formerly William Berry's. Description mentions Jones's Creek or Dover River . . . containing one hundred seventy acres of upland and fifty acres of marsh. Also a full moiety or half part of a tract called Kingston Upon Hull containing fifty acres. Also a full moiety or half part of land beginning at cor of John Auler's land . . . containing fifty acres. Being land of Robert French, great grandfather of Mary Sykes in and by his last will devised to eldest dau, Katharine who married John Shannon and left two daus: Mary, late wife of James Sykes, and Ann, wife of John Maxfield now living. Wit: Anna Maria Chew, Jas. VanDyke. 12 Nov 1772 (V:p61)

100. 23 Apr 1772 Indenture between Jonathan Cowpland of city of Philadelphia, inn holder and Mary, his wife and William Masters of the Northern Liberties, city of Philadelphia, distiller and Charles Lyon of same place, mariner. Consideration of three hundred twenty pounds conveys two equal undivided third parts of a parcel of land in forrest of Murtherkill Hund at head of Tanner's Branch or Colbreath's Marsh commonly called the Bear Swamp in Kent on Delaware. Beginning in line of Timothy Jenkins . . . also cor of survey made for Waitman Sipple . . . cor of late survey made to Henry Wells . . . cor of land belonging to Joseph Powell . . . land surveyed for heirs of Thomas Thomas . . . in Thomas Mumcy's line . . . and Joseph Rash's land . . . by Barry's Race Ground . . . cor of Nicholas Loockerman's land . . . laid out for five hundred fifty one acres. Same tract that Henry Wells, yeoman and Sarah, his wife, by deed 13 Feb 1765 (Book R, folio 22, etc) conveyed to Jonathan Cowpland in trust for use of himself, the said Charles Lyon, Thomas Bond, Junr and the said William Masters according to their proportions therein. Thomas McKean, Esq apptd atty. Wit: Peter Thomson, Jacob Cooper, Mark McCall. Ackn 11 Feb 1773 (V:p63)

101. 4 Dec 1772 Indenture between Jonathan Cowpland of city of Philadelphia, inn holder and Mary, his wife and William Masters of the Northern Liberties, city of Philadelphia, distiller and Thomas Bond Junr of city of Philadelphia, merchant. Consideration of one hundred sixty pounds convey one full equal and undivided third part of parcel of land in Murtherkill Hund at head of Tanner's Branch or Colbreath's Marsh commonly called the Bear Swamp in Kent on Delaware. Beginning in line of Timothy Jenkins . . . also cor of survey made for Waitman Sipple . . . cor of late survey made to Henry Wells also a cor of land of Joseph Powell . . . in line of land surveyed for heirs of Thomas Thomas . . . in Thomas Muncy's line . . . of Joseph Rash's land . . . by Berry's Race Ground . . . cor of Nicholas Loockerman's land . . . laid out for five hundred fifty one acres. Same tract that Henry Wells, yeoman and Sarah, his wife, by deed 13 Feb 1765 (Book R, folio 22, etc) did sell and release to Jonathan Cowpland in trust for the use of

himself, the said Thomas Bond, Charles Lyon and William Masters according to their several proportions of the land. Thomas McKean apptd atty. Wit:Peter Thomson, Jacob Cooper, Mark McCall. Ackn 11 Feb 1773 (V:p64)

102. 9 Feb 1773. Petition of William Ball sheweth that William and Samuel Coney obtained judgment and execution agst Samuel Ball, late of Kent on Delaware, store keeper and James Caldwell placed into execution two lots situate nr crossroads in Duck Creek Hund (subject to a deed mortgage made by Samuel Ball to your petitioner for six hundred pounds) and disposed of same to your petitioner for sum of fifteen shillings. Caldwell since out of office, William Ball prays that John Cook, Esq, present sheriff execute the deed. The within petition being read, the court orders the present sheriff to make over the land. A true copy test. (signed) Samuel Chew. (V:p65)

103. 9 Feb 1773 Indenture between John Cook, Esq. sheriff of Kent on Delaware and William Ball of city of Philadelphia, merchant. William Coney and Samuel Coney in the court of Common Pleas recovered agst Samuel Ball, store keeper, living at the crossroads within one mile of Duck Creek, a debt of ninety nine pounds twelve shillings eight pence and a half penny also four pounds two shillings ten pence for damages. James Caldwell by virtue of a writ seized in execution a certain messuage and lot of ground in Salisbury town and a number of lots at the crossroads in Duck Creek Hund containing six or seven acres of land. William Baker and John Bell stated the premises were insufficient in rents and profits to pay the debt in term of seven years. Caldwell sold the property at public vendue to William Ball (under the incumbrance of mortgage made by Samuel Ball and his wife, Elizabeth, on 19 March 1771) for sum of fifteen shillings. Beginning at cor of land of Thomas Ross . . . lot devised by Thomas Green to his dau, Marcy, wife of Howell Buckingham . . . cor of Richard Holliday's lot . . . cor of Finwick Fisher Esqrs land . . . on south side of Landing Road nr a new school house . . . to Samuel Ball's lot . . . laid off for fifteen acres and twenty nine perches and one half of a perch which James Green of Duck Creek Hund, farmer on 14 Mar 1768 conveyed to Samuel Ball (Book S, folio 87) and all that other half part or piece of land part of Gravesend beginning at cor of William Creighton's lot . . . remainder of James Green's land . . . line of Fenwick Fisher's land . . . cor of Thomas Ross's lot . . . containing sixty eight and three quarters of an acre and nine perches which James Green and Mary, his wife by deed on 5 Nov 1768 granted to Samuel Ball and William Ball (Book S, folio 93). Wit: Geo. Painter, Nath. Smithers. Ackn 10 Feb 1773 (V:p66)

104. 10 May 1764 Indenture between Joshua Carpenter of city of Philadelphia, gent and Allivia, his wife and Jasper Carpenter said city, cabinet maker and Mary,

his wife. Joshua and Jasper being sons of Samuel Carpenter, decd, of one part and John Reed of Philadelphia, merchant. Samuel Carpenter was seized in his life time of several parcels of land in counties of Newcastle, Kent and Sussex. For consideration of two hundred pounds, Joshua Carpenter and Allivia, his wife, and Jasper Carpenter and Mary, his wife, do each of them for him and herself and for his or her hiers hereby covenant promise grant and agree to and with the said John Reed or his heirs shall and will make or cause to be made and executed all and every other or further assurance deed or conveyance that shall be deemed needful and necessary by the said John Reed or his heirs by his or their council learned in the law for the further and better assuring and conveying the above premises. Wit: Robert Clerk, Matthew Biays, Edwd. Merefield, Andrew Edge. James Sykes, Gent apptd atty. Ackn 1 Oct 1773 (V:p67)

105. 11 Feb 1773 Indenture between Sarah Pemberton and Hannah Robinson, daus and devisees of George Robinson formerly of Saint Jones's hund alias Dover hund, Kent on Delaware and John Nickerson same co, gent. Consideration of one hundred fifteen pounds convey a parcel of land being part of tract called Great Pipe Elm situate in Dover hund, devised to them by their father. Beginning at cor of land conveyed by the two women to Jonathan Caldwell . . . containing fifty seven acres and eighty six perches of land. Saml. McCall and Mark McCall apptd attys. Wit: Chas Marim, Jno. Marim. Ackn 11 Feb 1773. (V:p68)

106. 29 Jan 1773 Indenture between Joshua Jamison late of Duck Creek Hund, Kent on Delaware, sadler and Thomas Jamison of same place, yeoman. Consideration of two hundred fifty pounds conveys lott or piece of ground nr the Cross Roads. Beginning at cor of Howell Buckingham's lott in right of Marcey, his wife, a devisee under will of Thomas Green, Senr, decd . . . containing thirty two poles or perches. Wit: Andrew Jamison, James Townsend, Tho. Brown. Ackn 10 Feb 1773. (V:p69)

107. 3 Feb 1773 Indenture between Benajmin Chew, Charles Ridgely and Benjamin Wynkoop, extrs of John Vining, late of Kent on Delaware, Esq and Phebe Vining of city of Philadelphia, widow and relict of John Vining who was seized in his lifetime of lott in city of Dover which he purchased from Richard Mott on 14 Dec 1757 laid out for five and three quarters acres and a small tract of land situate in Murther Creek Hund adj the town of Dover and Dover River or Jone's Creek containing about nine acres and sixty perches which he purchased of Robert Johnson on 13 Aug 1759. Vining made his will 13 Nov 1770 devising that properties in Pennsylvania, lower counties of Delaware, province of East and West Jersey and elsewhere be sold. Consideration of one thousand pounds best price that could be reasonably obtained and paid by Phebe Vining, now convey the afsd land

to her. Wit: Geo. Emlen, Junr, Jos. Mifflin, Thomas Rodney, John Chew. Ackn 23 Feb 1773 (V:p69)

108. 21 Aug 1772 Indenture between John Ware of Dover Hund, Kent on Delaware, blacksmith, William Ware of Sussex on Delaware, pilate(sic) and David Ware of city of Philadelphia, cord wainer of one part and Caesar Rodney, town of Dover, Esq of other part. William Winsmore on 8 Mar 1676/7 had survey made called Great Pipe Elm situate on north side of Hog Pen Branch, Dover Hund and enlarged by resurvey for Winsmore by Joshua Barkstead on 11th, 12th, 13th Oct 1683 and part of tract of about one hundred acres through sundry conveyances became property of William Ware who died intestate, father of above named John, William and David Ware and a dau named Mary who died of late without issue. John and David Ware by joint deed 29 Mar 1768 (Book R, folio 259) conveyed their shares to Rodney and William Ware by deed 1 Aug 1769 (Book S, folio 201) conveyed his share to Rodney, in which deeds is recited chain of conveyances from Winsmore to William Ware, Senr. The brothers now convey their sister, Mary's, one fifth part of land purchased by their father, William Ware from Benjamin Brown on 8 Feb 1745 (Book N, folio 95), to Rodney for consideration of fifty pounds. Wit: Stephen Lewis, John Bell, Junr, Joseph Alford, Samuel McCall. Ackn 11 Feb 1773. (V:p70)

109. 9 Dec 1772 Indenture between Joshua Clayton of Kent on Delaware, physician and Rachel, his wife and Samuel Chew same co, gent. Consideration of eight hundred fifty two pounds convey parcel of land situate in Murtherkill Hund beginning on south side of Walker's Branch . . . line of tract called Long Reach . . . laid out for two hundred eighty four acres and five perches. Caesar Rodney and William Killen apptd attys. Wit: John Chew, Richard Bassett. Rachel Clayton privately examined gave consent. Ackn ___ Feb 1773. (V:p71)

110. 27 Feb 1773 Indenture between Cox Gordon of Kent on Delaware and John Gordon same place. Griffith Gordon, father of Cox and John, was seized of tract called Lisbon in Jones' Hund and devised same to be divided by Caesar Rodney, Charles Marim and Caleb Luff between his two sons, Cox and John, and Letitia Gordon. On 9 Feb 1763, land was divided and allotted to the heirs. (Book Q, folio 127 & 128). Consideration of five hundred twenty pounds, Cox Gordon conveys ninety five and one half acres to his bro, John. Wit: John Chew, William Berry. Ackn 27 Feb 1773. (V:p71)

111. 27 Feb 1773 Indenture between Sarah Gordon of Kent on Delaware, widow of one part and John Gordon same place, yeoman. For divers good causes and considerations and sum of five shillings doth remise, release and forever quit claim

33

... to part of tract called Lisbon laid out for ninety five and one half acres. Wit: John Chew, William Berry. Ackn 27 Feb 1773. (V:p72)

112. 24 Feb 1773 Indenture between Francis Denney of Duck Creek Hund, Kent on Delaware and Joseph Denney of same place, farmer. Evan Jones, gent, of co afsd by will 21 Mar 1721 devised his dwelling plantation, part of tract called Benefield, to George Martin and Philip Denney for thirty years in partnership and to heirs of their body for fifty years and for ninety years to heirs of their body in joint partnership. George Martin died leaving son, George, who with Philip Denney, son of Philip Denney, the elder, also possessed the land during their natural life. George, son of George Martin, the elder, died without issue and Philip Denney, father of Francis Denney died intestate leaving seven children: Philip, Francis, Christopher, Mary, Rebecca, Margret and Elizabeth. Philip and Francis, admrs, d.b.n. of their father, Philip Denney, it appears that eight years of the middle term of fifty years in which the land was devised commence from 21st Mar next. Following appraisal of land by Thomas Tilton, Esq and Emmanuel Stout, gents, Francis Denney for consideration of one hundred seventy six pounds conveys his right, title and interest in tract Lisbon to Joseph Denney. Wit: Frans. Barber, Jas. Raymond. Ackn 24 Feb 1773 (V:p72)

113. 25 Feb 1773 Indenture between Joseph Denney of Duck Creek Hund, Kent on Delaware, yeoman and Francis Denney same place, yeoman. Francis Denney by deed dated day before this present indenture did as admr d.b.n. on estate of his father, Philip Denney (with his brother, Philip Denney, Junr) granted to Joseph Denney all that parcel of land called Benefield which belonged to his father, Philip Denney, decd, in his lifetime for a term of fifty years to commence from 21 Mar 1721 of which time a shorter term of twenty eight years to commence from 21 Mar next ensuing is still behind and belongs of right to est of his decd father, Philip Denney. Land was appraised by Thomas Tilton, Esq and Emmanuel Stour, gents for value of one hundred seventy six pounds and Joseph Denny is about to convey the land to Francis Denney for value given afsd now releases all title, claim, etc. Wit: John Ham, Robert McYarnnent. Ackn 25 Feb 1773. (V:p72)

114. 25 Feb 1773 Indenture between James White and Richard Dallener of Kent on Delaware, extrs of will of William Downs, decd and Archibald McSparren same place. Extrs obtained a court order to sell a small plantation of William Downs to discharge estate debts being part of tract called Clayton situate on west side of Ivy Branch. Land was sold at public auction to McSparren for sum of twenty five pounds five shillings. Beginning on Ivy Branch alias Jews Creek ... where road from Kings Road leading from McSparran's to William Rhodes mill crosses ... containing twenty five acres and seventy two perches. Wit: Warner

Mifflin, John Bell. Ackn 25 Feb 1773 (V:p74)

115. 1 February 1773 Indenture between Daniel Boazman and Sinna his wife of Kent on Delaware and Francis Jester same co. Consideration of three pounds eighteen shillings nine pence convey part of tract situate in Mispillion Hund beginning at cor of land called Good Luck . . . division line between Boazman and Jester . . . cor of Jehu Jester's land . . . laid out for twelve and three quarter acres. Wit: Major Anderson, Wm. Anderson. Sinah Boazman privately examined gave consent. Ackn 24 Feb 1773. (V:p74)

116. 12 Feb 1773 Indenture between William Porter of St. Jones's (alias Dover Hund), Kent on Delaware, farmer and Ann Hardin of Murthkill Hund, same co, widow. Consideration of twenty five pounds conveys parcel of land and swamp which was surveyed for James Dill on 17 Dec 1754 under warrant granted 27 Nov 1754 who on 12 May 1768 was conveyed to Jessey Beauchamp who conveyed same to William Porter. Beginning at cor of land possessed by Peter May . . . with land of Christopher Wyse . . . sapling of Jacob Wooter's land . . . William Dill's land . . . laid out for sixty nine and one half acres and usual allowance of six acres. Wit: Simon W. Willson, John Comegys. Ackn 25 Feb 1773 (V:p75)

117. 1 Mar 1773 Indenture between Cornelius Hanzer of Fork of Dover Hund, Kent on Delaware, yeoman and Nehemiah Hanzer same place, yeoman. Warrant was granted 9 Nov 1734 to William Hanzer formerly of said place, father to parties herewith, survey was made by Hugh Durborow, surveyor on 21 Nov 1737 for a tract of two hundred acres called Jolley's Neck in fork of Dover River (Book N, folio 189). Hanzer devised the tract to his son, Cornelius, who is conveying twenty five acres to his bro, Nehemiah for consideration of fifteen pounds. Vincent Loockerman apptd atty. Wit: Vincent Loockerman, Junr, Thomas North. Ackn 5 Mar 1773. (V:p75)

118. 5 Mar 1773 Indenture between Cornelius Hanzer of forest of Dover Hund, Kent on Delaware, yeoman and Benjamin Wells of Little Creek Hund, same co, yeoman. Warrant was granted 9 Nov 1734 to William Hanzer formerly of said place and survey was made by Hugh Durborow, surveyor on 21 Nov 1737 for a tract of two hundred acres called Jolley's Neck in forest of Dover Hund. Beginning at head of Dover River and on Chance's Branch . . . cor of land laid out for Nicholas Powell . . . land laid out to Samuel Manlove . . . laid out for two hundred acres. Cornelius hath conveyed twenty five acre part to Nehemiah Hanzer, now conveys the residue for sum of forty five pounds. Samuel McCall apptd atty. Wit: Mark McCall, Peter Stout. Ackn 5 Mar 1773. (V:p76)

119. 26 Feb 1773 Indenture between John Cullin of Kent on Delaware, yeoman and William Cullin same place, yeoman. Consideration of five pounds and the love good will and affection which John Cullin doth bear unto and especially for the performent(sic) of William Cullin, conveys parcel of land in Mispillion Hund including present dwelling plantation of William Cullin, part of tract called Saw Mill Range. Beginning in the line of land of Mathias Davis nr the store house of William Cullin . . . to division line between William and Jonathan Cullin . . . to land sold by William Dill and uxor to Cullin . . . cor of division between William, George and Jonathan Cullin . . . containing seventy six acres and seven eighths, more or less. John Cullin to have use to the timber for fuel or firewood during his lifetime. Wit: Wm. Dill, Isaac Beauchamp. Ackn 26 Feb 1773 (V:p77)

120. 26 Feb 1773 Indenture between John Cullin of Kent on Delaware, yeoman and George Cullin (son of John Cullin) same place, yeoman. Consideration of love good will and affection which he hath and doth bear unto and especially for the performent(sic) of George Cullin and also in consideration of five pounds conveys a parcel of land in Mispillion Hund on southwest side of Cullin's Branch including present dwelling plantation of George Cullin, a part of tract called Saw Mill Range. Beginning at a marked oak for division between George and Jonathan Cullin . . . landing road leading by dwelling of George Cullin . . . line run by the London Company . . . containing about seventy two and five eighths acres. To use of John Cullin so far as timber for fuel or rails and other repairs during his natural life and that he fall no green or growing timber. Wit: Wm. Dill, Isaac Beauchamp. Ackn 27 Feb 1773 (V:p78)

121. 26 Feb 1773 Indenture between William White of Murtherkill Hund, Kent on Delaware, yeoman and Tryphena, his wife and James Craig of town of Dover, taylor. Consideration of twenty five pounds convey parcel of land part of tract called Old Fields Range as conveyed by Thomas Moore to William White on 16 Nov 1769 (Book S, folio 224), laid out for twenty five acres of land. Wit: John Williams, Thomas Moor. Ackn 26 Feb 1773. (V:p79)

122. 26 Feb 1773 Indenture between John Williams oldest son of James Williams late of Mispillion Hund in Kent on Delaware, decd and Henry Whitacre(Whitaker) same place, yeoman. By proceedings of the orphan's court men by appointment for that purpose brought to evaluation and adjudged to be property of John Williams who is now selling part to raise money to satisfy the other heirs. Consideration of two hundred nineteen pounds conveys land beginning at cor of Moses Whitaker's land . . . laid off for one hundred forty six acres as by the draught thereof under hand of David Caldwell, surveyor. Wit: Saml. McCall, George McCall. Ackn 26 Feb 1773. (V:p80)

123. 23 Feb 1773 Indenture between Thomas Nixon of town of Dover, Kent on Delaware, merchant and Moses Jackson of Murtherkill Hund, yeoman. Consideration of two hundred three pounds conveys all parcel of land which by deed on 30 May 1772 (Book V, folio 1) was conveyed by Charles Ridgely, Esq as adm d.b.n. of James Rash unto Thomas Nixon. Said land is called Betty's Folly being part of larger tract called Barn's Chance orig granted to Lewis Johnson situate in Murtherkill Hund laid out for one hundred acres. Wit: Saml. McCall, Mark McCall. Ackn 24 Feb 1773. (V:p80)

124. 10 Feb 1773 Indenture between William Killen of town of Dover, Kent on Delaware, atty at law and Alexander McDonald of Mispillion Hund, yeoman. Consideration of forty three pounds ten shillings conveys parcel of land part of larger tract called Pathalia Plains orig laid out for Alice Peak situate in forest of Mispillion hund and by sundry means and conveyances became property of William Killen. Beginning at a cor oak on ridge of land late possessed by John Williams, decd . . . line of land possessed by Daniel Smith . . . land possessed by Phinehas Banning . . . land called Long Acre . . . tract this day conveyed by William Killen to heirs and representatives of James McDonald, decd, namely Alexander McDonald, Sarah Curry and Mary Fleming . . . with line thereof to the beginning laid off for fifty eight acres and twenty two square perches. Wit: Saml. McCall, Mark McCall. Ackn 24 Feb 1773. (V:p81)

125. 10 Feb 1773 Indenture between William Killen of town of Dover, Kent on Delaware, attorney at law and Alexander McDonald, yeoman; Sarah Curry the wife of Archibald Curry; and Mary Fleming wife of Robert Fleming, all of Mispillion Hund, heirs and representatives of James McDonald, late of said co, decd. William Killen by his bond obligatory to James McDonald on 29 Mar 1755 did covenant to grant all that part of land called Pathalia Plains orig surveyed for Alice Peak and through various conveyances has become property of Killen. McDonald has died intestate leaving issue above named heirs. Consideration of ten pounds, Killen conveys the land beginning at cor of land possessed by Mary and Thomas Williams and also part of the whole tract conveyed by Killen to Alexander McDonald . . . to line of Long Acre belonging to the London Land Company . . . land possessed by William Barker . . . land belonging to London Land Company called Plains of Jericho . . . laid out for two hundred five acres and eighty six squares. To have and to hold one undivided moiety to Alexander McDonald and the other undivided moiety between Sarah Curry and Mary Fleming. Wit: Saml. McCall, Mark McCall. Ackn 24 Feb 1773 (V:p82)

126. 9 Feb 1773 Indenture between William Killen of town of Dover, Kent on Delaware, attorney at law and Charles Ridgely of town and co afsd, Esq.

Consideration of thirty eight pounds thirteen shillings five pence conveys parcel of land situate in Murtherkill Hund called Brother's Portion part of which is the Town land of Dover. Beginning at cor of land of Charles Ridgely part of tract purchased as twenty five acres ... stone in line of Brother's Portion and an ancient tract called Denbigh ... by side of Dover Town land commonly called The Slipe ... laid off for seven and a half acres. Wit: Richd. Smith, William Rhodes. Ackn 26 Feb 1773. (V:p82)

127. 13 Jan 1773 Articles of agreement between Thomas Hill of Kent on Delaware, yeoman and Silas Snow of same place. Hill obliges himself, heirs, extrs and admrs to convey to Snow parcel of land containing one hundred fifty acres whereon Thomas Hill now dwells, bounded by lands of Joseph Hill, Thos. Collins, David Willson and John Moor at such time Snow pays to Hill sum of two hundred fifty pounds part of consideration of four hundred sixty three pounds with interest in manner following. One hundred fifty pounds on 1st Apr next; one hundred pounds on 1st Jan 1774; sixty three pounds on 1st Jan 1775; fifty pounds on 1st Jan 1776; fifty pounds on 1st Jan 1777; fifty pounds on 1st Jan 1778; Thomas Hill to have liberty to live in house to 1st Mar next. Wit: Richd. Sawyer. Ackn 13 Jan 1773. (V:p83)

128. 1 Apr 1772 Indenture between Job Willoughby of Murtherkill Hund, Kent on Delaware, cordwainer and Elizabeth his wife and Charles Ridgely of town of Dover, Esq and practitioner in phisick. Warrant dated 2 June 1746 granted to James Herring said co a survey was made by William Killen, surveyor, on 21 Nov 1752 containing two hundred six acres of land. Beginning at cor of land of Thomas Cox ... cor of Richard White's land ... cor of Abraham Stradley's land ... land of Philemon Cubbage ... of James William's land. By another warrant dated 27 Feb 1739 for James Herring and survey was made by his heirs on 7 Dec 1770 by Samuel McCall, surveyor, bounded as beginning at same cor ... to heirs of Samuel Ross ... road leading from Black Swamp Bridge to Choptank Bridge which road divides Murtherkill and Mispillion Hunds and from Black Swamp Bridge to Maryland line ... land of James Williams ... containing eighty and nine tenths acres. Herring at time of his death left a widow still living (who has married Samuel Willoughby) and left issue four children: Elizabeth, wife of Job Willoughby; George, Curtis and Mary and as oldest son has two shares, Elizabeth Willoughby is vested in one fifth in her own right who along with husband, Job is about to mortgage her part. Condition being before 1st day Apr 1773 the just and full sum of thirty seven pounds be paid.. Wit: Nicholas Vining, Ezel. Cowgill. Elizabeth Willoughby privately examined gave consent. Ackn 24 Feb 1773 (V:p83)

129. 18 Feb 1773 Indenture made between John Wheelton of Little Creek Hund, Kent on Delaware, carpenter and Mary, his wife who is one of daus of Silas Crispin late of said place, bricklayer, decd and Garret Sipple of Murtherkill Hund, gent. Joseph Crispin, taylor, formerly Little Creek Hund on 20 Feb 1723 purchased part of tract called Shrewsbury from Robert Gordon containing one hundred twenty acres situate in afsd hund adj land called Simpson's Choice (Book H, folio 87). Land became property of Silas Crispin, decd, who left four daus: Mary Wheelton, Tabitha, Elizabeth and Sarah and also widow, Tabitha, still living. John Wheelton had resurvey made 15th this inst and find beginning . . . to stone for cor in line of Simpson's Choice (land along side formerly of John Foster now to heirs of John Hunn, Esq. decd) . . . now contains one hundred twenty four and three quarters acres. By warrant of 15 Mar 1745 a survey was made by William Killen, surveyor, on 1 June 1749 for Silas Crispin of ninety acres of marsh and allowance adj first described tract. Consideration of eighty two pounds five shillings convey all undivided one fourth part of two thirds excepting one third laid off to widow, part to be conveyed about thirty six acres. Wit: Saml. McCall, Sarah McCall, Junr. Mary Wheelton privately examined gave consent. Ackn 24 Feb 1773. (V:p85)

130. 27 Feb 1773 Petition of Elizabeth Skidmore extx of will of Samuel Skidmore of Kent on Delaware, decd, sheweth that James Boyer and others obtained judgement and executions agst Thomas Skidmore, late of said co and Thomas Collins, Esq, late sheriff of co by virtue of writs took into execution and disposed at public vendue all right and title of Thomas Skidmore to tract of one hundred seventy one acres to Samuel Skidmore for sum of two hundred sixty pounds which has been paid and Collins has not made deed. Further sheweth that Samuel Skidmore died before conveyance was made and devised the land to his dau, Mary Skldmore. Petitioner prays the court to order present sheriff, John Cook, to execute a deed. Petition being read, court orders John Cook to execute a deed of conveyance. (V:p86)

131. 5 Mar 1773 James Boyer recovered a certain debt of four hundred twenty four pounds also fourty one shillings and three pence damages agst Thomas Skidmore and Thomas Collins, sheriff, was ordered to seize and place in execution one hundred seventy one acres of land which was sold at public vendue to Samuel Skidmore for sum of two hundred sixty pounds, he being highest bidder. Samuel Skidmore died before deed was made but by will on 6 Jan 1771 (Book L, folio 94) devised the land to his dau, Mary Skidmore, dau of Elizabeth Merony. John Cook, present sheriff, conveys all right, title, interest and claim of Thomas Skidmore to land called Bartlets Lot situate in Murtherkill Hund released to him by his bro, Samuel Skidmore in division of real est from their father, Thomas Skidmore, the elder. (Book R, folio 46). Beginning on boundary of Bartlet's Lot . . . on Mill

Branch ... line of John Hines, decd ... containing one hundred seventy one acres. Wit: Caleb Furbee, Geo. Painter. Ackn 5 Mar 1773 (V:p86)

132. 8 Jan 1773 Indenture Tripartite between Caleb Luff of Kent on Delaware, gent; Margaret Rodney of said co, widow; and Nathaniel Luff, now of Philadelphia, yeoman (only son of Caleb Luff). In consideration of sum of five shillings paid by Margaret Rodney to Caleb Luff and for natural love and affection which Caleb Luff hath for Nathaniel, his only son, and other goods causes, etc., Caleb Luff releases and conveys tract of land to Margaret Rodney (excepted which is hereinafter excepted) all tract called Kingston Upon Hull situate on east side of St. Jone's Creek, Dover Hund. Beginning and running with land formerly of Robert Jones's ... land callerd Town Point ... containing four hundred fifty acres and fifty acres of marsh between the land and creek orig granted to John Briggs and Mary Philips by Sir Edmond Andrews, Knight Etc. by patent 14 Aug ____ and by Margaret Rodney by deed 11 Feb 1763 granted to Caleb Luff in fee also parcel of marsh situate on north side of St. Jones's Creek beginning at oak of Town Point ... containing two hundred acres which was deeded by John Williams and Rachel, his wife, on 18 Aug 1753 to Caleb Luff ... excepting and reserving out of the conveyance of these tracts one hundred sixty acres of Kingston Upon Hull sold by George Nowell now decd to sundry persons. Wit: Timothy Caldwell, Will. Killen. Ackn 24 Feb 1773. (V:p88)

133. 1 Feb 1773 Indenture Tripartite between Thomas Summers, Kent on Delaware, husbandman; George Painter said co, gent; and Thomas Peterkin of same co, gent. Witnesseth for docking and barring all estates tail and for settling the parcel of land and in consideration of sum of one hundred sixty pounds paid to Thomas Summers by Thomas Peterkin and by good and common recovery by George Painter, Summers conveys parcel of land beginning in line of land called Fairfield ... cor of land of Michael Cary Aaron ... cor of land of Jonathan Dewese ... Benjamin Rasin's land ... containing one hundred twenty eight acres ... said premises by John Summers, decd, by will on 2 Apr 1770 devised to Mary, his wife, for her lifetime, remainder to Thomas Summers, his son, and Mary on 1 Dec 1771 granted the estate to Thomas, her son. Wit: Samuel Chew, Will. Killen. Ackn 24 Feb 1773. (V:p89)

134. 23 May 1757 I, Samuel Griffith of Kent on Delaware stand firmly bound unto Preston Berry in just sum of three hundred pounds. Samuel Nicholas late of co afsd did by deed of sale convey to Griffith one hundred acres of tract called Manlove Berry and land being mortgaged in the Loan Office and Griffith posted a bond jointly with Preston Berry to Nicholas for near forty pounds. Condition being that Preston Berry discharge afsd bond part to Nicholas and also discharge the land of

the Loan Office then Samuel Griffith will convey with sufficient deed the one hundred acres of land. If Preston Berry discharges only part of the bond and discharges only part of the loan, and not discharge the whole, then Griffith obliges himself to repay to Preston Berry all such part as shall be by them paid then this present obligation to be void. Wit: Joseph Powel, Elizabeth Griffeth. Ackn 27 Feb 1773. (V:p90)

135. 15 May 1772 Indenture between Edward Tilghman the younger now of city of Philadelphia eldest son of Edward Tilghman of Queen Anns Co, Maryland Esq and Elizabeth, his wife, now decd, dau of Samuel Chew formerly of Kent on Delaware Esq and Benjamin Chew of city of Philadelphia, Esq. Samuel Chew about 1744 died instate seized in fee parcel in Duck Creek Hund of about nine hundred eighteen acres called White Hall. In 1748 in partition of est of Samuel Chew, a part was allotted to Elizabeth Tilghman beginning and running to . . . part of tract allotted to his dau, Ann, then wife of Samuel Galloway but since purchased by Benjamin Chew . . . laid out for two hundred forty two acres. Elizabeth Tilghman died intestate leaving three children: Edward, party to these presents; Elizabeth who married Richard Tilghman of Queen Ann's Co, Maryland and died intestate leaving only child called Richard; and Ann. Edward Tilghman the elder in right of his late wife, Elizabeth, had a life estate in the land and surrendered his interest to his son, Edward Tilghman, the younger; and to his dau, Ann; and to grandson Richard Tilghman. Edward the younger secured partition of above tract and other lands of his mother but lands were not sufficient for division and court valued the lands to Edward Tilghman, the younger who was to pay the other heirs a legal share. For consideration of six hundred ninety four pounds conveys two hundred forty two acres of tract White Hall. Will Killen and James Vandyke, Esqrs, apptd attys. Wit: Thos Buckmaster, William Tilghman. Ackn 12 May 1773. (V:p90)

136. 14 May 1773 Indenture between Charles Kimmey of Browns Neck, Mispillion Hund, Kent on Delaware, yeoman and Mary his wife of one part and Johnson Eareckson of Kent Island, Maryland, yeoman. Consideration of ninety pounds conveys parcel of land in Brown's Neck which Thomas Hall formerly conveyed to William Pegg (Book M, folio 20) who on 15 Feb 1770 sold land to Charles Kimmey, (Book S, folio 278) laid out for fifty acres. Wit: Saml. McCall, Mark McCall. Mary Kimmey privately examined gave consent. Ackn 14 May 1773. (V:91)

137. 10 May 1773 Indenture between William Carpenter of St. George's Hund, Newcastle on Delaware and Mary his wife and Powel Cox of Murtherkill Hund, Kent on Delaware, gent. By virtue of warrant made 21st of 12th mo 1681, a survey was made 22d of 2nd mo 1683 to Peter Gronendyke, Esq called Cittinbourn of

four hundred twenty acres situate on north side of Murther Creek. Beginning at cor of Duke of York's Mannor ... confirmed to Peter on 5th day 5th mo 1684. On 13th 1st mo 1690, Peter assigned land to John Hillyard (Book C, folio 73) who in a swap of lands with Mark Manlove, Esq, sought to rectify mistakes in orig patent and survey but great part was omitted and Manlove by deed of gift 9 Aug 1727 (Book I, folio 93/94) conveyed part said to be three hundred acres to his son, William Manlove. Description mentions land of ____ Ringgold who owned part of the tract. William Manlove died intestate leaving issue three children all of age: William, Margaret and Kesiah (who married John Wheelor), who made division assisted by Thomas Clarke, Esq., John Emerson and Waitman Sipple, Junr and releases were passed in 1751. Margaret conveyed her part to bro, William on 12 Aug 1751 (Book O, folio 105). Errors were found in deeds to Thomas Whittington and Daniel Robinson, and from Robinson and Patience, his wife and Whittington jointly to William Carpenter who is vested in the whole land of Mark Manlove, Esq. In consideration of nine hundred pounds William and Mary Carpenter convey all above described three hundred acres. Mary (Molley) Carpenter privately examined gave consent. Wit: William Thomas, Arther Whiteley. Ackn 12 May 1773 (V:p92)

138. 12 May 1773 Indenture between Benjamin Clarke of Dover Hund, Kent on Delaware, yeoman and Daniel Wright Newnam of Little Creek Hund, yeoman. Consideration of forty pounds conveys parcel of land in the fork of Dover Hund lately property of Masculine Clarke, decd, father of Benjamin Clarke. Beginning at cor oak of land late of Charles Williams, decd ... to hickory of Jane Carbine's land ... part sold by David Clarke to Daniel Wright Newnam ... laid out for twenty seven acres three roods fifteen square perches. Wit: Robert Hodgson, Edward Fisher. Ackn 12 May 1773. (V:p93)

139. 15 Feb 1773 Indenture between Andrew Doz of city of Philadelphia, gent and Ezekiel Goddin of Mispillion Hund, Kent on Delaware, yeoman. Survey was made on 22nd day of 12th mo 1685 of four hundred acres of land to George Cullin called Angleton situate in Mispiillion Neck & Hund on or near branch called Fishing Creek. George Cullin on 10 Sept 1697 by deed (Book C, folio 194) granted one hundred acres to James Howel now property of Cornelius Dewees and George Cullin being indebted to John Dubroise, merchant, and being convicted thereof, Thomas Bedwell, then sheriff, together with twelve jurors legally held an inquisition on the other three hundred acres, took same in execution and sold same to John Dubroise by record 11 Apr 1699 (Book C, folio 228) who on 8 Feb 1702 sold the tract to Joseph Pidgion, merchant and also Joseph Pidgion, son and heir of father, Joseph, by deed 24 May 1727 granted same to Lewis Deweese (Book I, folio 220) who in 1739 (Book M, folio 24) granted same to son, Cornelius Dewees

who owned the whole tract. Part became property of Govey Trippet who conveyed same to Isaac King, Junr and also Cornelius Dewees by deed of 11 Feb 1746 (Book N, folio 122) granted all and residue of said tract to Isaac King, Senr, lying northward of Fishing Creek and adj tracts Increase and Richmore and part that Isaac King, Junr bought from Govey Trippet. Isaac King, Senr devised on 15 June 1749 one half to include his mansion dwelling plantation to wife, Ann, and other moiety to son, Isaac King, Junr. who died intestate without any division and indebted to Andrew Doz and other persons, his land was seized in execution and sold to Andrew Doz. Mark McCall, surveyor, settled division lines between Andrew and Ann King on 19 Oct 1772. Doz lately conveyed part to James King now conveys residue to Ezekiel Goddin for consideration of one hundred ten pounds, part of tract Angleton beginning on Parnel's Branch . . . to line of Richmore orig surveyed for Richard Williams . . . to line of Increase orig surveyed for Baptist New Comb . . . laid off for one hundred twenty nine acres one hundred fifty two and a half perches. Saml. McCall and Mark McCall apptd attys. Wit: John Wood, John Morris. Ackn 13 May 1773. (V:p94)

140. 8th Mar 1772 Indenture between Vincent Loockerman the elder of Kent on Delaware, merchant and Molleston Fisher same co, husbandman. Consideration of one hundred thirty pounds conveys tract called Fisher's Delight situate on Murtherkill Creek in Mispillion Hund containing three hundred twenty five acres. Orig surveyed for Adam Fisher, decd father of Molleston Fisher and on 15 Apr last past were granted by Molleston to Vincent Loockerman in fee. Conveyance subject to payment of money due or grow due for pincipal and interest to trustees of General Loan Office on a mortgage made by Molleston Fisher. Wit: Will. Killen, Timothy Jenkins. Ackn 14 May 1773. (V:p95)

141. 9 Feb 1773 Indenture: Whereas by last will of Robert Hall of Little Creek Hund, Kent on Delaware, on 16 Jan 1770 gave authority to Jerusha, his wife, to dispose of his real est for payment of debts. Jerusha has married Thomas Cahoon same place and they advertised for sale two hundred acres of the land with nineteen and three quarter acres of branch and fifty acres of marsh and was sold to Thomas Collins, he being highest bidder for seven hundred five pounds. Thomas Cahoon and Jerusha, his wife, now convey to Thomas Collins for sum of one thousand one hundred five pounds land beginning at stone in line of John Frazier's land . . . laid out for two hundred fourty eight acres and one hundred fourty three perches of fast land and branch cripple, also fifty acres of marsh adj the above. Wit: Charles Cahoon, Thomas Parkison. French Battell or John Pryor apptd to ackn above deed in court. Ackn 13 May 1773. (V:p96)

142. 25 July 1769 Indenture between Samuel Ball of Duck Creek Hund, Kent on

Delaware, merchant and William Ball of city of Philadelphia, province of Penn., silversmith and Edward Skidmore of Kent on Delaware, waggoner. Consideration of fourty pounds now conveys a lott of ground nr the Crossroads on northwest side of new Ballt Street. Beginning at cor of Thomas Wild's lott . . . laid out for three acres of land, part of tract Samuel and William Ball bought of James Green. Nicholas Vandyke apptd atty. Wit: Tho. Brown, John White. Ackn 13 May 1773. (V:p97)

143. 15 Feb 1773 Indenture between above named Edward Skidmore of one part and John Darrach, David Kennedy and James Darrach. Consideration of thirty pounds conveys the above described parcel of land. Nicholas Vandyke apptd atty. Wit: Tho. Brown, Thomas Shaw. Deborah Skidmore, wife of Edward, hereby becomes party and joyns with her husband in the execution of this deed. Wit: Tho. Brown, Grace Hendrickson. Ackn 13 May 1773. (V:p97)

144. 11 Feb 1772 Indenture between James Caldwell, high sheriff of Kent on Delaware and Thomas Buckmaster same place, mariner. Caldwell was directed to expose to sale for benefit of John Pryor, two tracts of land contained in a deed from Benjamin Warren and Elizabeth, his wife, and Alexander Huston and Ann, his wife, to Isaac Killam, decd on 9 Feb 1766 now in possession of Catharine Killam adm of Isaac Killam. Caldwell by virtue of writ exposed the two tracts to public vendue and sold same to Thomas Buckmaster for one hundred ninety pounds, he being highest bidder. Caldwell now conveys the one hundred acres of land part of tract called Whitwells Delight formerly sold by Thomas Skidmore to John Fullerton also another tract laid off for three hundred acres called Mill Neck excepting one hundred acres devised by Stephen Simons to dau, Mary. Wit: Richardd Bassett, Geo. Painter. Ackn 28 May 1773. (V:p98)

145. 12 May 1773 Indenture between Thomas Buckmaster of Kent on Delaware, yeoman and Elizabeth Warren the elder, widow of Benjamin Warren, late of Kent Co, yeoman, and John, Benjamin, Samuel, Zipporah, Mary and Elizabeth Warren, sons and daus of decd. Thomas Buckmaster by obligation made 11 Feb 1772 became bound to Benjamin Warren in sum of five hundred pounds with condition that Buckmaster should convey parcel of land late property of Isaac Killam. Benjamin Warren died intestate before deed was passed, now his above heirs for sum of two hundred fifty pounds paid to Buckmaster receive a conveyance of one hundred acres called Whitwells Delight and also three hundred acres called Mill Neck excepting one hundred acres devised by Stephen Simons to dau, Mary. Wit: Thomas Rodney, Samuel Chew. Ackn 28 May 1773. (V:p99)

146. 22 Feb 1773 Indenture between Peter King of Kent on Delaware, yeoman

and Ann King, his wife and William Dunning, yeoman. Consideration of one hundred ten pounds conveys two hundred sixty one acres and one hundred fifty four perches situate in forest of Murderkill Hund called Grubby Ridge (formerly surveyed for Curtis Evans pursuant to warrant 2nd 6th mo 1746 containing two hundred forty eight acres and allowance). Beginning nr Dunning's fence in a line of the Cave . . . to land called Whortleberry Ridge. Wit: Jacob Morgan, Robert Bostick. Ann King privately examined gave consent. Ackn 26 May 1773. (V:p100)

147. 26 May 1773 Indenture between David Maxwell and Susanna his wife of Kent on Delaware and Joseph Downham, farmer and Ann Wooderson same place. Robert Maxwell had surveyed tract called Maxwell's Adventure containing one hundred eighty seven and a half acres with allowance of six percent on 27 June 1759 in pursuance of warrant 10 May same year and devised to his eldest son, David Maxwell, one moiety to be laid off adj Andrew Caldwells and Richard Downham's land. Consideration of thirty pounds paid by Ann Wooderson David Maxwell conveys ninety three and three quarters acres of the land to Joseph Downham during his natural life with reversion to Ann. Beginning at cor of Andrew Caldwell, Richard Downham and Isabel Craigs lands . . . John Chamber's land. Wit: James Howell, James Scoten, Junr. Susanna Maxwell privately examined gave consent. Ackn 26 May 1773. (V:p101)

148. 12 Jan 1773 Jonathan Rees of Bedford Co and Spring Hill Township in province of Penn. appoints trusty friend, Joseph David, Junr of Little Creek Hund, Kent on Delaware, his atty to appear in court with petition to appoint five freeholders to divide the lands of Timothy Irons late of Kent Co, decd (who was my brother) and should they find the land insufficient to divide, then the court to appoint three freeholders to value same. My atty to accept the land at appraised value and to pay any moiety who shall lawfully claim any part . . . also to take out letters of adm on my brother's estate. Wit: Richd. Smith, William Barns. Ackn: 27 May 1773. (V:p101)

149. 23 July 1772 Indenture between John Harmason late of Kent on Delaware, miller but now of city of Philadelphia, shop keeper and Sarah, his wife and Miers Fisher of same city, atty at law. Consideration of two hundred fifty pounds conveys parcel of land in Mispillion Hund situate on each side of Drawbridge Road. Description mentions land of Joseph Warner . . . land of Thomas Peterkin . . . Covil Tumlins line . . . containing ninety six acres being same land which Edward Fizrandolph and Mary, his wife, by deed 27th 2nd mo 1769 conveyed to John Harmason. Wit: Samuel Fisher, Charles Logan. Sarah Harmason privately examined gave consent. Caesar Rodney and George Read apptd attys. Wit to power of atty: Jacob Rush, Joseph Wharton. Ackn: 11 Aug 1773. (V:p102)

150. 7 Aug 1773 Indenture between John Rash, Junr of Murtherkill Hund, Kent on Delaware, yeoman and Mary, his wife and John Baning of town of Dover, said co, sadler. Consideration of one hundred pounds convey parcel of land in afsd hund called Howel's Lott, same released by Henry Rash to John Rash in division of the land of their father, Samuel Rash, on 23 May 1772. Description mentions Barn's Branch . . . land of William Pearse. Wit: Benjamin Rasin, Samuel Nicholas. Mary Rash privately examined gave consent. Ackn: 10 Aug 1773. (V:p102)

151. 13 Sept 1773 Indenture between John Freeman of Kent on Delaware and Francis Barber of same place. John Freeman by writing obligatory is firmly bound to Francis Barber in sum of two hundred pounds. Condition of payment of one hundred pounds is on demand. In consideration of above debt and for better securing payment thereof conveys parcel of land in Murtherkill Hund the same conveyed by Moses Freeman, father to John, on 5 Aug 1756 (Book O, folio 346). Description mentions Horse Pen Swamp . . . line of John Willson . . . laid out for one hundred twenty three acres. Wit: Jacob Stout, James Raymond. (no date of ackn given) (V:p102)

152. 12 Aug 1773 Indenture between James Gordon of Murtherkill Hund, Kent on Delaware, taylor and Elijah Sipple of same hund. Consideration of one hundred pounds conveys parcel of land in Mispillion Hund where Elijah Sipple doth live being tract conveyed by Thomas Bowman as adm of William Merchant, decd to Gordon on 11 Aug 1768 (Book S, folio 43). Beginning at a cor division post . . . part sold by Gordon to Christopher Sipple, not yet conveyed . . . also in line of Solomon Edmondson's land called The Breeches . . . cor of land formerly conveyed by Anthony Rawlings to William Manlove now claimed by Sampson Lewis . . . cor of land of William Pegg now of Charles Kimmey . . . laid out for seventy nine acres and one hunded thirty five perches. Wit: George McCall, Jonathan Sipple. Ackn: 12 Aug 1773. (V:p103)

153. 11 Aug 1773 Indenture between William Hudson of Mispillion Hund, Kent on Delaware, yeoman and Elizabeth, his wife and Isaac Lowber same hund & co, yeoman. Dispute has arisen and subsisted between John Robinson and Henry Molleston, both decd, and still subsists between William Hudson (in right of John Robinson) and heirs of Henry Molleston respecting title to certain marshes between Murther Creek and Baucumbrig Creek adj lands of said parties to these presents. Description mentions land of late Henry Molleston now of Jonathan Molleston . . . a marsh surveyed for John Betts in 1694 by William Morton, surveyor for three hundred acres now belonging to Jonathan Molleston . . . laid out for sixty acres and usual allowance, and by the Commissioners of Property adjudged to William Hudson in right of John Robinson. Consideraton of sixty

pounds now conveys said marsh to Isaac Lowber. Wit: Mark McCall, George McCall. Elizabeth Hudson privately examined gave consent. Ackn: 11 Aug 1773. (V:p103)

154. 10 Aug 1773 Indenture between Elizabeth Lewis of city of Philadelphia in Penn, Robert Mcmullan, John McMullan of Newcastle on Delaware, taylors, all of one part and Vincent Loockerman the elder of Kent on Delaware, merchant. Whereas a tract of land was conveyed by William Buckwell to John Register who conveyed same to Nicholas Nixon who conveyed the land to William McDonnald who died with will devising the tract to his five sons: William, Bryan, Jeremiah, Joseph and Thomas McDonnald to be divided into six parts, two shares to William. Bryan died intestate without issue. William and Jeremiah sold to Vincent Loockerman. Joseph had issue of three sons: William, Joseph and Jeremiah. William died a minor without issue and Joseph and Jeremiah sold to Loockerman. Thomas died intestate without issue whereby two thirds of the land descended to Joseph, the elder. Afsd Elizabeth, dau of William, the elder is entitled to some part and Robert and John McMullan, two son of MaryMcMullan, also dau of William, the elder is also entitled. Beginning . . . line of land formerly belonging to Daniel Rodney . . . containing two hundred ten acres called Register's Range. Other part begins at cor of Brinckle's Range . . . containing one hundred five acres. Consideration of ten pounds paid by Loockerman. Wit: Jno. Smithers, John Rash. Ackn: 10 Aug 1773. (V:p104)

155. 30 July 1773 Indenture between Henry Rash of Kent on Delaware, yeoman and Mary, his wife, and William Pearse same place, yeoman. Consideration of one hundred twenty pounds conveys parcel of land called Howell's Lott, a part of the land of Samuel Rash, father of Henry and his bro, John Rash. Division was made through releases to each other but seven acres released by John to bro, Henry, is in this grant left out as it has been found to be part of William Bogg's estate laid off to Joseph Boggs. Description mentions division line between the bros and also a tract called Dundee . . . laid off for eighty nine and one half acres. Samuel McCall and Mark McCall apptd attys. Wit: Thos. Hanson, Ann Gaskin. Mary Rash privately examined gave consent. Ackn 10 Aug 1773. (V:p104)

156. 13 Mar 1773 Indenture between Caesar Rodney of town of Dover, Esq. and James Train of Murtherkill Hund, both of Kent on Delaware and Train Caldwell same place, yeoman. Roger Train formerly of said co was sieized in tract of land called Rhode's Forest found to contain in part two hundred fifty five and a half acres, having six children: Hamilton (father to above James), James, Sarah, Mary, Esther and Bathsheba and made will 9 Nov 1736 devising all lands to two sons, Hamilton and James equally omitting heirs and assigns so devise was good only for their natural lives. James died first and Hamilton discovering the intent of the will

purchased shares from sisters, Sarah and Mary both then living (Esther and Bathsheba being decd) he then became vested in their two sevenths part and also their one fourth part of the two sevenths of Esther and Bathsheba together with two sevenths as oldest son of father, Roger Train, together with one fourth part of Esther and Bathsheba brought eleven fourteenth parts of the whole land to be property of the heirs after Hamilton's decease and the other three fourteenths parts the property of James and his heirs as though Roger Train had died intestate. Hamilton Train has since decd leaving James, only child, first above named and James Train, son of Roger, is indebted to Caesar Rodney as trustee of General Loan Office who had execution made by sheriff to Caesar Rodney by deed 4th Aug last past who with James Train has entered into bond of arbitration to be made between them by William Killen, Esq, Paris Chipman and Samuel McCall and Train Caldwell has purchased part allotted to Caesar Rodney who with James Train joins in deed to the purchaser. Consideration of one hundred eight pounds paid to Caesar Rodney and five shillings paid to James Train for fulfilling his contract. Beginning at a division stone for the tract Gainsborough now belonging to Warner Mifflin . . . to main Tidbury Branch . . . land formerly of George Craigs now Paris Chipmans . . . laid out for ninety acres. Together with all and singular improvements, etc., excepting a barn which James Train shall remove to his own land and what winter grain may be thereon he shall peaceably save and carry away. Wit: Sarah Mcall, Sarah McCall, Junr. Ackn 10 Aug 1773. (V:p105)

157. 20 Mar 1773 Indenture between Joseph Rogers of Kent on Delaware, yeoman and Catherine, his wife and Thomas Hanson same co, Esq. By virtue of warrant and survey a grant was made for John Newell on 28th 7th mo 1683 called The Reserve situate on north side of Dover River on southeast side of Isaac Webb's Branch in Murtherkill Hund laid out for four hundred acres. John Vining, Esq, by deed acquired the land and in his will of 13 Nov 1770 ordered all lands sold by his extrs, Benjamin Chew, Charles Ridgely and Benjamin Wynkoop who sold five hundred fifty one and a half acres of The Reserve to Joseph Rogers., who with his wife, Catherine, for sum of six hundred pounds conveys a part of afsd tract. Description mentions land called Brecnock . . . land called Great Geneva . . . laid off for two hundred acres reserving crop of wheat growing on premises with free ingress and egress to cut, reap, save and stack and to carry away at some reasonable time of the year. Wit: John Pryor, James Fitzgarril. Catherine Rogers privately examined gave consent. Ackn 10 Aug 1773. (V:p105)

158. 10 Feb 1773 Indfenture between Jonathan Pleasontine of St. Jone's alias Dover Hund, Kent on Delaware, yeoman and Amey his wife of one part and Coe Gordon same place, yeoman. A patent under Great Seal of province of Pennsylvania by Richard Hill, Isaac Norris and James Logan, commissioners, on

20 Sept 1715 to John French for tract situate in Murtherkill Hund laid out for five hundred eighty eight acres. French on 10 Sept 1717 granted the land to John Brinckloe (Liber E, folio 304) who by will on 10 May 1720 devised to Mary and Letitia Crawford the forest tract purchased from Colonel John French of Newcastle on Delaware, commonly called The Cave. Mary Crawford married John Pleasontine, father of Jonathan and Letitia married Daniel Stevens. Mary and John Pleasontine and Daniel Stevens divided the land who with wife Letitia, deeded one moiety to Mary and John on 13 Feb 1744 containing two hundred ninety four acres (Book N, folio 58). Jonathan Pleasontine is only child and surviving heir of Mary and John and conveys the moiety in consideration of five hundred pounds. Wit: Hanah Gordon, John Chew. Ruhamay (Amey) Pleasonton examined privately gave consent. Ackn: 11 Aug 1773. (V:p106)

159. 5 Aug 1773 Indenture between Daniel Bozeman of Kent on Delaware, yeoman and Sinah, his wife and Joseph Standley of same co, yeoman. Consideration of one hundred pounds conveys parcel of land on south side of Marshy Hope the dwelling plantation of Bozeman, twelve and three quarters acres excepted which were sold to Francis Jester. Description mentions Mark Marrett's line . . . laid out for one hundred thirty six and one quarter acres. Also conveys tract adj old tract called Good Luck beginning in line of Francis Jester's land . . . to Mager Henderson's land . . . to Widow Staten's land . . . to John Smith's land. Wit: Zadock Crapper, Thos. Sheriff. Sinah Bozman privately examined gave consent. Ackn: 11 Aug 1773. (V:p107)

160. 9 Aug 1773 Indenture between William Hudson of Mispillion Hund, Kent on Delaware, yeoman and Elizabeth, his wife and Henry Killen, same hund, yeoman. Consideration of nine hundred fifty pounds fifteen shillings conveys all described parcels of land and marsh in Mispillion Neck, part of real est formerly of John Robinson, decd, which became property of Jonathan Robinson, afterwards sold but not conveyed by Jonathan to Daniel Robinson, father to Elizabeth Hudson. Premises were sold by sheriff to William Hudson at suit of Jonathan Robinson to satisfy him the purchase money for which he sold the premises to Daniel Robinson but also to fulfill a deed of confirmation to William Hudson. Beginning at a cor of land of William Molleston . . . post in line of Robert Winsmore to Henry Molleston . . . land of the heirs of John Hall . . . land late conveyed by William Hudson to Isaac Lowber . . . being both parts of tract called Bett's Purchase . . . containing two hundred thirty five acres and one hundred eleven square perches of land and marsh being all part of Bett's Purchase except twenty two acres and seventy five square perches of marsh on Baucombrig Creek surveyed for William Hudson in right of John Robinson by Samuel McCall, surveyor, to settle a dispute between John Robinson and Henry Molleston. Also a part of granted premises

being a tract of salt marsh also surveyed for William Hudson containing four hundred two acres and one hundred forty five perches of land and marsh. Wit: Mark McCall, George McCall. Elizabeth Hudson privately examined gave consent. Ackn: 12 Aug 1773. (V:p107)

161. 9 Aug 1773 Indentue between Henry Killen of Mispillion Hund, Kent on Delaware, yeoman and Susannah, his wife, and William Hudson, same place, yeoman. Consideration of five hundred fifty pounds fifteen shillings conveys parcel of land late devised by Robert Killen, Esq. to son, Henry Killen. Beginning at cor oak of land late of James McNatt . . . land surveyed for Aaron Stuart . . . land surveyed for heirs of William Berry . . . land of Philis Meredith . . . land of heirs of George Fleming . . . containing three hundred five acres and one hundred sixty one square perches. Wit: Mark McCall, George McCall. Susannah Killen privately examined gave consent. Ackn 12 Aug 1773. (V:p108)

162. 12 Aug 1773 Indenture between Obediah Voshell of Kent on Delaware, farmer and Elizabeth, his wife and Jonathan Neall same co, house carpenter and joyner. John Brown was seized in tract of land in fee called The Downs. By virtue of his will he devised to son, John Brown, one hundred fifty acres lying at west end of tractl; and to his wife, Elizabeth Brown, one hundred acres lying at east end of tract. Residue to be divided among his daus: Elizabeth, wife of Obediah Voshell, Junr; Rachel, wife of Govey Trippit and Mary Brown according to division made by William Killen, James Caldwell and Waitman Sipple on 20 and 21 Apr 1759 circumscribed in following manner. Beginning at a cor stake between The Downs and tract called Ousby orig surveyed for Thomas Heathord . . . land laid off to Rachel Trippit . . . with her land that Jonathan Neall has lately purchased . . . containing one hundred acres. Consideration of two hundred pounds Obediah Voshell, the elder and Elizabeth, his wife, convey her share of the tract as devised to her by her former husband, John Brown. Wit: Simon Willson, John Comegys. Elizabeth Voshell privately examined gave consent. Ackn 12 Aug 1773. (V:p108)

163. 12 Aug 1773 Indenture between Michael Offley of Appoquinimink Hund, in Newcastle on Delaware, husbandman and David Lewis of Duck Creek Hund, Kent on Delaware, husbandman. Consideration of five hundred thirty pounds conveys parcel of land in Duck Creek Hund, Kent Co beginning at cor of Gravesend and Shurmer's Survey in the Manner line on rd from Duck Creek to Georgetown nr Molleston Curry's tan yard . . . from the western door of William Griffin's house . . . to two acres condemned for William Griffin's mill . . . line of Matthew Griffin's land . . . land of Daniel David . . . containing two hundred sixty three acres and thirty seven perches. Wit: William Rees, David Thompson. Ackn 12 Aug 1773. (V:p109)

164. 11 Aug 1773 Petition of Michael Offley of Newcastle on Delaware sheweth that he purchased from James Wells a plantation in Duck Creek Hund, Kent on Delaware, adj land of Molleston Curry and others, one other tract adj William Griffin and others containing forty acres, and all the estate and interest of William Pugh in land and marsh on side of road leading from Thorofare to Duck Creek Town except fifty acres thereof, for sum of five hundred and twenty pounds, all the late property of William Pugh, decd intestate and the petitioner was given letters of admin and has paid James Wells the consideration of one hundred fifty two pounds twelve shillings ten pence and deed has not been made. He prays the court to authorize John Cook, present sheriff, to execute the deed. (signed) Michael Offley. The petition being read to the court and considered is granted whereupon court ordered John Cook, Esq to execute the deed. (V:p109)

165. 12 Aug 1773 Indenture William McKean, the younger had common recovery in court of Common Pleas agst William Pugh, late of Appaquinimink Hund, Newcastle on Delaware, a debt of eighty pounds fifteen shillings six pence as sixty two shillings ten pence as damages. The estate was insufficient to pay the debt and a writ was issued to James Wells, then sheriff, to seize the lands and place in to execution according to the writ. Pugh's land being in Duck Creek Hund, Kent on Delaware, adj lands of Molleston Curry and others, also another tract in same place adj William Griffin and others, containing forty two acres and also all estate and interest of William Pugh in the land and marsh belonging to his father, Roger Pugh, decd, except fifty acres devised by Roger Pugh to heirs of James Egbert, decd. The messuage and two tracts were exposed to sale and sold to Michael Offley for five hundred twenty pounds, he being the highest bidder, he having paid James Wells the sum of one hundred fifty two pounds twelve shillings ten pence and deed not passed. The court authorized John Cook, present sheriff to execute the deed for two hundred sixty three acres and thirty seven perches of land. (see above petition for description of land, etc.). Wit: Geo. Painter, Jsnoorr (?). Ackn 12 Aug 1773. (V:p110)

111. 28 Dec 1772 Power of Attorney: I, John Poole of Rowan County, province of North Carolina, planter, nominate, constitute, ordain and appoint my trusty friend, Thomas Blackshare of Kent County in province of Pennsylvania, planter my true and lawful attorney to ask, demand, recover and receive for me and in my name and to my use and behoof giving and granting by these presents to my said attorney my sold and full power and authority . . . (signed) John Poole. Wit: Edwd. Hughes, Train Caldwell. Ackn 12 Aug 1773 (V:p110)

112. 12 Aug 1773 Bond: John Revel of Mispillion Hund, Kent on Delaware, is firmly bound to Southy Brincklee of same place yet a minor (son of Southy

Brincklee late decd by being drowned) in the sum of two hundred forty eight pounds one shilling three pence to be paid. Amelia, wife of the above bounden John Revel is a daughter of Doctor Spencer Cole formerly of Mispillion Hund who married Sarah Brincklee and by survey became vested in land and marsh on north side of Murther Creek and died leaving one son and four daus: Spencer, Penelope, Sarah, Mary and Amelia Revel. Spencer Cole, Junr died in his minority without issue and the four sisters became vested in the whole and also became jointly vested in part of estate of John Brincklee late decd. Penelope married Reynear Williams; Sarah married John Peterkin; Mary married Joshua Clarke and Amelia married first Southy Brincklee who drowned and had son, Southy Brincklee, the minor, and has married John Revel and desirous that her son inherit one half value of her one fourth part after decease of John Revel. All parties have agreed to valuation which is equal to sum in above obligation. Revel is entitled during his lifetime and after his decease, one half or one hundred twenty four pounds seven pence should be paid to Southy Brincklee, minor. Wit: Joshua Clark, John Furchas. Ackn 25 Aug 1773. (V:p111)

113. 25 Aug 1773 Indenture between Robert Hodgson of Murtherkill Hund, Kent on Delaware, yeoman and Priscilla, his wife and William Kirkley same place, yeoman. Consideration of one hundred pounds conveys small parcel of ground in forest in hund afsd part of tract called Wedmore formerly property of James Bedwell who conveyed same to Hodgson laid out for three acres. Wit: Jonathan Willson, Mark McCall. Priscilla Hodgson privately examined gave consent. Ackn 24 Aug 1773. (V:p111)

114. 13 Aug 1773 Indenture between Thomas Collins of Kent on Delaware and Thomas Muncy same place, miller. Consideration of three hundred twenty five pounds conveys tract, mill and plantation lying in Mispillion Hund. Beginning at mouth of Brown's Branch . . . intersects Manlove's Branch . . . containing one hundred thirty(sic) five and three quarter acres with the mill and condemned land thereto belonging laid out for two acres condemned for use of Richard Brinckle's mill 6 Feb 1746. Wit: John Brinckle, Thos. Skillington. Ackn 13 Aug 1773. (V:p111)

115. 24 Aug 1773 Indenture between Jonathan Emerson of Murtherkill Hund, Kent on Delaware, Esq and John Dill same place, yeoman. Consideration of the rents and covenants hereinafter mentioned and reserved on part of John Dill to be paid and performed and sum of five shillings to Emerson who has sold two lotts in town of Frederica at head of Murtherkill, Nos. 27 & 28. Yielding and paying to Emerson yearly on the 29th day 9th mo sum of three pounds - first payment to be made on 29th Sept next and if in arrears, Emerson may proceed by law to recover

the rent. Wit: David Caldwell, George Mellechop. Ackn 27 Aug 1773. (V:p112)

116. 24 Aug 1773 Indenture between James Thomas, John Murphey and Comfort his wife of Kent on Delaware and Richard Quinnally of Dorchester Co in Maryland and Mary his wife of one part and Jonathan Morgan of Kent Co. By warrant in 1743 a survey was made for Daniel Thomas on 2nd Apr 1746 for tract of land in Mispillion Hund containing one hundred ninety eight and one quarter acres with usual allowance adj land said to belong to James Anderson, Robert Smith and other land called Bright's Glade. Daniel Thomas died leaving issue among whom were James Thomas, Comfort and Mary to whom part descended. Consideration of fifty pounds convey the undivided part of land afsd described. Wit: Daniel Benson, James Nutter. Ackn 26 Aug 1773. (V:p112)

117. 30 Oct 1773 Appointment: To Caesar Rodney of Kent on Delaware, Esq. Know that reposing special trust and confidence in your loyalty, integrity and ability, we have assigned and appointed . . . Caesar Rodney to be second justice of our Supreme Court to be held for our said government . . . in testimony thereof we have caused these our letters to be made patent. Witness: John Penn, Esq., Governor and Commander in chief of counties abovesaid and province of Pennsylvania. A true copy test. (V:p112)

118. 14 June 1773 Indenture between Benajmin Chew of city of Philadelphia, Esq; Charles Ridgely of Kent on Delaware, Esq., and Benjamin Wynkoop, of city afsd, merchant, extrs named in last will of John Vining, late of Kent Co, decd, Esq. one one part and John Pennell said co of Kent, miller. John Vining in his lifetime was seized in divers lands tenements and hereditaments in province of Pennsylvania, lower counties of Delaware and East and West Jersey whereas the water mills and parcels of land hereinafter mentioned are part and being so seized authorized his extrs to sell same. Consideration of twelve hundred fifty pounds convey all that water corn mill and saw mill and forty seven and three quarter acres situate on both sides of Isacc's Branch in Murtherkill Hund being part of two tracts called Shoemakers Hall and The Reserve. Beginning at cor of Joseph Rogers land . . . to stake in Kings Road . . . cor of land late of Robert Reynolds . . . always reserving out of the conveyance of this grant and all future owners, occupiers or possessors of all that part of The Reserve lying or being below the Kings Road afsd two fit and convenient places for horses and cattle to be lead or driven to Isaac's Branch to drink and other such uses. Wit: Thomas Candby, William Tilghman, George McCall, Will Killen. Ackn 25 Aug 1773. (V:p113)

119. 27 Aug 1773 Petition of Henry Stevens sheweth that by virtue of writ of venditione exponas to James Wells, then sheriff of Kent on Delaware, at suit of

Richard and Peter Footman, merchants of city of Philadelphia, property of Peter Stout, decd, was exposed to public sale and petitioner became highest bidder, conveyance has not been made. Pray the court may direct John Cook, present sheriff, to execute a deed of conveyance. (signed) Henry Stevens. Petition being read to the court, considered and is granted and John Cook is ordered to do so. (V:p114)

120. 13 Aug 1773 Indenture between John Cook, high sheriff of Kent on Delaware, Esq and Henry Stevens of Little Creek Neck & Hund. Whereas John Hall, formerly of afsd co was seized in his lifetime of sundry parcels of land, vizt. One called Willson's Choice; one other part of Betts Endeavor; one other part of Chippon Norton; one other part of land called Brubshaw or Brooksbay; one other part of Willing Brook; also parcel lying between Brook's Bay and Chippon Norton and also parcel of salt marsh between the Bayside and part of said lands. Hall in will dated 31 Oct 1732 (Book H, folio 44) devised one third part of his estate after payment of debts to his wife, Letitia Hall and remaining two thirds parts equally among his five children: Hannah, Ellioner, John, Robert and Letitia Hall. Ellioner and John Hall died intestate without issue and remaining bro and sisters became vested in the decd two fifths part. Hannah Hall married Robert Bellach and had issue only son, John Bellach. Letitia Hall married John Bell of Dover then shop joiner, and Robert Hall, John Bell and Letitia, his wife, procured a writ of partition agst John Bellach. The sheriff partitioned the land and allotted part to John Bellach beginning at cor of land of Stokely Sturgis . . . cor of land late of James Trail . . . cor of land of Charles Hillyard in right of a conveyance by John Hall to his dau, Elizabeth, wife of Charles Hillyard . . . laid out for three hundred five acres. And also the marsh situate on Green's Creek . . . with line of marsh late of Daniel Needham . . . containing forty two acres. John Bellach by deed 15 Dec 1763 (Book Q, folio 170) conveyed to Peter Stout all of the three hundred five acres of land and also forty two acres of marsh excepting fifty two acres Bellach formerly conveyed to Charles Hillyard and also excepting ten acres of tract to adjoin Stokely Sturgis and land of James Trail, the two parcels containing sixty two acres so in fact that only two hundred forty three acres besides the forty two of marsh were deeded to Stout who by writing obligatory for part of the consideration money to Bellach who assigned same to Thomas Parke then of town of Dover. Also Peter Stout was indebted to William Plumbstead by bond which remained unpaid. Stout died intestate and wife, Rebecca married with Jabez Jenkins and Thomas Parke also died intestate and his widow, Ann Parke by letters of admin transferred the said obligation to Richard and Peter Footman who with extr of estate of William Plumbstead, vizt: Mary Plumbstead, Archibald McCall and Judah Foulk secured judgments agst est of Peter Stout then in hands of Jabez Jenkins and his wife, Rebecca, directing the sheriff to levy a debt of one thousand three hundred pounds

and three pounds one shilling eleven pence damages. Estate was not sufficient to pay the debt and James Wells, sheriff, was ordered to place into execution and expose to public sale the lands of John Bellach. James Stevens being highest bidder purchased the property for sum of seven hundred and fifty pounds but no deed of conveyance was made, now by order of court, John Cook, present sheriff conveys the land as described afsd. Wit: Saml. McCall, Thos. Hickey. Ackn 27 Aug 1773. (V:p114)

121. 23 Aug 1773 Indenture between William Powel of Murtherkill Hund, Kent on Delaware, yeoman and Martha his wife and John Boggs of same place, cordwainer. A tract called Long Reach situate on Isaac Webb's Branch, part formerly property of Mark Bardon; who by will devised part to John Bryan bounded as follows: Beginning at ancient cor white oak standing in mill pond of Isaiah Wharton . . . cor of land of James Gardner formerly of Robert French . . . across the land of John Boggs . . . land of Mark Cowdratt . . . containing seventy four and a half acres. John Bryan died without issue, land became property of remaining heirs of Mark Bardon and Mark Harper petitioned court for a division which could not be made and was valued to William Powel as an heir who with his wife, Martha, for consideration of one hundred fifty pounds conveys the tract to John Boggs. Wit: William Owen, Saml. McCall. Martha Powel privately examined gave consent. Ackn 25 Aug 1773. (V:p115)

122. 27 Aug 1773 Indenture between Benjamin Rasin of Kent on Delaware, yeoman and Rachel, his wife of first part; Jonathan Cullen of same co, husbandman and Anne his wife only dau of Benjamin Rasin, of second part and Zadock Crapper same co, Esq. of third part. Consideration of ten pounds paid to Rasin by Cullen and also for five shillings paid by Zadock Crapper to Benjamin Rasin who with wife, Rachel convey to Crapper all parcels of land situate in Mispillion Hund, Kent Co adj land of Edward Fitzrandolph, Michael Carey Aaron, Cashena Candy and Thomas Bowman containing one hundred twenty two acres also all other parcel of land adj first parcel containing sixty six acres and one hundred forty seven square perches. And also other parcel adj first described tract and land of Michael Carey Aaron, containing one hundred fifty acres. The first two tracts of land described afsd were by Benjamin Rasin and Rachel, his late wife, by deed 23 Nov 1770 were conveyed to John Tucker who with his wife, Margaret, by deed same day and year last reconveyed the same to Benjamin Rasin. The parcel of one hundred fifty acres was by Cashena Candy and Susanna, his wife, by deed 22nd day 2nd mo 1771 to Benjamin Rasin. For use of Benjamin Rasin for term of his natural life and after the decease of Benjamin Rasin to Jonathan Cullen and Anne, his wife for and during their joint life and to the use of the survivor and after the death of such survivor to the heirs of the body of Anne Cullen, then to the use and behoof of the

right heirs and assigns of Benjamin Rasin. Benjamin Rasin for himself and Rachel, his wife, agree with Zadock Crapper and his heirs in manner and form following, that is to say Benjamin Rasin and Rachel, his wife, and any other person or persons having claim, etc, shall and will from time to time upon request of Zadock Crapper execute and suffer or cause to be made reasonable acts for the better and more perfect assurances and conveyances in the law. Wit: Phillip Barratt, Matthias Davis. Rachel Rasin privately examined gave consent. Ackn 27 Aug 1773. (V:p115)

123. 16 Nov 1772 Indenture between Reynear Williams of Kent on Delaware, doctor in physick and Ann his wife and Joshua Clark same place, yeoman. Consideration of one hundred twenty seven pounds six shillings eleven pence half penny conveys one hundred twenty two acres and seventy two perches of land strict measure situate in Mispillion Hund westernmost part of tract called Bridge Town. Beginning on the side of the Improvement Branch . . . cor of Isaac Mason's land. Wit: John Clark, Reynear Williams, Senr. Anne Williams privately examined gave consent. Petition of 25 Aug 1773 made by Joshua Clark sheweth that Reynear Williams the younger of Sussex Co on Delaware and Ann, his wife, by deed dated 16 Nov 1772 conveyed a parcel of land to your petitioner who has paid the consideration money, but Reynear Williams never acknowledged said deed and is now dead. Petitioner prays the court to authorize the extrs to acknowledge same. The within petition being read to the court and considered is granted and ordered that Ann Williams and Littleton Townsend, extrs of Reynear Williams, Junr, acknowledge in open court the conveyance. Ackn 25 Aug 1773. (V:p116)

124. 25 Aug 1773 Petition of Martha Griffin, adm of goods and chattles, etc. of Samuel Griffith late of Kent Co, decd, most humbly sheweth Samuel Griffith, her husband,   did bind himself in a bond in sum of three hundred pounds on 3 May 1757 to Preston Berry for conveyance of one hundred acres of land. Griffith is since dead and no conveyance has been made. Petitioner prays court to grant permission to execute a deed for the land in discharge of the bond. (signed) Martha Griffeth, adm. Petition being read to the cour and considered is thereupon granted. (V:p117)

125. 25 Aug 1773 Indenture between Martha Griffeth of Kent on Delaware, adms of Samuel Griffeth, late of said co, who died intestate, and Preston Berry same co, inholder. Samuel Griffeth and Preston Berry by writing obligatory on 12 May 1757 bound themselves to Samuel Nicholas for payment of thirty nine pounds one shilling ten pence for conveyance of one hundred acres of land. Nicholas by deed 12 May 1757 (Book P, folio 10) granted to Griffeth his former dwelling plantation which Nicholas purchased from John Virdin, Junr situate on south side of Bishop's

Branch called Manlove's Berry. Samuel Griffeth on 23 May 1757 did bind himself to Preston Berry under penalty of three hundred pounds condition being that if Preston Berry should discharge first above mentioned bond to Nicholas and clear out the one hundred acres, then Griffeth would make over and convey the one hundred acres of land. Griffeth is since dead and no conveyance has been made Preston Berry has fully discharged the said bond and loan office afsd now Martha Griffeth by authority of the court conveys the land. Description mentions Preston Berry's land . . . land of William Rhodes . . . and land of John Virdin. Wit: Saml. McCall, Joseph Meredith. Ackn 25 Aug 1773. (V:p117)

126. 10 Aug 1773 Indenture between Andrew Jamison of Duck Creek Hund, Kent on Delaware, farmer and Alexander Jamison same place, farmer. Consideration of two hundred pounds Andrew and Mary, his wife, convey plantation in possession of Alexander Jamison situate in hund and co afsd. Beginning at an oak of John Dawson's land . . . of Henry Moore's land . . . land claimed by James Steel . . . in line of Pearmain's Choice . . . cor of John Graydon's now William Cahoon's land . . . land called Christiana . . . to John Joy's land . . . containing one hundred ninety four acres. Wit: Finwick Fisher, Allen McLeane. Mary Jamison privately examined gave consent. Ackn 25 Aug 1773 (V:p118)

127. 24 Aug 1773 Indenture between James Voshall of forest of Murtherkill Hund, Kent on Delaware, yeoman and Maryanne, his wife and John Rash, Junr, same place, son in law to James Voshall. Consideration of fifty pounds convey parcel of land in forest of Murtherkill Hund on which Voshall does dwell which he purchased from Thomas Irons, Esq. Beginning at cor oak of John Freeman's . . . of land formerly of Thomas Morris . . . laid out for fifty acres. Wit: Willm McMin, Saml. McCall. Mary Anne Voshall privately examined gave consent. Ackn 24 Aug 1773. (V:p118)

128. 26 Aug 1773 Indenture between Anne Sipple of Mispillion Hund, Kent on Delaware, widow of Christopher Sipple, late decd, and James Gordon of same place, taylor. James Gordon on 13 Oct 1770 entered into an alienation bond to Christopher Sipple for conveyance of tract of land in Mispillion Hund in Brown's Neck adj lands of William Pegg and Jonathan Sipple said to contain one hundred acres deemed to be part of Longford but is found to be part of Ancaster and is a parrt of same land James Gordon purchased from Thomas Bowman admr of est of William Marchant. No deed was ever made to Christopher Sipple nevertheless, Anne Sipple by order of the court sold the land to pay debts to James Gordon for fifty two pounds and now makes conveyance of same. Wit: Geo. Painter, Mark McCall. Ackn 26 Aug 1773 (V:p118)

129. 25 Aug 1773 Indenture between William Pickrell and Ann, his wife of Mispillion Hund, Kent on Delaware, yeoman and Peter Calloway same place, yeoman. Consideration of one hundred forty pounds conveys tract of land in same hund afsd containing ninety eight acres. Wit: John Banning, George Saxton. Ann Pickrell privately examined gave consent. Ackn 25 Aug 1773. (V:p119)

130. 26 Aug 1773 Indenture between Warner Mifflin of Kent on Delaware, Esq, admin of goods and chattles of John Jackson late of said co decd, husbandman and Daniel James, yeoman. John Jackson was seized in part of tract called The Plains situate in Murtherkill Hund. Beginning and with the land late of Reverend George Gillespie . . . in Rutty's old field . . . containing seventy five acres. John Jackson's est was insufficient to pay several large debts and Mifflin by order of orphan's court exposed the land at public vendue and sold same to Daniel James for consideration of eighty five pounds six pence. Wit: Caleb Furbee, Henry Stevens. Ackn 26 Aug 1773 (V:p119)

131. 12 Aug 1773 Indenture between Reynear Williams of Mispillion Hund, Kent on Delaware, yeoman and Penelope, his wife; John Revel of same place, yeoman and Amelia, his wife; John Peterkin of city of Philadelphia, taylor and Sarah, his wife, all of one part and Joshua Clark same hund and co, yeoman. A survey made 12 Jan 1680 by Richard Noble for Thomas Skidmore for land called Richman's Worth situate in hund and co afsd said to contain four hundred acres of fast land. A part of tract by sundry conveyances has become property of John Hammett long decd. During his lifetime a survey was made on small tract of vacant land thereto adj and two tracts became property of Dr. Spencer Cole, decd, who made survey on small piece of vacant land of twenty seven and three quarter acres on 18 May 1749 which adj above two tracts. Dr. Cole died leaving issue: Penelope Williams, Sarah Peterkin, Amelia Revel and Mary wife of Joshua Clark and also one son named Spencer, to whom all the lands were devised, is now decd without issue leaving his sisters sole heirs. An accurate survey late made by Mark McCall at direction of Samuel McCall, surveyor. Beginning at mouth of Cole's Ditch . . . with marsh surveyed for Daniel Robinson now property of heirs of William Masten . . . to land surveyed for Daniel Durham now of Winlock Hall . . . land called Wadford now of heirs of William Walker orig surveyed for Thomas Groves . . . laid out for three hundred seven acres and twenty two square perches. The above named heirs now convey their three fourth parts of described tracts to Joshua Clark for consideration of four hundred sixty six pounds thirteen shillings nine pence. Wit: John Clarke, John Furchas. Penelope Williams, Sarah Peterkin and Amelia Revel privately examined gave their consent. Ackn 12 Aug 1773. (V:p120)

132. 30 Oct 1773 Appointment: To Samuel Chew of Kent on Delaware, Esq.,

know that reposing special trust and confidence in your loyalty, integrity and ability, we have assigned and appointed and by these presents appoint you third justice of our Supreme Court. Witness: John Penn, Esq, Governor and Commander in Chief of counties afsd. and province of Pennsylvania at Newcastle. A true copy test. (V:p120)

133. 20 Feb 1772 Indenture between Reynear Williams of Kent on Delaware, farmer and Reynear Williams same co, doctor of physick. Reynear Williams, the elder, in his lifetime made his will 5 Dec 1743 and devised a part of tract of land called Bridge Town situate in Mispillion Hund, part being six hundred acres to son, Aron Williams; and to son, Reynear Williams, three hundred acres of above tract. Aron died before division was made leaving one son, Reynear Williams, Junr and doctor of physick. The afsd Reynear Williams, farmer, and Reynear Williams, Junr have agreed to a division by three honest men which was done and Reynear, the farmer, doth fully clearly quit claim to Reynear, doctor, all right and title to land and marsh awarded. Description mentions Williams' Branch . . . tract called Angleford . . . containing four hundred sixty eight acres of land and marsh also one hundred twenty five acres containing by metes and bounds one hundred and thirty seven acres, twelve acres thereof excepted as sold by Reynear, farmer to Isaac Mason. Conveying in the whole five hundred ninety three acres. Wit: David Caldwell, Edward Fisher. Ackn 13 Aug 1773 (V:p120)

134. 12 Aug 1773 Indenture between John Peterkin of city of Philadelphia, taylor and Sarah, his wife; Joshua Clark of Mispillion Hund, Kent on Delaware, yeoman and Mary, his wife; John Revel of same hund and co, yeoman and Amelia, his wife, all of one part and Reynear Williams same hund and co, yeoman. A division of real est of John Brinklee, Esq, decd by Robert Killen, Edward Fisher, David Peterkin, Thomas Bowman and Isaac King, freeholders, appointed by orphans court on 20 May 1766, there was allotted to heirs of Doctor Spencer Cole a part known as Brinklees Island consisting of fast land with marsh adj. Description mentions Randel's Ditch . . . Strunt Creek . . . Great Pond . . . Great Fishing Gut . . . widow of Brinklee . . . containing two hundred ninety six acres of land and marsh by the draught annexed by David Caldwell, surveyor. Wife of Reynear Williams and Sarah, Mary and Amelia being four daus and only surviving children of Cole who now for consideration of two hundred seventy pounds convey their three fourths part to Reynear Williams. Wit: John Clark, John Furchas. Sarah Peterkin, Mary Clark and Amelia Revel privately examined gave their consent. Ackn 12 Aug 1773 (V:p121)

135. 25 Aug 1773 Indenture between Jonathan Emerson of Motherkill Hund, Kent on Delaware, Esq and John Crumpton same place, yeoman. Consideration of five

shillings and rents and covenants mentioned conveys lott No.Two in town of Frederica at head of Murtherkill. Crumpton to pay on 29th day of 9th mo sum of two pounds beginning 29 September next. Wit: Isaac Dawson, Roert Hodgson. Ackn 25 Aug 1773. (V:p122)

136. 27 Aug 1773 Indenture between Jonathan Emerson of Murtherkill Hund, Kent on Delaware, Esq and Frances Manny (Francis Many) same place, merchant. Consideration of five shillings and rents and covenants mentioned conveys lotts No. Twenty Five and No. Twenty Six in town of Frederica at head dof Murthkill. Manny to pay on 29th day of 9th mo and every year thereafter sum of three pounds beginning 29 September next. Wit: Phillip Barratt, John Dill. Ackn 27 Aug 1773. (V:p122)

137. 23 Aug 1773 Indenture between Henry Hudson of Cedar Creek Hund, Sussex on Delaware, yeoman and Sarah, his wife and William Killen of town of Dover, Kent on Delaware, attorney at law, of one part and Thomas Calloway of Mispillion Hund, same co, yeoman. By virtue of warrant dated 8 Mar 1738 a survey made by George Stevenson, surveyor on 8 Apr 1748 of tract of land situate on Brown's Branch of four hundred eighty one acres and allowance and by division in the survey into two parcels: one to Pemberton Brown of two hundred sixty one acres and to Daniel Brown of two hundred twenty acres, said lands laid out long before to their father, Daniel Brown, decd but niether warrant or survey is to be found. Pemberton Brown died with a will devising his land to his one son, Daniel Brown, who died intestate without issue vesting the land to his sister, Elizabeth Brown who married William Russell. She is decd without issue whereas John Carlisle and Sarah Hudson, half bro and sis, are entitled in right under half blood. John Carlisle by deed 26 Feb 1772 granted to William Killen his undivided share who with Sarah Hudson are entitled to the whole. A survey was made by Mark McCall by order of Samuel McCall, surveyor, and is found to begin nr head of Indian Branch being cor of land called Drapersberry now in possession of Elijah Sipple called Trinacria . . . to land formerly of Daniel Brown but now of Jonathan Sipple . . . containing two hundred seventy six acres. Consideration of two hundred pounds paid in hand by Thomas Calloway, Henry Hudson and his wife, Sarah, and William Killen convey one moiety or one hundred thirty eight acres. . Wit: Thos. Sheriff, Jonathan Sipple, Mark McCall. Sarah Hudson privately examined gave consent. Ackn 25 Aug 1773. (V:p122)

138. 23 Aug 1773 Indenture between Henry Hudson of Sussex on Delaware, yeoman and Sarah, his wife and William Killen of town of Dover, Kent on Delaware, atty at law and Elijah Sipple of Mispillion Hund, same co. By virtue of warrant dated 8 Mar 1738 a survey made by George Stevenson, surveyor on 8 Apr

1748 of tract of land situate on Brown's Branch of four hundred eighty one acres and allowance and by division in the survey into two parcels: one to Pemberton Brown of two hundred sixty one acres and to Daniel Brown of two hundred twenty acres, said lands laid out long before to their father, Daniel Brown, decd but neither warrant or survey is to be found. Pemberton Brown died leaving one son, Daniel and a dau, Elizabeth. To son, Daniel, he devised all lands who is since decd without issue and Elizabeth Brown became vested in the title and married William Russell but died without issue. John Carlisle and above named Sarah Hudson, his sister, half bro and sis to Elizabeth became heirs in half blood and John Carlisle by deed 26 Feb 1772 conveyed his undivided share to William Killen (Book T, folio 214) whereby William Killen and Sarah Hudson became legally entitled to the whole. A survey made 16th day this inst by Mark McCall by order of Samuel McCall is bounded as follows (see above deed for description) For consideration of two hundred pounds Henry Hudson and Sarah, his wife, and William Killen convey the following moiety, separated from other moiety conveyed this date to Thomas Calloway, of one hundred thirty eight acres. Wit: Jonathan Sipple, Mark McCall, Thos. Sheriff. Sarah Hudson privately examined gave consent. Ackn 25 Aug 1773. (V:p123)

139. 27 May 1773 Indenture between Phebe Vining of city of Philadelphia, widow and Samuel Chew of Kent on Delaware, Esq. Consideration of twelve hundred pounds conveys all that messuage and several lots of land situate on east side of Dover Square and extending eastward to Jones Creek otherwise called Dover River containing fifteen acres and twenty perches lately part of est of John Vining and were conveyed by his extrs to Phebe (Book V, p69). Wit: James Sykes, Benjamin Wynkoop. Charles Ridgely and John Chew apptd attys. Ackn 10 Nov 1773. (V:p124)

140. 13 Nov 1773 Indenture beween Samuel McCall of town of Dover, Kent on Delaware, practitioner in physick and Sarah his wife and James Hutchins of Kent Island, Queen Ann's co, province of Maryland, merchant. Consideraton of two hundred thirty five pounds ten shillings convey parcel of land situate in forest of Murtherkill on north side of Tanners Branch of Choptank River. By virtue of warrant 28 July 1759 granted to William Merrit who assigned same to Samuel McCall on 30 Oct 1761 and was surveyed by William Killen, depty surveyor, on 23 Nov 1761 found to contain one hundred forty eight acres and allowance. Beginning . . . by Benjamin Jones's land . . . Benjamin Start's land . . . with Moses Freeman's land . . . cor of land late possessed by William Hall now of James Hutchins . . . laid out for one hundred forty eight acres. Wit: Mark McCall, George McCall. Ackn 13 Nov 1773 (V:p124)

141. 1 Jan 1773 Indenture between James Howel of Rowan County, province of North Carolina, farmer, one of sons of James Howel, late of Kent on Delaware and George Blackiston of Kent Co, province of Maryland, gent. Joseph Howel of Kent on Delaware next bro in age to James Howel as his atty in conjunction with two younger bros, David and Thomas conveyed to George Blackiston all their parts of real est of their father, James Howel, decd and also conveyed the part that the father devised to James, the younger, by their deed 4 Nov last with mention of the title of John and Richard Gloverconveyed to George Blackiston by French Battel and James Stevens. Now James Howel makes this conveyance for all that part of John Thompsons Patent which was devised to him by his father except part in possession of Brian Seeney which George Blackiston refuses to purchase. Consideration of three hundred thirty three pounds fifteen shillings already paid to Joseph Howel for use of James Howel. Description mentions land of William Kirkley . . . tracts Hazard and Tantanbourrow and is also a cor of Wedmore . . . land in possession of heirs of Robert Bohanon . . . containing one hundred thirty three and a quarter acres. Samuel McCall and Mark McCall apptd attys. Wit: Sarah McCall, George McCall. Ackn 11 Nov 1773 (V:p125)

142. 11 Nov 1773 Indenture between Isaac Carty of Duck Creek Hund, Kent on Delaware, yeoman and Samuel Griffith same place, yeoman. Consideration of twenty seven pounds ten shillings conveys small piece of land situate in hund and co afsd part of tract called The Partnership purchased by Isaac from John Dickinson, Esq. Beginning at cor of land of John Patterson . . . laid out for two acres and one hundred twenty five square perches. Wit: Saml. McCall, Robert Hamilton. Ackn 12 Nov 1773. (V:p125)

143. 13 Nov 1773 Indenture between Philemon Dickinson of Bellville in Hunterdon County, Province of New Jersey, Esq. and Mary, his wife and John Dickinson of Fairhill in co of Philadelphia in province of Pennsylvania, Esq. Consideration of fifteen hundred pounds conveys parcel of land and marsh in Dover Hunt, Kent on Delaware. Beginning on the line of division between lands of John and Philemon Dickinson . . . containing one hundred ninety nine acres and one hundred fifty seven square perches. Wit: Caesar Rodney, James Sykes. Ackn 13 Nov 1773. (V:p125)

144. 11 Nov 1773 Indenture between Patrick Hugg of Mispillion Hund, Kent on Delaware, shoemaker and Johnson Earickson of Queen Ann's Co, province of Maryland on Kent Island, yeoman. Consideration of sixty seven pounds ten shillings conveys parcel of land in hund and co afsd conveyed by William and Rachel Pegg to Patrick Hugg on 25 Aug 1772 (Book V, folio 8). Beginning at cor of land sold by Pegg to Charles Kimmey . . . now of Johnson Earickson . . . to cor

of land sold by Pegg to Elizabeth Brown . . . line of James Gordon's land . . . laid out for forty seven acres and thirty square perches. Wit: Saml. McCall, Mark McCall. Ackn 11 Nov 1773 (V:p126)

145. 9 Nov 1773 Petition of William Morris sheweth that he has purchased a small parcel of land at public vendue late property of Manasseh Cain sold at suit of Robert Hodgson by writ on 31 Aug 1762 directing William Rhodes, then sheriff, to execute sale of the one hundred acres. Rhodes is out of office and petitioner prays that court authorize John Cook, present sheriff, to execute a deed for the land. (signed) William Morris. The within petition being read to the court and considered is granted. Test: Samuel Chew. (V:p126)

146. 9 Nov 1773 Indenture between John Cook, sheriff of Kent on Delaware, Esq and William Morris of Murtherkill Hund same co, tanner. Robert Hodgson, Junr obtained judgment agst Manasseh Cain in sum of twenty pounds and damages of forty one shillings three pence. William Rhodes, then sheriff, seized in execution one hundred acres of land appraised by David Caldwell and John Bell - Rhodes sold the land at public vendue to James Colgun who had purchased the land before from Cain and eloped from co before paying the consideration to the sheriff who had to pay the debt to the plaintiff, the land was still on his hands for want of buyer and again sold same at public vendue to William Morris for forty pounds eighteen shillings. Whereas James Cain was indebted to Owen Cain (being both brothers to Manasseh Cain) and also indebted to other persons in co eloped from his place of abode. A writ of attachment was issued from the court and on motion from council for the plaintiff, John Banning, John Pryor and French Battel, gents, were apptd to make distribution of money from sale of James Cains goods and chattels lands and tenements. The sheriff sold small parcel of land in forest of Murtherkill Hund containing about fifty acres the property of James Cain to William Morris twenty five pounds five shillins, he being highest bidder. John Cook, present sheriff, for consideration of forty pounds eighteen shillings paid to William Rhodes, Esq, for land of Manasseh Cain and further sum of twenty five pounds five shillins paid to John Cook for land of James Cain now conveys the two parcels of land. Wit: Armisell Lockwood, Richard McNatt. Ackn 10 Nov 1773. (V:p126)

147. 2 Nov 1773 Indenture between John Cook, Esq, high sheriff of Kent on Delaware and Thomas Keith of Little Creek Hund, yeoman. Whereas Thomas Harwood, Elizabeth Harwood, Charles Hopman and Rachel Toy by deed on 6 Feb 1768 (Book R, folio 244) conveyed to Randel Alston two parcels of land parts of tract called Chester situate in afsd hund on both sides of Kings Road on south side of Alston's Branch. Beginning at cor of land late of Israel Alston . . . laid out for one hundred fifty acres. Randel Alston became indebted to Thomas Collins for sum

of four hundred ninety pounds with bond obligatory therefore was seized with a sore lingering disease and died. Thomas Collins securing judgement, a writ was issued directing the sheriff to take into execution the goods, chattles, land and tenements of Randel Alston, decd, and expose to public vendue. Property was sold to Thomas Keith for sum of four hundred forty pounds and the sheriff now conveys same. Wit: Saml. McCall, James Starling. Ackn 11 Nov 1773 (V:p127)

148. 12 Nov 1773 Indenture between George Manlove of Mispillion Hund, Kent on Delaware, gent and Thomas Russum, son of Peter Russum late of Kent Co, decd. Whereas Elizabeth, his wife and extx and John Furchase, extr, by deed 12 Nov 1773 in open court made over to George Manlove a parcel of land situate in Mispillion Hund part of tract called William's Choice. Beginning at a new marked oak in line of Furchase's land . . . line of Joseph Parson's land . . . laid out for thirty acres and one hundred forty eight square perches. George Manlove for consideraton of twenty seven pounds sixteen shillings conveys said tract to Thomas Russum. Wit: Isaac Dawson, John Revell. Ackn 11 Noc 1773. (V:p127)

149. 20 Oct 1773 Indenture between John Faries of city of Philadelphia, cordwainer only surviving son and heir of John Faries of Kent on Delaware, decd and William Jones of township of Oxford, Philadelphia co, farmer. Consideration of thirty pounds conveys parcel of land in Little Creek Hund, Kent Co, beginning at cor of land late of William Smith . . . intersection of Smith's and Loockerman's land . . . containing one hundred fifty nine and a quarter acres and allowance of six percent. Said land was surveyed for John Faries on 13 July 1753. Wit: Jacob Rush, Evan Jones, John Murduch. Thomas Parry of Kent Co, brewer, apptd atty. Ackn 10 Nov 1773. (V:p128)

150. 13 Nov 1773 Indenture between Jonathan Pleasanton of Jones Hund, Kent on Delaware, gent and his wife, and John Dickinson of Fair Hill in the Northern Liberties of Philadelphia, Esq. Whereas disputes have arisen between parties above named concerning a parcel of marshy swamp branch or cripple situate in hund afsd, bounded to southeastward by land formerly of William Berry, part whereof now belongs to Jonathan Pleasanton and to northward by land formerly of Walter Wharton and by land called commonly Bartletts Point both now belonging to John Dickinson containing about twenty six acres. Parties afsd have agreed to divide the disputed land between them. Pleasanton and wife in consideration of five shillings conveys one full equal half part or moiety of said land to be divided by a ditch through the middle of the property to be dug by Pleasanton and Dickinson. Wit: William Howel, Shadrack Bostick. Ackn 13 Nov 1773. (V:p128)

151. 21 Sept 1772 Indenture between Martha Griffin of Duck Creek Hund, Kent

on Delaware, widow of Samuel Griffin of same place, and Samuel Griffin of the hund and co afsd, husbandman (one of sons of Samuel Griffin, decd) and Mary, his wife, Josiah Meredith same place, husbandman and Elizabeth, his wife and one of daus of said Samuel Griffin, decd, and Isaac Griffin same place, husbandman of one part and John Pattison same place, husbandman. In consideration of five hundred eighty six pounds convey a moiety or half part of tract conveyed by Benjamin Chew, Esq. to Samuel Griffin on 2 Jan 1769 part of tract called Manor of Frieth. Beginning nr a white oak cor of Isaac Carty's land . . . containing four hundred seventy six and a quarter acres. Wit: Molleston Correy, William Pattison. Ackn ----Nov 1773. (V:p129)

152. 13 Nov 1773 Indenture between John Dickinson, Esq. of Fairfield in Northern Liberties of Philadelphia and Jonathan Pleasonton of Jones Hund, Kent on Delaware, gent. Whereas disputes have arisen between parties above named concerning a parcel of marshy swamp branch or cripple situate in hund afsd, bounded to southeastward by land formerly of William Berry, part whereof now belongs to Jonathan Pleasanton and to northward by land formerly of Walter Wharton and by land called commonly Bartletts Point both now belonging to John Dickinson containing about twenty six acres. Parties afsd have agreed to divide the disputed land between themselves. John Dickinson in consideration of five shillings conveys to Pleasanton one full equal moiety or half part of the said swamp, branch or cripple which is to be divided by a ditch dug through the middle of the tract by Dickinson and Pleasanton. Wit: William Howel, Shadrack Bostick. Ackn 13 Nov 1773. (V:p129)

153. 10 Nov 1773 Indenture between William Brown of forest of Mispillion Hund, Kent on Delaware, shopkeeper and Henry Carter of Queen Ann's Co, province of Maryland, yeoman. Consideration of two hundred pounds conveys several parcels of land. First tract begins at cor white oak of land late of Edward Dill, decd . . . with land of William Green . . . containing one hundred ten acres and allowance called by name of Grassy Ridge. Second is a four acre tract adj afsd land. Third begins at cor of John Johnson's land . . . containing one hundred twenty acres. Above described three tracts wer conveyed by William Morris to John Edwards by deed on 17 May 1762 (Book R, folio 41). Also a fourth tract being conveyed being land conveyed by Samuel Newell and Sarah, his wife, to John Edwards on 7 Sept 1759 in forest of Murtherkill Hund orig surveyed for Newell 3 Oct 1758 beginning at cor oak of Thomas Newell's land . . . line of Michael Greenly . . . Thomas Hudson's land . . . said to contain one hundred four and a half acres. Fifth parcel of land was conveyed by Thomas Newell and Rachel, his wife, to John Edward 7 Sept 1759 surveyed for Thomas Newell 30 Sept 1757 beginning at cor of land late of Richard Bandy, decd . . . cor of William Green's land . . . possessed by Thomas

Edwards . . . cor of James Anderson's land . . . containing one hundred forty acres. Five tracts set forth were property of late John Edwards sold in execution by the sheriff to William Brown for eighty four pounds, he being highest bidder and James Caldwell, sheriff, on 29 May 1772 deeded the land to Brown. Wit: Jno. Smithers, John Clayton. Ackn 11 Nov 1773. (V:p130)

154. 12 Nov 1773 Indenture between Elizabeth Russum and John Furchase of Mispillion Hund, Kent on Delaware, extx and extr of Peter Russum, decd and George Manlove of same co. Peter Russum was seized in parcel of land in Mispillion Hund and by last will 12 Aug 1772 devised that part of the land should be sold. Beginning at an oak in line of Fruchase's land . . . line of Joseph Parson's land . . . laid out for thirty acres and one hundred forty eight square perches, said land was sold at public vendue to Manlove for consideration of twenty seven pounds. Wit: Isaac Dawson, John Evell. Ackn 11 Nov 1773. (V:p130)

155. 20 Nov 1773 Indenture between William Green of Mrtherkill Hund, Kent on Delaware, husbandman and Hannah, his wife and Powell Cox same place . Consideration of two hundred forty pounds conveys parcel of land laid out for Edward Dill pursuant to warrant of 28 Apr 1739. Beginning at cor of another tract of Dill's . . . in Richard Banning's line . . . nr John Read's line . . . oak of William Morris's land . . . containing two hundred eighty three and a quarter acres. John Banning and Joseph Prior of town of Dover apptd attys. Wit: William Rhodes, Mary Green, Nathl. Smithers. Hannah Green examined privately gave consent. Ackn 24 Nov 1773. (V:p131)

156. 10 Nov 1773 Indenture between William Morris of Kent on Delaware, tanner and cordwainer and Armwell Lockwood same place, farmer. William Morris is seized of parcel of land part of Springfield in forest of Murtherkill Hund on north side of Cuthbeth Marsh surveyed for Thomas Hawkins, conveyed to Hugh Durborow who conveyed to Owen Cain, decd, leaving three children as heirs and two children, Manassah and James became in debt so Manassah's part was taken into execution by William Rhodes, sheriff and James Cain's part was taken by attachment and sold by John Cook, sheriff to Wiliam Morris. In consideration of twelve pounds conveys part of afsd lands containing twenty four acres and one hundred forty eight square perches. Wit: Richard McNatt, Richd. Bassett. Ackn 10 Nov 1773. (V:p131)

157. 11 June 1773 Indenture between John Willson of town of Dover, Kent on Delaware, tanner and William Rodney of Dover Hund, gent. Consideration of seventy five pounds convey parcel of land in neck of hund afsd part of Great Pipe Elm orig surveyed for William Winsmore, part hereby granted late property of

Thomas Willson, father of John. Beginning at cor of land of George Stevens . . . land of heirs of John Pemberton . . . containing thirty acres and one hundred six square perches. Samuel McCall, Mark McCall apptd attys. Wit:George McCall, James Moon. Ackn 11 Nov 1773. (V:p132)

158. 24 Nov 1773 Indenture between William Dill of Kent on Delaware, yeoman and admtr of Edward Dill, decd, unadministered by Mary Dill, now also decd, and William Mastin same co, yeoman, eldest son and heir of William Mastin, the elder, yeoman, decd. Edward Dill was seized in part of tract called Fairfield situate in Mispillion Hund. Beginning on east side of Kings Road and Pemberton's savannah . . . containing three hundred forty and a half acres, also parcel, part of larger tract beginning . . . on south side of plantation late of Nathaniel Tomlin . . . containing one hundred fifteen and three quarter acres. Edward Dill's personal est was insufficient to pay his debts and maintain his children in their minority. Mary Dill petitioned orphan's court for permission to sell the land and at public vendue was sold to William Mastin, the elder, for sum of one hundred sixty pounds. Mastin died leaving issue William Mastin, eldest son, and five other children. The land could not be divided and was valued to William Mastin, eldest son. William Dill for further sum of five shillings now conveys the land. Wit: Will. Killen, Walter Mileham. Ackn 24 Nov 1773. (V:p132)

159. 24 Nov 1773 Indenture between Jacob Morgan of Kent on Delaware, hatter and Marthew (Martha), his wife and Isaac Whitacre same place, farmer. Consideration of one hundred sixty one pounds convey parcel of land situate in Brown's Neck adj land of Elijah Berry and Grace, his wife. Beginning at cor of Robert Bostick's land . . . by the said Whitacres fence . . . containing eighty one and a quarter acres. Wit: Peter King, Jos. Russell. Martha Morgan privately examined gave consent. Ackn 24 Nov 1773. (V:p133)

160. 23 Nov 1773 Indenture between Levin Charles of Kent on Delaware, farmer and Mary, his wife, and Edward Gibbs same place, merchant. Consideration of fifty pounds conveys his one fourth part of parcel called Elizabeth's Lott, the whole into four equal parts, the est of John Clampit, decd, father to Mary afsd. which fell to her under the law. William Rhodes apptd atty. Wit: Zadock Crapper, Henry Clampitt. Mary Charles privately examined gave consent. Ackn 24 Nov 1773. (V:p133)

161. 24 Nov 1773 Indenture between John Tumblin of Kent on Delaware, shop joyner and Cecelia Tumblin, his wife, and Edward Gibbs same place, merchant. Consideration of three hundred fifty eight pounds conveys parcel of land called Cambridge. Beginning at a stone cor of Gibbs other land nr to his house. . . land of

widow Piper . . . cor of Jacob Morgan's land . . . containing one hundred nineteen acres seventy nine perches. Wit: Edward Gibbs, John Dickinson, Junr. Cecelia Tumblin privately examined gave consent. Ackn 24 Nov 1773. (V:p134)

162. 24 Nov 1773 Indenture between Edward Gibbs of Kent on Delaware, merchant and Elizabeth, his wife and John Dickinson same co, farmer. Consideration of six hundred sixty nine pounds conveys parcel of land on Murther Creek in Murtherkill Hund. Description mentions William Rhode's land . . . land formerly belonging to John Craig . . . containing three hundred nine acres being part of two tracts, one called Farmsellsworth orig surveyed to Daniel Brown, the other called The Exchange orig surveyed to Peter Groundike. Said premises conveyed by Mark Manlove, Junr to Isaac King on 26 Aug 1763 (Book Q, folio 167) who with Martha, his wife, conveyed to Samuel Carpenter on 17 May 1766 (Book K, folio 91) who conveyed same to Edward Gibbs on 10 May 1769 (Book S, folio 172). Wit: Jacob Morgan, Eneas Gibbs. Elizabeth Gibbs privately examined gave consent. Ackn 24 Nov 1773. (V:p135)

163. 24 Nov 1773 Indenture between Katharine Tanner one of heirs of Christian Tanner formerly of Kent on Delaware, decd and Vincent Loockerman, Junr of Dover Hund, gent. Whereas George Hinds, Mary Dean, Susannah Lucas and David Tanner by deed on 13 Feb 1768 (Book S, folio 274) conveyed all their right and title to small parcel of land called fifty acres and part of tract called Content situate in Dover Hund to Nicholas Loockerman, gent, now decd. Katharine Tanner one of the heirs now conveys her share to Vincent Loockerman an heir under will of Nicholas Loockerman, for consideration of twenty five shillings. Samuel McCall and Mark McCall apptd attys. Wit: Joseph David, Rob. Blackshare. Ackn 26 Nov 1773. (V:p136)

164. 24 Nov 1773 Indenture between Jacob Morgan of Kent on Delaware, hatter and Martha, his wife and Robert Bostick same co, farmer. Consideration of fifty two pounds conveys parcel of land situate in Brown's Neck on main branch of Murther Creek. Beginning at cor of land called Seaton . . . containing twenty six and a quarter acres. Wit: Peter King, Thomas Russell. Martha Morgan privately examined gave consent. Ackn 24 Nov 1773. (V:p136)

165. 23 Nov 1773 Indenture between Samuel McCall of town of Dover, Kent on Delaware, practitioner in physick and Sarah his wife and Mark McCall same place, surveyor and eldest son of Samuel and Sarah. In consideration of love good will and affection also for sum of five shillings convey parcel of land called Hour Glass situate in forest of Murtherkill Hund resurveyed to Samuel McCall on 29 May 1770 by warrant granted 18 Sept 1769 directed to William Killen to execute by

John Jakens(?), surveyor general. Beginning at a red oak for land of George Soward . . . and James Gorrel(?) . . . land surveyed for Thomas Blackshare . . . now of Thomas Nixon . . . land called The Tappahannah . . . survey made for Thomas Vanderford . . . land of Matthias Steelman . . . land of James Gorrel(?) . . . containing two hundred forty nine acres and one hundred eight square perches. Wit: Warner Mifflin, George McCall. Sarah McCall privately examined gave consent. Ackn 25 Nov 1773. (V:p137)

166. 25 Nov 1773 Indenture between George Goforth of Kent on Delaware, cordwainer and Celia, his wife and William Killen, atty at law. Consideration of one hundred three pounds conveys that messauge and lot whereon the messauge standeth situate on east side of Kings Road from Dover to Three Runs. Beginning at a lot of land late of James Morton, decd . . . lot of Mathew Boggs . . . containing five acres. Wit: John Pryor, Joseph Pryor. Celia Goforth privately examined gave consent. Ackn 26 Nov 1773. (V:p137)

167. 15 Nov 1773 Indenture between Moses Hall of Sussex on Delaware, taylor and Easter, his wife, John Catts of Kent on Delaware, yeoman and Mary his wife of one part and Walter Mileham same co, farmer. Whereas Peter Miner by deed 1st Feb 1742 conveyed to Thomas Fitzsimmonds a parcel of land called Miner's Folly situate nr Marshyhope, Mispillion Hund. Beginning at cor of land of John Sipple's . . . Waitman Sipple's land . . . laid out for forty five acres, said deed (Book N, folio 89). Thomas Fitzsimmonds died intestate leaving children: Shokely, Sassy, Thomas, Elenor, and Anne Mitcham, Ester Hall and Mary Catts. Land was never divided and above parties to this deed are now about to convey their interest in consideration of four pounds. William Berry and Peter Torbet apptd attys. Wit: Simon W. Wilson, John Hillyard. Easther Hall and Mary Catts privately examined gave their consent. Ackn 15 Dec 1773. (V:p138)

168. 15 Dec 1773 Indenture between Walter Mileham and Ann, his wife; Moses Hall of Sussex on Delaware and Easther, his wife and John Catts of Kent on Delaware. For consideration of sixty pounds conveys portion, part or parcel of land and plantation part of Hookfield in forest of Mispillion Hund which was bought by Thomas Fitzsimmons late of Kent Co from John Cade of Sussex Co 6 Feb 1753 (Book O, folio 191). Beginning at cor of land of heirs of Stephen Catts and the heirs of Willilam Downs . . . cor of Alexander Whitley's land . . . Timothy Long's land . . . laid out for ninety two acres. Wit: Thos. Skillington, Simon W. Wilson. Ann Mileham and Esther Hall privately examined gave consent. Ackn 15 Dec 1773. (V:p138)

169. 23 Nov 1773 Indenture between John Nickerson of Dover Hund, Kent on

Delaware, yeoman and Mary, his wife and Charles Marim, same place, yeoman. Whereas John Marim was seized in tract of land of one hundred seven acres and seventy six perches, part of Little Pipe Elm and also of one hundred sixty six acres and forty six perches, part of Edenton, and died leaving issue of whom Mary Nickerson is one entitled to one third part of Little Pipe Elm and one sixth part of Edenton. Charles Marim has purchased residue of each and Charles and John desiring to divide have had Samuel McCall, surveyor, make division on 28 Sept 1769. John and Mary Nickerson now release that part beginning on Pipe Elm Branch which formerly divided lands of Joshua Nickerson and John Marim . . . with tract called Tinhead Court orig surveyed for John Glover. Samuel McCall and Mark McCall apptd attys. Wit: William Rodney, John Marim. Mary Nickerson privately examined gave consent. Ackn 14 Dec 1773. (V:p138)

170. 24 Nov 1773 Indenture between John Williams eldest son of James Williams late of Mispillion Hund, Kent on Delaware, decd and John Cox of forrest of said hund, yeoman. Whereas by proceedings of orphans court, one third of James Williams land was allotted to Mary, widow, in right of dower and she has married Henry Wells, Junr who eloped from his native place indebted to sundry persons and said thirds were taken into execution and sold to John Cox for and during the natural lives of Henry and Mary Wells and John Williams at time of Mary Well's death will be entitled to two shares of said dower now conveys same. Consideration of fifty eight pounds conveys his undivided dividends. Situate on head of Murther Kill called the Black Swamp adj road leading from Choptank Bridge to Johnnycake Landing . . . containing ninety four acres. Wit: William Dill, Robert Bostick. Ackn 24 Nov 1773. (V:p140)

171. The proper ear mark for horses, cattle, sheep and hoggs of John Chambers is, viz: the right ear a short crop, the left ear a crop and slit. Recorded at request of the said John Chambers, the nineteenth day of February Annoque Domini Seventeen hundred and sventy four. (V:p140)

172. 24 Nov 1773 Indenture between Jemima Dill of Kent on Delaware, spinster and George Lamdin same co, husbandman. By virtue of warrant and survey laid out to William Dill late of same co, husbandman, decd, a parcel of land in forest of Murtherkill. Beginning at the land late in possession of John Dill, Junr . . . by improvement of late William Dill . . . in John Baynard's line . . . land late in possession of John Sap . . . land now or late of Job Willoughby . . . containing one hundred sixty four and three quarter acres and allowance. William Dill died intestate leaving Nathan Dill, only son, and three daus: Jemima, Elizabeth and Mary Dill. Nathan Dill died intestate without issue. In consideration of nine pounds, Jemima Dill conveys her one third part of undivided whole. Wit: James

Tilton, Robert Greenlee. Ackn 25 nOV 1773. (V:p140)

173. 3 Nov 1773. Appointment: To Richard McWilliams, Caesar Rodney, Samuel Chew and David Hall, justices of our supreme court of courties of Newcastle, Kent and Sussex on Delaware, know that reposing special trust and confidence in your loyalty integrity and ability, we have assigned you our justices to enquire by the oaths and solemn affirmations respectively of honest and lawful men, (instructions given for determination and punishment of crimes, capital or felonies). (signed) John Penn. (V:p141)

174. 25 Nov 1773 Indenture between John Nickerson of Dover Hund, Kent on Delaware, yeoman and Mary, his wife and William Rodney same place, yeoman. Aaron Hart by deed conveyed to Samuel Hanson part of tract called Great Pipe Elm containing one hundred ten acres who with his wife, Sarah, on 3 July 1771 (Book T, folio 226) sold land to William Rodney excepting out a small piece or parcel of ground adj the run of Pipe Elm Branch for a watering or drinking place. Rodney with Lydia, his wife on 21 Sept 1772 granted same to John Nickerson, who by will of his brother, George Nickerson was equally entitled with John Marim, his sister's son, and eldest son of Charles Marim unto another piece whereby John Nickerson and John Marim by mutual agreement and releases made have divided the said parcel on which said division John Nickerson was found to have ninety eight acres and one hundred fifty square perches. Right to the property have been found to be in Sarah Pemberton and her sister, Hannah Robinson, daus of George Nickerson, who have conveyed their share to John Nickerson on 23rd day this inst and a twenty acre part of the fifty seven acres and eighty square perches to John Marim whereby there remains thirty seven acres and eighty six square perches belonging to John Nickerson who in consideration of twelve hundred fifty two pounds seven shillings six pence conveys all right title and interest in the several parcels of land united in one body. Beginning at cor of land late possessed by Stephen Paradee and Jonathan Caldwell . . . to part conveyed by Laurance Robinson to Daniel Pleasonton . . . to twenty acres conveyed by John Nickerson and wife, Mary, to John Marim . . . containing two hundred forty six acres and seventy six square perches. Wit: Cha. Marim, John Marim. Mary Nickerson privately examined gave consent. Ackn 14 Dec 1773. (V:p141)

175. 17 Nov 1773 Indenture between William Mullin surviving heir of James Mullin and Margaret his wife who was one of daus of Benjamin Shurmer formerly of Kent on Delaware and Isaiah Wharton of Murtherkill Hund same co, farmer, Whereas survey was made on 27 Sept 1742 by virtue of warrant 27 July 1731 for Benjamin Shurmer of tract of land situate between Isacc Webb's Branch and Walker's Branch. Description mentions tract Longina(?). . . containing one hundred

thirty two and three quarter acres. William Mullin in right of his mother is entitled to one fifth part and Isaiah Wharton has purchased four fifths parts from other heirs, Mullin in consideration of sixty pounds conveys his share. Samuel McCall and Mark McCall apptd attys. Wit: Joseph Pryor, Sarah McCall. Ackn 24 Nov 1773. (V:p142)

176. 26 Nov 1773 Indenture between James Hutchings the younger of Queen Ann's Co, province of Maryland, gent and Thomas Emory same co. Consideration of twelve hundred fifty pounds conveys all these several parcels of land. A parcel situate on Cow Breath Marsh in forest of Murtherkill Hund, Kent on Delaware, beginning at second boundary of Bushberry . . . containing two hundred two acres of land part of which is Bushberry orig granted to Abraham Bush 28 March 1736 containing one hundred sixteen acres and residue is part of Long Mead granted to John Long 6 June 1735 containing eighty six acres. Also that other parcel called Mead's Addition, description mentions land late of Ephraim Shaw . . . containing one hundred fifty four acres. Wit: Isaac Lowber, Henry Killen. Ackn 26 Nov 1773. (V:p143)

177. 17 Nov 1773 Indenture between Miriam King and John Furchase, she being relict and widow of James King late of Mispillion Hund, Kent on Delaware and both his admins and Peter King, same co, yeoman. Whereas Andrew Doz of city of Philadelphia, merchant by deed on 24 Nov 1772 (Book V, folio 15) conveyed one hundred thirty acres of Angleton to James King. Beginning at mouth of Cullen's Branch . . . line of tract called Middletown . . . land of Caleb Luff . . . part of tract Increase. Estate of James King was found insufficient to pay debts and the admins sold the land at public vendue to Peter King for sum of two hundred ten pounds. Wit: Silas Snow, Joseph David. Ackn 25 Nov 1773. (V:p143)

178. 24 Nov 1773 Indenture between William Anderson of Kent on Delaware and Margaret his wife and Francis Jester of same co. Whereas Anderson and Jester in partnership have bought a parcel of land from heirs of Ebenezer Hawthorn and by contract of their own divided the said land of one hundred twenty nine acres. Anderson paid his share and took fifty three acres and Jester took seventy six acres. Anderson's part beginning at a stump of James Rawley's land . . . he now conveys for consideration of sixty six pounds five shillings. Wit: Joseph Lister, Sarah Tharp. Ackn 26 Nov 1773. (V:p144)

179. 21 Sept 1772 Indenture between William Rodney of Kent on Delaware, gent and Lydia his wife and John Nickerson same co, gent. Whereas Samuel Harper the elder of Kent Co, gent, conveyed to William Rodney (Book T, folio 226) a parcel of land part of Great Pipe Elm in Dover Hund. Beginning on Pipe Elm Branch . . .

to land formerly belonging to Stepen Pardee, decd . . . containing one hundred ten acres. William Rodney and Lydia his wife convey the land for sum of five hundred fifty pounds. Wit: John Hart, James Stevens. Lydia Rodney privately examined gave consent. Ackn 14 Dec 1773. (V:p144)

180. 24 Nov 1773 Indenture betweern John Nickerson of Dover Hund, Kent on Delaware, yeoman and Mary his wife and John Marim, son of Charles Marim, same place, yeoman. Consideration of forty pounds paid by Charles Marim on behalf of his son, they now convey parcel of land in St. Jones's Neck part of tract surveyed and resurveyed for William Winsmore and resurveyed for George Robinson known as Great Pipe Elm. Part of tract was purchased by Joshua Nickerson from Lawrence Robinson, one of sons of George Robinson but it has been learned that Lawrence Robinson had no estate in the land and has of late been purchased by John Nickerson and Charles Marim from Sarah Pemberton and Hannah Robinson, daus of George Robinson, and deed of conveyance was made solely to John Nickerson though part belonged to John Marim, the greater part thereof by will of George Nickerson, son to Joshua Nickerson and said John Nickerson and Mary his wife now convey and release the said part to John Marim. Beginning at cor of land of David Pleasonton . . . laid off for twenty acres of land. Wit: Charles Marim, Willm. Rodney. Mary Nickerson privately examined gave consent. Ackn 14 Dec 1773. (V:p145)

181. 23 Nov 1773 Indenture between John Nickerson of Dover Hund, Kent on Delaware, yeoman and Mary his wife and John Marim same place, yeoman. Whereas John Nickerson and John Marim are equally entitled to a parcel of land called Great Pipe Elm situate on Pipe Elm Branch by virtue of will of George Nickerson, decd, who was brother to John Nickerson and no division has been made between the parties, they are now releasing to each other the land contained in bounds of their said tract by lines they have agreed upon after a survey hath been first made. John Nickerson and Mary his wife in consideration of the other moiety released to them by John Marim and sum of five shillings convey land beginning at cor of land of David Pleasontons late of Lawrence Robinson, etc. Wit: Charles Marim, Wm. Rodney. Mary Nickerson privately examined gave consent. Ackn 14 Dec 1773. (V:p145)

182. 23 Nov 1773 Indenture between John Marim of Dover Hund, Kent on Delaware, yeoman and John Nickerson same place, yeoman. Whereas John Marim and John Nickerson are jointly entitled to a parcel of land part of a tract called Great Pipe Elm situate on Pipe Elm Branch by virtue of will of George Nickerson, decd, bro of John Nickerson and no division has been made between said parties they are now about to compleat(sic) the same by releasing to each other the land

contained within the bounds of their said part respective of lines agreed upon after a survey hath been first made. John Marim for consideration of other moiety to him released by John Nickerson and Mary his wife and for sum of five shillings conveys all land on the south and east side of a certain line. Beginning at a stone in line of David Pleasonton (late Lawrence Robinson's) . . . etc. Wit: Chas. Marim, Wm. Rodney. Ackn 14 Dec 1773. (V:p146)

183. 24 Nov 1773 Indenture between Charles Marim of Dover Hund, Kent on Delaware, yeoman and Ruhannah his wife and John Nickerson same place, yeoman and Mary his wife. Whereas John Marim formerly of said place, decd, was seized of one hundred seven acres and seventy six perches of land part of tract called Little Pipe Elm and also one hundred sixty six acres and forty six perches part of Edenton and died leaving Mary Nickerson as heir entitled to one third of Little Pipe Elm and one sixth of Edenton and as Charles Marim has purchased residue of each, now he and John Nickerson design to divide and pass releases between each other. They jointly called Samuel McCall, surveyor to survey and make division on 28 Sept 1769 and Charles Marim and his wife, Ruhannah, convey the part laid off for John Nickerson and his wife, Mary, to them. Beginning at the branch formerly divividing lands of Joshua Nickerson and John Marim . . . containing in bounds thirty two acres and one hundred twenty five square perches part of Little Pipe Elm and also twenty eight acres and fourteen square perches of Edenton. Wit: Charles Ridgely, William Rodney. Ruhannah Marim privately examined gave consent. Ackn 14 Dec 1773. (V:p146)

184. 14 Dec 1773 Triparte Indenture between James White the elder of Kent on Delaware, yeoman and James White the younger same co, yeoman and son of afsd James White and Levi Muncy of same co, husbandman. Whereas James the elder for sum of five shillings paid by James the younger and five shillings paid by Levi Muncy and for diverse other good causes and considerations, James the elder does alienate release and confirm to Muncy all that messuage water corn mill and one hundred acres of land on south side of Brown's Branch and also seven acres of land on the same branch . . . to Muncy in trust nevertheless to and for the several uses intents and purposes herein after mentioned . . . for use of James White the elder during his natural life and after his decease, to use of James White, the younger, and that within one year after he attains age twenty one to convey a moiety of three hundred acres and part of larger tract called Hunting Quarter unto his bro, Robert White. Upon non performance of James the younger then the property shall remain to use and behoof of Robert White. Wit: John Clarke, William Lister. Ackn 14 Dec 1773. (V:p147)

185. 16 Nov 1773 Indenture between David Finney of Newcastle on Delaware and

John Joy of Duck Creek Hund, Kent on Delaware, yeoman. Whereas a resurvey was made to Robert French, gent of Newcastle Co he being grandfather of David Finney on 9 Apr 1703 for tract of land called Golden Grove which was executed from est of George Martin, then decd. In consideration of one hundred pounds Finney conveys the parcel of land called Golden Grove beginning at a stump in James Severson's field . . . also cor of Robart's Chance . . . by survey to contain two hundred nine acres. Finwick Fisher, Esq apptd atty. Wit: James Vandyke, John Lewis, John Davis. Ackn 14 Dec 1773. (V:p147)

186. 15 Dec 1773 Writ of Execution and Indenture. John Cook, high sheriff of Kent on Delaware sends greeting: Whereas Caesar Rodney and Thomas Nixon, trustees of General Loan Office in court of Common Pleas did recover agst Thomas Skillington admr of goods and chattles of David Hall of forest of Mispillion Hund, planter, decd, unadministered by Mary Hall late admx a certain debt of seventy pounds also two pounds eighteen shillings and ____ pence and John Cook by virtue of writ issued and executed seized the land of David Hall part of Gravesend. Description mentions stake of John Hardin's land . . . containing one hundred acres of land with thirty acres more adj on Hardin's which premises were mortgaged by Hall to John Vining and John Brinckle, Esqrs, late trustees of General Lona Office. Sheriff sold the land at public vendue to Thomas Skillington for ninety four pounds thirteen shillings one penny and now conveys same to him. Wit: Allen McLeane, Elijah Chance. Ackn 15 Dec 1773. (V:p148)

187. 25 Nov 1773 Indenture between John Cook, high sheriff of Kent on Delaware and Thomas Irons of Little Creek Hund, gent. Whereas Owen Irons was possessed of small parcel of land about sixty two acres in forest of Murtherkill Hund beginning at cor of land formerly surveyed to Penelope Freeman . . . land surveyed for Thomas Morris . . . part of this tract late conveyed to James Voshell . . . said land surveyed for Owen Irons who was indebted to sundry persons and to Morris McBride who obtained judgment and the sheriff by writ from court of Common Pleas sold the land to Thomas Irons for twenty pounds. John Cook now conveys the land. Wit: Samuel McCall, John Haslet. Ackn 15 Dec 1773. (V:p149)

188. 23 Aug 1773 Indenture between John Pennell of Kent on Delaware, miller and Benjamin Chew of city and co of Philadelphia, Esq and Charles Ridgely of Kent Co, Esq and Benjamin Wynkoop of Philadelphia, merchant. Whereas John Pennell by writing of agreement on 8 Mar last past with Charles Ridgely, one of extrs of John Vining on behalf of himself and other extrs stands indebted to same in sum of five hundred pounds to be paid at certain times. The money is the residue of twelve hundred fifty pounds purchase money for certain mills and thirty five acres of land. Witnesseth that as well for better security for payment of debt and

sum of five shillings, Pennell conveys all that water corn mill and saw mill and forty seven acres and three quarters of land on both sides of Isaac's Branch in Murtherkill Hund. Pennell to pay sum of five hundred pounds in form following: One hundred sixty six pounds thirteen shillings four pence on 1st May next ensuing and equal payments on same day in 1775 and 1776. Wit: George McCall, Will. Killen. Ackn 16 Dec 1773. (V:p149)

189. 1 Nov 1773 Indenture between Obediah Voshall, Senr and Elizabeth, his wife and Obediah Voshall, Junr and Elizabeth, his wife, Govey Trippet and Rachal his wife, Richard Lewis and Mary his wife, and John Brown all of Murtherkill Hund, Kent on Delaware being heirs and devisees of John Brown, decd, of one part and Jonathan Neall of hund and co afsd. By virtue of warrant on 22nd 12th mo 1681 granted to Bryan O'Neall, survey was made 23rd 12th mo 1683 by Joshua Barkstead for tract called The Downs containing four hundred acres adj tract called Owsbey orig surveyed for Thomas Heathard and by sundry conveyances down from Bryan O'Neall land became property of John Brown except fifty acres sold by John Severson to Robert Cumings. Brown so seized and another tract adj called Williams Choice, he on 5 Jan 1728/9 made his will (Book 7, folio 259) devising to his son, John Brown one hundred fifty acres to include his part of William's Choice whereon he lived. To his wife, Elizabeth, he devised one hundred acres and residue of about one hundred sixty acres to his three eldest daus: Rachal, Elizabeth and Mary. William Killen, surveyor, James Caldwell and Waitman Sipple laid off the parts and Elizabeth, widow, now wife of Obediah Voshall, Senr. Obediah Voshall, Junr and Elizabeth have long since conveyed their parts to Daniel Robinson who conveyed same to Perkins Donnabels(?) who conveyed same to Jonathan Neall. Richard Lewis and Mary his wife on 13 Feb 1770 conveyed their part to Neall. Govey Trippet and Rachal his wife on 13 May 1772 conveyed their part andf Obediah Voshall, Senr and Elizabeth, his wife on 12 Aug last past conveyed the one hundred acres devised to her by her former husband, decd. Survey was made erroneously and as Neall has now purchased the whole tract the heirs all join in to rectify all mistakes by this conveyance. Samuel McCall and Mark McCall apptd attys. Wit: James Tilton, John George, William Mannering, Andw. Caldwell. Elizabeth Voshall, Senr & Jr, and Rachel Trippet and Mary Lewis privately examined gave their consent. Ackn 10 Feb 1774. (V:p150)

190. 20 Nov 1773 Indenture between William Ball of city of Philadelphia, merchant and Elizabeth his wife of one part and Ezekiel Needham of Duck Creek Hund, Kent on Delaware, practitioner of physic. Consideration of twenty eight pounds conveys parcel of ground situate in the Crossroads on southeast side of a tract laid out twenty four feet wide for a street called Ball's Street. Beginning at cor of Ezekiel Needham's dwelling lott . . . lot in tenure of Howell Buckingham in right

of Mary his wife a devisee under will of Thomas Green . . . to Thomas Jamison's lott . . . to William Ball's lott part of now occupied by William Pearse . . . containing about sixty four square perches. William Killen and Richard Bassett, Esqrs, apptd attys. Wit: Geo. Emlen, Junr., Wm. Baker, Thos. Skillington, Mathw. Manlove. Ackn 10 Feb 1774. (V:p151)

191. 20 Nov 1773 Indenture between George Manlove of Mispillion Neck & Hund, Kent on Delaware and Mary his wife and Jacob Cremeen same place, taylor. Consideration of one hundred twenty pounds convey situate on School House Branch part of tract Cowpein or Cowpan . . . laid off on 27 July last past by Mark McCall, surveyor for Samuel McCall, surveyor for county at reqiest of George Manlove for one hundred acres. Wit: Sarah Christopher, Matthew Manlove. Mary Manlove privately examined gave consent. Ackn 15 Dec 1773. (V:p151)

192. 15 Dec 1773 Indenture between Thomas Skillington of Duck Creek Hund, Kent on Delaware, innkeeper and John Cook of same co, Esq, who by deed on 15 Dec 1773 did as high sheriff grant to Thomas Skillington as highest bidder a parcel of land in forest of Murtherkill Hund part of tract Gravesend. Description mentions . . . stake by John Hardin . . . containing one hundred acres with thirty acres more adj. Said land on 11 June 1760 mortgaged by David Hall, decd, to John Vining and John Brinckle, Esqrs, trustees of General Loan Office and a writ issued by Caesar Rodney and Thomas Nixon, present trustees, the land was taken in execution and sold to Thomas Skillington who is now about to reconvey the land to John Cook. Consideration of one hundred pounds. Wit: Allen McLeane, Elijah Chance. Ackn 15 Nov 1773. (V:p152)

193. 13 Nov 1773 Indenture between William Ball of city of Philadelphia, goldsmith and Elizabeth, his wife and Samuel Morris of hund of Apequinimink and co of Newcastle on Delaware, yeoman. Consideration of thirty pounds conveys lot of ground on north side of forest road leading to Robert Holliday's store and landing in Duck Creek Hund, Kent on Delaware. Beginning at cor of Howell Buckingham's lott in right of his wife, Mary, devisee under will of Thomas Green . . . to stone in line of William Ball's lott . . . containing one acre of ground. Wit: David Shoemaker, Augustine Biddle. Ackn 10 Feb 1774. (V:p152)

194. 17 Sept 1773 Indenture between William Ball of city of Philadelphia, goldsmith and Elizabeth, his wife and Allexander Workwell of Duck Creek Hund, Kent on Delaware, harness maker. Consideration of thirty pounds conveys lott of ground situate near the Cross Roads in Duck Creek Hund beginning at cor of lot late of William Creighton, decd . . . to William Ball's land . . . containing one acre of ground. Wit: Allen McLeane, John White. Ackn 9 Feb 1774. (V:p153)

195. 10 Dec 1773 Indenture between John Fothergill, London, doctor in physick; Daniel Zackary, London, goldsmith; Jacob Hagan, Silvanus Grove and William Heron of London, merchants, surviving trustees of a proprietorship commonly called Pennsylvania Land Company of London by Jacob Cooper, Samuel Shoemaker and Joshua Howell of Philadelphia, merchants and their attys, of the one part and Joseph Calloway of Mispillion Hund, Kent on Delaware, yeoman. An act for vesting certain estates in Pennsylvania, New Jersey and Maryland belonging to Pennsylvania Land Company remaining unsold in Thomas Hyam, Thomas Reynolds and Thomas How, surviving trustees for the said partnership to settle the estates vested in John Fothergill, David Zachary, Devereux Bowly, Luke Hind, Richard How, Jacob Hagan, Silvanus Grove and William Heron . . . for sum of twelve pounds one shilling nine pence convey to Joseph Calloway a messuage and tract of land in Mispillion Hund part of Long Acre surveyed for Nicholas Bartlet by Joshua Barkstead, said part conveyed being two small pieces. Description mentions Thomas Barker's part . . . Alexander McDonald's . . . containing forty seven acres and eighty nine square perches. Wit: John Rattledge, Samuel Shoemaker, Junr. Ackn 9 Feb 1774. (V:p153)

196. 23 Nov 1773 Indenture between John Nickerson of Dover Hund, Kent on Delaware, yeoman and Mary his wife and Charles Marim of same place, yeoman. Whereas John Marim was seized in fee of one hundred seven acres and seventy six perches of land part of tract called Little Pipe Elm and also in one hundred sixty six acres and forty six perches of land part of tract called Edenton. He died leaving issue of whom Mary Nickerson is one now entitled to one third part of Little Pipe Elm and one sixth part of Edenton. Charles Marim has purchased residue of each and he and John Nickerson design to divide and pass releases between each other. They jointly called Samuel McCall, surveyor to survey and make division on 28 Sept 1769 and now John Nickerson and his wife, Mary, to release to Charles Marim part laid off to him and for sum of five shillings convey that part . . . seventy four acres and one hundred eleven perches part of Little Pipe Elm and also one hundred thirty eight acres and thirty two perches of Edenton. Wit: Wm. Rodney, John Marim. Mary Nickerson privately examined gave consent. Ackn 2 Dec 1773. (V:p155) NOTE: A notation on the binding states "This Deed is already recorded . . . here by mistake".

197. 1 Feb 1774 Indenture between John Fothergill, London, doctor in physick; Daniel Zackary, London, goldsmith; Jacob Hagan, Silvanus Grove and William Heron of London, merchants, surviving trustees of a proprietorship commonly called Pennsylvania Land Company of London by Jacob Cooper, Samuel Shoemaker and Joshua Howell of Philadelphia, merchants and their attys, of the one part and John Dillen of province of Maryland gent. Thomas Hyam, Thomas

Reynalds and Thomas How surviving trustees settled the estates vested in John Fothergill, Daniel Zachary, Thomas How, Devereaux Bowly, Luke Hind, Richard How, Jacob Hagan, Silvanus Grove and William Heron. Messauge plantation and land is part of Casbron(?) situate in Brown's Neck, Mispillion Hund now conveyed for fifty six pounds three shillings three pence laid out for one hundred forty eight acres and twenty perches to John Dillen. Description mentions orig survey of Henry Stevens . . . late purchase of N___ Goddein . . . and of Cottenham. Wit: Alexdr. Rutherford, Mark McCall. Ackn 9 Feb 1774. (V:p155)

198. 27 Nov 1773 Indenture betweern John Baning of Kent on Delaware, merchant and Edward McIllvoy of same co, husbandman and Samuel Ball now of Newcastle on Delaware but late of Kent Co. Samuel Ball has contracted with Edward McIllroy for sale and conveyance of lot of ground situate at place called Cross Roads beginning at a post on south side of Landing Road . . . containing two acres for sum of sixty pounds paid by Edward McIllroy to Samuel Ball. Whereas in further execution of contract, Samuel Ball by bond or obligation on 22 May 1770 became bound to Edward McIllroy in penal sum of one hundred for the making and signing of a good and lawful deed for the said lot of ground. Samuel Ball is confined to jail in Kent Co by one or more writs from county court and has prayed to be discharged from impriorment under an act of relief for insolvent debtors. Court did discharge him and set over to John Baning all his effects real and personal estate for benefit of his creditors and the said lot is now vested in John Baning who for the sixty pounds now conveys the lot. Wit: Thos. Hickey, Mary Beauchamp, Simon Jeffrey, Hayly Bell. Ackn 10 Feb 1774. (V:p156)

199. 7 Feb 1774 Petition of Jonathan Sipple sheweth that John Baning was highest bidder at a vendue held by James Wells, late sheriff, of lands late of Stephen Brown in Brown's Neck and by attachment by Joseph Caldwell and thereby became the purchaser of said lands for four hundred eighty five pounds and the petitioner has purchased the lands from John Baning and no deed has been made and petitioner prays the court to authorize John Cook, present sheriff, to do so.(signed) Jonathan Sipple. The petition being read to the court and considered is granted and John Cook is ordered to execute same. (V:p157)

200. 9 Feb 1774 Indenture between John Cook, high sheriff of Kent on Delaware and Jonathan Sipple of Brown's Neck, Mispillion Hund. Whereas by writ of attachment by Joseph Caldwell agst Stephen Brown who was seized in fee of two parcels of land, one on Brown's Branch as laid off by George Stevenson, surveyor, in 1748 containing two hundred twenty acres and other parcel laid off for one hundred fifty four acres and thirty perches. James Wells, then sheriff of said co seized the lands and placed same in execution and said lands were sold to John

Baning for sum of four hundred eighty five pounds who conveyed his rights of purchase to Jonathan Sipple who has petitioned the court to have present sheriff convey the land which is now made. Wit: Edward Fisher, John Crumpton. Ackn 9 Feb 1774. (V:p157)

201. 24 Jan 1774 Indenture between William Killen of Kent on Delaware, atty at law and James Moore same place, yeoman. Consideration of four hundred pounds conveys parcel of ground in forest of Murtherkill Hund beginning at a red oak standing by road from plantation late of Hugh Durborow to plantation late of Daniel Gooding. . . containing two hundred acres. Said premises now in occupation of William Burroughs and heretofore belonging to James Moore and by virtue of writ were granted and conveyed by Thomas Collins, late sheriff, to Killen on 5 June 1766. Wit: Saml. McCall, George McCall. Ackn 9 Feb 1774. (V:p158)

202. 9 Feb 1774 Levin Charles of Kent on Delaware and Mary his wife and Kemmel Godsin of Dorchester Co in Maryland. Whereas Joseph Nicolls late of Kent Co decd by his will devised to above Mary a parcel of land situate in Mispillion Hund purchased by Nicolls of Joseph Chadwick containing forty nine and one quarter acres part of tract called Fairfield also one other parcel containing seven acres and sixty four perches adj first one purchased from Winlock Wheelor part of tract called Clayten. Consideration of eighty five pounds convey two parcels beginning on brow of hill on cor of that purchased from Chadwick . . . land of the widow Warrington . . . mulberry tree of Benjamin Benston . . . parcel purchased of Wheelor . . . containing in the whole sixty one acres and one hundred four perches of land, one acre excluded for heirs of Patience Smothers, decd, to be laid off in a square to include the improvements of said Smothers. Wit: Thomas Soward, William Berry. Mary Charles privately examined gave consent. Ackn 9 Feb 1774. (V:p158)

203. 2 Nov 1773 Indenture between David Lewis of Duck Creek Hund, Kent on Delaware, yoeman and his wife and William Griffith same place, miller. Consideration of twenty four pounds conveys a lot of ground in hund afsd called Pugh's Lott surveyed for Roger Pugh and since the property of his son, William Pugh, now both decd which with other lands have been conveyed to Lewis by the sheriff for satisfaction of William Pugh's debts. Description mentions door of William Griffith's house . . . laid off for four acres of ground. Mark McCall apptd atty. Wit: Samuel Griffith, Nathl. Gordin(?). Ackn 9 Feb 1774. (V:p159)

204. 15 Jan 1774 Indenture between Vincent Loockerman, Junr of Dover Hund; Kent on Delaware, gent and Jesse Newport of forest of Murtherkill Hund. Whereas Nicholas Loockerman, late of said co, on 1 Sept 1740 obtained warrant and survey

for tract of land of nine hundred thirty nine and three fourths acres which Landing Road passes through from Forest Landing on Dover River to forest of afsd hund, passing by smith shop of Thomas Hale and tract surveyed for Loockerman by name of Starlight(?) and Loockerman by will vested the residue in afsd Vincent Loockerman, Junr who is about to convey all land to westward and northward of the Landing Road in consideration of seventy pounds paid. Wit: Treadwell Manlove, Sarah McCall. Ackn 9 Feb 1774. (V:p159)

205. 26 Jan 1774 Indenture between Gove Clampit of Kent on Delaware, yeoman and David Gibbs of same co, merchant. Consideration of one hundred thirty pounds conveys all right title interest property claim and demand to all his father. John Clampit's lands he died possessed of excepting what Jonathan Emerson has taken by a late survey which remains yet undivided. John Baning and Joseph Pryor, gents, apptd attys. Wit: Elijah Berry, Aneas Gibbs. Ackn 9 Feb 1774. (V:p159)

206. 9 Feb 1774 Indenture between Absalom Virdin and Sarah, his wife of Kent on Delaware and Arnald Hudson same place, yeoman. Whereas they convey part of tract Absalom Virdin bought of Rubin Wallace part of land called Butinton adj land of Hudson's dwelling plantation. Description mentions William Summers clearing . . . laid off for eighteen and two quarter acres and thirty perches. Consideration of fifteen pounds fifteen shillings. Wit: Richard McNatt, Eliphaz Morris. Ackn 9 Feb 1774. (V:p160)

207. 2 Feb 1774 Indenture between William Clampit of Murtherkill Hund, Kent on Delaware, yeoman and Jonathan Emerson same place, Esq. Whereas Clampit by deed on 26 Aug 1746 under hand of Thomas Green, then sheriff, purchased tract surveyed for Christopher Tapham on 11 June 1739 by Thomas Noxon, surveyor, containing five hundred eighteen acres and allowance, which was sold to pay Tapham's debts. Tract Bishop's Choice included some part of Tapham's survey and by a lawsuit Clampit released the part to Emerson and it appeared the residue belonged to Clampit who had conveyed one hundred acres to Ebenezer Clampit and also about eighty one acres to John Clampit and thirty four and three quarter acres to Andrew Henderson, the residue of the tract about one hundred eighty five acres belongs to William Clampit who is indebted to sundry persons and that sundry execution was obtained agst him and to satisfy all writs, Jonathan Emerson has agreed to pay all debts and Clampit hereby makes a deed of mortgage and as security for consideration of sum of five hundred pounds as payments to his creditors grants and conveys the residue of his land . . . agrees to pay on 2nd of Feb every year until whole sum is paid by Feb 1776. Wit: James Howell, Saml. McCall. Ackn 8 Feb 1774. (V:p160)

208. 3 Nov 1773 Indenture between William Clampit of Murtherkill Hund, Kent on Delaware, yeoman and Jonathan Emerson same place, Esq. Whereas survey was made for Benoni Bishop called Bishop's Choice in Kent Co joining on north side of Murther Creek and joining on several sides if Bishop's Branch of which tract Jonathan Emerson is legally seized. A survey made for Christopher Tapham on some more ancient lands included part of Bishop's Choice and William Clampit became possessed of greater part thereof and also claimed that part of Bishop;s Choice which raised long dispute between he and Emerson. By determination of Caesar Rodney, Charles Ridgely and Robert Killen, Esqrs, and Joseph Howel and Samuel McCall, arbitrators, agreement and division was made and Clampit and Emerson acknowledge the proper lines and Clampit hereby releases all claims to the land that falls within Emerson's part. Wit: William Powell, Saml. McCall. Ackn 8 Feb 1774. (V:p161)

209. 3 Feb 1774 Indenture between William Killen town of Dover, Kent on Delaware, atty at law and Alexander McDonald of forest of Brown's Neck, Mispillion Hund and Phinchas Baning same place. William Killen is proper owner of land called Pathelia Plains in Brown's Neck of which Phinchas Baning, carpenter, claimed having held a part heretofore purchased found of late to be part of Pathelia Plains. Beginning at a cor black gum being a line tree of same tract possessed by Daniel Smith . . . with land late conveyed by Killen to McDonald . . . tract belonging to the London Company called Long Acre . . . of which Phinehas Baning . . . part in possession of Thomas Barker . . . containing sixteen acres and one hundred thirty three square perches. William Killen's part sold to McDonald begins at same place . . . to land possessed by Thomas and Mary Williams . . . containing fifty eight acres and seventy two perches. McDonald has purchased a part of Long Acre from the London Company for use of Phinehas Baning containing eight acres and fifty three square perches and another piece McDonald purchased from the Company for himself containing five acres and thirty five square perches. Phinehas Baning requests that Killen and McDonald join in a deed in order to save the expense of plurality of deeds. Killen in consideration of twelve pounds twelve shillings five pence and also Alexander McDonald for consideration of fifty five pounds eight shillings eight pence convey the above described parcels of land. Wit:Thos. Tilden, Saml. Chew. Ackn 9 Feb 1774. (V:p161)

210. 9 Nov 1773 Indenture between Thomas Collins of Duck Creek Hund, Kent on Delaware, gent and Joseph Parsons of Mispillion Hund, same co, yeoman. Whereas William Morris as atty for Hannah Dury of Island of Barbados granted conveyances to Collins for sundry tracts of land situate in Mispillion Hund. Thomas Collins by bond in writing obligatory on 11 Apr 1767 engaged himself to convey legally unto Ephraim Reynolds, Ezekiel Williams and William Catts as

much of the land they possessed by virtue of surveys made by Henry Reynolds under whom they before had claimed by new rights but agreed to purchase the ancient titles for their parrts. Ephraim Reynolds by bond made 9 Jan 1768 obliged himself to convey his part to Joseph Parsons. Description mentions Fairfield . . . land of John Falconer, decd . . . containing one hundred one and a half acres. Thomas Collins has not made conveyance to Ephraim Reynolds for his part of land above and Reynolds would have been enabled to convey same to Parsons before Reynolds moved to Carolina. Thomas Collins for covenants and contracts between himself and Ephraim Reynolds now conveys all above said land to Joseph Parsons. Wit: James Sterling, Pierce Jones. Ackn 9 Feb 1774. (V:p162)

211. 11 Apr 1767 Know all men by these presents that I, Thomas Collins, Kent County on Delaware am held and firmly bound to Ephraim Reynolds, Ezekiel Williams and William Catts in sum of six hundred pounds . . . condition that Thomas Collins make over all his right, title, interest and demand to two parcels of land situate in Mispillion Hund laid out for six hundred acres or such part claimed by above parties by their surveys. . . two tracts laid out for John Manlove and Thos Heather . . . then above obligation to be void. Wit: William Carpenter, William Downs. Ackn 9 Feb 1774. (V:p163)

212. 9 Jan 1768 Know all men by these presents that I, Ephraim Reynolds, Kent County on Delaware, yeoman, am held and firmly bound to Joseph Parson same place, yeoman, in sum of two hundred pounds . . . condition being that above Ephraim Reynolds shall reasonably request of Joseph Parsons to alienate makeover and convey parcel of land beginning at cor black oak . . . estate of Joshua Wheeler, decd . . . land called Fairfield belonging to est of John Falconer, decd . . . containing one hundred one and five eighths acres it being one moiety of tract situate between Ivy Branch and Fork Branch surveyed for Henry Reynolds and William Sterele on 20 June 1759. Wit: James White, Wm. Brown. Ackn 9 Feb 1774. (V:p163)

213. 25 Nov 1773 Indenture between Rebecca Evans and Elizabeth Clark, both of city of Philadelphia, spinsters (same being daus and surviving issue of William Clark of same city, gent, decd by Rebecca his first wife which William Clark was only son and heir of William Clark sometime of city of Dublin in kingdom of Ireland, late of Sussex on Delaware, decd by Honor, his wife, also decd), of one part and William Bradley of Kent on Delaware, yeoman. Consideration of fifty pounds conveys parcel of land situate on Mispillion Creek bounded on east by land of Levin Crapper, Esq and on west by land of Joseph Oliver. Description mntions Sawmill Range . . . improvement of Isaiah Bradley, decd . . . with a line mentions Booth's . . . containing one hundred twenty nine acres, part of Sawmill Range

granted to Henry Bowman who died seized thereof intestate and adm was in due form of law committed to William Clark, the grandfather, obtained an order to make sale of the tract to pay Bowman's debts amounting to seven hundred pounds and Sawmill Range was appraised to said William Clark adm for two hundred pounds whereupon the land descended to Rebecca Evans and Elizabeth Clark. Wit: Matthew Manlove, S. Shoemaker. Ackn 24 Feb 1774. (V:p163)

214. 23 Feb 1774 John Cook, Esq. high sheriff of Kent on Delaware send greeting whereas Arnold Hudson and Ezekiel Anderson by recovery agst Isaac Jones and Hannah his wife who by name of Hannah Smith was admx of Robert Smith, decd, a debt of twelve pounds fourteen shillings two pence half penny and four pounds adjudged as damages. John Cook seized and placed in execution a parcel of unimproved land and marsh belonging to Robert Smith of one hundred twenty nine acres and sold same to Hudson and Anderson for sum of fifteen pounds. Description mentions white oak of John Clifton's land . . . cor of John Smith's land called Point Lookout. Wit: Thos. Tilton, Samuel Chew. Ackn 23 Feb 1774. (V:p164)

215. 22 Feb 1774 Indenture between Edward McIllroy. Senior, Kent on Delaware, husbandman and Edward McIllroy, Junr, yeoman and only son of said Edward first named. For the natural love and affection he hath and beareth to Edward, Junr., his son and for the better maintainance livelihood, conveys a lot near the Cross Roads in Duck Creek Hund. Beginning at a cor stake . . . on the side of road leading toward Maryland . . . laid out for one acre of land. Wit: F. Battell, Richard Bassett. Ackn 24 Feb 1774. (V:p164)

216. 24 Feb 1774 Petition of Thomas Smith of city and co of Philadelphia, merchant, by William Killen, his atty, humbly sheweth that a writ at the suit of John Clayton as assignee of Thomas Parke agst Mark Manlove, Junr, of Kent Co, yeoman . . . debt of thirty four pounds eleven shillings eight pence and forty two shillings nine pence for damages. . . Thomas Collins, Esq, then sheriff of Kent Co seized and placed in execution one hundred fifty acres of land of Mark Manlove's in right of his wife, Violet bounded on south west by Double Run Branch on the north west by land called Caroon Manor . . . on northeast by land called Clapham and on south by Long Branch . . . sold at public vendue to petitioner for sum of twenty six pounds ten shillings. Thomas Collins, late sheriff, has not conveyed the land . . . petitioner humbly prays that your Worships order John Cook, present sheriff to execute the deed. The within petition being read to the court is granted. A True Copy . . . (signed) Samuel Chew. (V:p165)

217. 24 Feb 1774 Indenture between John Cook, high sheriff of Kent on Delaware

and Thomas Smith of city and co of Philadelphia, merchant. John Clayton lately in court of Common Pleas recovered agst Mark Manlove, Junr. a debt of thirty four pounds eleven shillings eight pence and forty two shillings nine pence like money for damages. By virtue of writ issued Thomas Collins, Esq., then sheriff of Kent Co seized and placed in execution one hundred fifty acres of land of Mark Manlove's in right of his wife, Violet. (Description of premises given in petition above). Same was sold at public vendue to Thomas Smith for sum of twenty six pounds ten shillings. Thomas Collins hath not conveyed the land during his continuance in office and Smith by petition by William Killen, his atty, asked the court to order John Cook, present sheriff to execute the deed which is now conveyed. Wit: Zadok Crapper, Samuel Chew. Ackn 24 Feb 1774. (V:p165)

218. 24 Feb 1774 Petition of Jonathan Emerson of Kent on Delaware most humbly sheweth that a writ at suit of Robert Montgomery agst Vincent Emerson of Kent Co, yeoman, otherwise of Worcester Co in province of Maryland, directing the sheriff to sieze the land of Vincent Emerson on south side of Indian Creek in Murtherkill Hund nr Johnny Cake Landing containing forty eight acres of land part of St. Collam, also part of same tract containing three hundred acres as well as a debt of four hundred pounds who Robert with Thomas Montgomery, decd, were assignees of John Keaton who recovered afst Vincent also two pounds eighteen shillings nine pence adjudged for damages. James Wells, Esq, then sheriff, seized the lands which were sold at public vendue to your petitioner in sum of seven hundred fifty pounds who has paid and satisfied the sheriff, James Wells, who has been removed from office and no deed has been executed. Petitioner prays that your Worships order present sheriff, John Cook, to execute the deed. The petition being read to the court and considered, is granted. A True Copy. (signed) Samuel Chew. (V:p166)

219. 24 Feb 1774 Indenture between John Cook, high sheriff of Kent on Delaware and Jonathan Emerson of same co. Whereas the sheriff by virtue of writ was ordered to seize and place in execution all lands of Vincent Emerson of Worcester Co, province of Maryland, a parcel of land situate on south side of Indian Branch in Murtherkill Hund. Beginning at a place nr Johnny Cake Landing . . . cor of land belonging to John Sipple . . . containing forty eight acres . . . part of St. Collum. Also all other tract part of said St. Collum beginning . . . to cor of land belonging to Mark Manlove . . . land of late of one Harper . . . containing three hundred acres of land. Also for debt of four hundred pounds and fifty pounds which Robert Montgomery with Thomas Montgomery, decd, as assignees of John Keaton recovered agst Emerson as well as two pounds eighteen shillings nine pence in damages. Sheriff sold the property at public vendue to Jonathan Emerson for sum of seven hundred pounds and hath not conveyed the deed. John Cook, present

sheriff, now conveys afsd parcels of land. Wit: James Sykes, Samuel Chew. Ackn 24 Feb 1774. (V:p166)

220. 23 Feb 1774 Petition of Solomon Wallace late of Kent on Delaware humbly sheweth that John Vining and John Brinckle, Esqrs, trustees of the General Loan Office obtained judgement agst Mark Smith, Senr, for sum of two hundred ten pounds and William Rhodes, then sheriff, by virtue of write seized one hundred fifty acres and exposed same to public vendue, selling the land to petitioner for two hundred pounds who therefore prays the court will order John Cook, present sheriff, to execute a deed of conveyance. The petition being read to the court, considered, is granted. A True Copy. (signed) Samuel Chew. (V:167)

221. 25 Feb 1774 Indenture: I, John Cook, high sheriff of Kent on Delaware, send greetings. Whereas by virtue of writ lately issued out of court of Common Pleas, William Rhodes, then sheriff, commanding him that of goods, chattles, lands and tenements of Mark Smith, Senr in hands of Robert Young, be caused to be levied and made as well as a debt of two hundred ten pounds which John Vining and John Brinckle, Esqrs, trustees of the General Loan Office secured agst him as well as forty one shillings three pence adjudged for damages. Rhodes placed in execution a parcel of land previously mortgaged of one hundred fifty acres, Mark Smith's dwelling plantation, being same Hugh Durborough deeded 11 Aug 1727 to Mark Smith, and sold same to Solomon Wallace for sum of two hundred ten dollars. John Cook with the authority granted now conveys the said land. Wit: Jacob Stout, Richd. Smith. Ackn 25 Feb 1774. (V:p168)

222. 23 Feb 1774 Petition of John Bell of Kent on Delaware humbly sheweth whereas by virtue of writ directed to Thomas Collins, then sheriff, commanding him to place in execution a parcel of unimproved land, property of David Caldwell conveyed to him by his father, Andrew Caldwell, Esq. containing one hundred sixty two acres and sold at public vendue to your petitioner for sum of one hundred pounds and Thomas Collins is now out of office and no deed has been made, your petitioner prays this court will order John Cook, present sheriff, to execute same. The petition being read to the court, considered, is granted. A True Copy. Samuel Chew. (V:p168)

223. 22 Feb 1774 Indenture between John Cook, Esq, high sheriff of Kent on Delaware and John Bell late of town of Dover, innkeeper but a farmer. Whereas David Caldwell was indebted to John Bell who in common recovery secured judgement agst him directing Thomas Collins, then sheriff, that of the goods and chattles, lands and tenements of Caldwell, he should cause said debt to be levied. Sheriff seized and placed into execution a tract of land in forrest of Murtherkill

Hund part of The Exchange containing one hundree sixty acres as it was conveyed to David Caldwell by his father, Andrew Caldwell, Esq, but subject to mortgage to General Loan Office, said land was sold at public vendue to John Bell for one hundred pounds, he being highest bidder, and Thomas Collins is no longer in office and no deed has been conveyed. John Cook by order of the court now conveys the land. Wit: John Martin, John Cox. Ackn 22 Feb 1774. (V:p169)

224. 23 Feb 1774 Petition of Robt. Hodgson humbly sheweth that a writ directed to James Caldwell, then sheriff of Kent on Delaware, land of David Caldwell was seized at suit of trustees of General Loan Office and sold to your petitioner on 3 Apr 1773 and James Caldwell is out of office and no deed has been made, your petitioner humbly prays the court to authorize John Cook, present sheriff to execute same. Petition being read to court, is considered and granted. A True Copy. Samuel Chew. (V:p169)

225. 23 Feb 1774 Indenture between John Cook, high sheriff of Kent on Delaware and Robert Hodgson of Murtherkill Hund, gent. Whereas Andrew Caldwell by deed conveyed to son, David Caldwell, a parcel of rough land part of tract called The Exchange adj to land part of said whole tract on which Robert Hudgson now dwelleth, said to be one hundred sixty two acres but by recent survey and after clearance of former sales, it is found to contain one hundred eighty two and a half acres and David Caldwell on 12 Sept 1760 mortgaged same to General Loan Office for sixty pounds and also gave bond with judgment for same and he not discharging same, a writ on judgment made directed James Caldwell, then sheriff, to seize and place in execution the parcel of land which was sold at public vendue to Robert Hodgson for sum of two hundred twenty seven pounds seventeen shillings seven pence and no deed was made. Now, John Cook by order of the court executes deed for the parcel of land. Wit: Jacob Stout, John Clarke. Ackn 24 Feb 1774. (V:p169)

226. 22 Feb 1774 Indenture between Richard Jester of Kent on Delaware and Rebeckah, his wife and William Jester same place. Consideraton of fifty pounds conveys parcel of land in Mispillion Hund beginning at cor of Ebenezer Hathorn's land . . . William Jester's other land . . . cor of Langarels land . . . laid out for one hundred ninety two and a half acres with allowance of six percent for roads, etc. Wit: James Rawley, Zadok Crapper. Ackn 23 Feb 1774. Rebecah Jester privately examined gave consent. (V:p169)

227. 23 Jan 1774 Indenture between John White of forest of Murtherkill Hund, Kent on Delaware, yeoman and Isabell, his wife and James Craige of town of Dover, said co, taylor. Consideration of one hundred sixty one pounds ten shillings

conveys parcel part of tract resurveyed to John White on 1st and 2nd Sept 1773 by virtue of warrant of resurvey dated 2 Dec 1772. Beginning on west side of Wild Cat Swamp . . . cor tree of land formerly surveyed for Dennis Conner and Charles Cottenham but now of Wheeler Meredith . . . by Thomas Hatfield's improvements . . . land late of John Oldfield . . . cor for Benedict Brice's land . . . land called Oldfield's Range . . . part conveyed by William White to James Craige . . . laid off for one hundred sixty one acres and ninety one square perches. Wit: John Gray, Peter Torbert. Isabell White privately examined gave consent. Ackn 24 Feb 1774. (V:p170)

228. 2 June 1773 Indenture between Sarah Pemberton, widow and Hannah Robinson, spinster, sisters, children of George Robinson formerly of St. Jone's Hund alias Dover Hund, Kent on Delaware and Jonathan Caldwell of same hund and co, yeoman. Whereas survey was made for William Winsmore called Great Pipe Elm situate in Dover Hund on south side of Little Creek adj lands formerly surveyed for Daniel Jones and Richard Levick. George Robinson purchased a great part of whole tract which was called the School House tract which he devised to daus: Sarah and Hannah and was taken into possession by Stephen Paradee (he having obtained warrant for vacant land lying between Great Pipe Elm, Byefield and Shoulder of Mutton, he included part of Pipe Elm in his survey thereby excluding the said devisees. Said part begins on prong of Pipe Elm Branch . . . nr Buck's Bridge . . . will of William Winsmore by his devise to Abel and Mathew Wilson . . . formerly Daniel Jones's land called Byefield . . . Richard Levick's land called Shoulder of Mutton . . . this part contains one hundred eighteen and a half acres. Above described land became property of Margaret, wife of Daniel Lewis, and dau to Stephen Paradee, Esq. and Daniel Lewis afterwards purchased a part of Pipe Elm from some person it seems had no right to sell, a part of the purchase is cleared and fenced and begins at cor of land belonging to William Rodney purchased from Samuel Hanson and formerly of Abel and Mathew Wilson . . . found to contain eleven and a half acres. After death of Daniel Lewis leaving sundry children, his widow, Margaret, married Jonathan Caldwell and Sarah and Hannah brought suit of ejectment agst him and he purchased the land from them in consideration of one hundred seventy five pounds and they now convey same. Samuel McCall and Mark McCall apptd attys. Wit: Hannah Hart, John Bell. Ackn 24 Feb 1774. (V:p170)

229. 17 Apr 1773 Indenture between Levin Crapper, Esq. of Sussex on Delaware and Joseph Oliver, mariner of same place. Consideration of seventy two pounds nineteen shillings conveys parcel of land in Mispillion Hund, Kent on Delaware, on north side of Mispillion Creek opposite John Brown's former dwelling plantation, to eastward of Joseph Booth's former dwelling plantation, being part of Sawmill

Range conveyed to Joseph Oliver by Purnal Wattson on 30 May 1771 and on day following by Joseph Oliver to Levin Crapper, Esq., laid off for one hundred fifteen acres. William Killen apptd atty. Wit: Levi Oliver, William Primrose. Ackn 23 Feb 1774. (V:p171)

230. 4 Feb 1771 Indenture between Samuel Skidmore of Kent on Delaware, physician and Charles Ridgely same place, Esq. Consideration of seven pounds, ten shilings conveys lot of land in town of Dover and part of large lot marked on town plat No. 31 which was property of Thomas Skidmore, decd, father of Samuel. Description mentions Joseph Pryor's lot . . . Gaol Lot. Wit: Andw. Caldwell, Caleb Sipple. Ackn 24 Feb 1774. (V:p172)

231. 23 Feb 1774 Indenture between Joseph Oliver of Sussex on Delaware, mariner and Nathan Adams of Kent on Delaware, merchant. consideration of nine pounds conveys parcel of land on Mispillion Creek part of tract called The Improvement. Beginning on part of land formerly belonging to Henry Molleston, decd . . . nr Mill Stone Landing . . . containing one quarter of an acre of land. Wit: David Hilford, Richard McNatt. Ackn 23 Feb 1774. (V:p172)

232 Nov 1774 Petition of John Cox of Mispillion Hund, Kent on Delaware, humbly sheweth that your petitioner purchased from James Caldwell, late sheriff of Kent Co, a certain messuage, plantation or tract of land situate on south west side of of main head of Mispillion Creek called Black Swamp adj road leading from Choptank Bridge over the Black Swamp to Johnny Cake Landing and allotted by the court to Mary Williams, widow of James Williams who died intestate as her right of dower and she later married Henry Wells, Junr who has eloped from his native place. Said dower was seized taken into execution and sold to Nimrod Maxwell who transferred his right of purchase to your petitioner who has paid the sheriff sum of thirty six pounds. James Caldwell is removed from office and petitioner prays court to command John Cook, present sheriff, to execute deed for same. Petition being read to court, considered, is granted. A True Copy. Samuel Chew. (V:p172)

233. 22 Feb 1774. I, John Cook, high sheriff of Kent on Delaware, send greetings. Whereas Timothy Caldwell assignee of James Caldwell recovered agst Henry Wells, Junr, yeoman, a judgement of debt of one hundred twenty pounds and two pounds one shilling six pence as damages. James Wells, then sheriff, seized parcel of land of Wells placing in execution a dowery in ninety acres of land and also eighty two acres without improvements which is not sold but the ninety acres of dower was sold at public vendue to Nimrod Maxwell for thirty six pounds who transferred his right of purchase to John Cox who petitioned the court to command

present sheriff, John Cook, to execute deed for same. For consideration paid, sheriff now conveys the afsd described land. Wit: John Edwards, Robert Hodgson. Ackn 22 Feb 1774. (V:p173)

234. Appointment: To Richard McWilliam of Newcastle on Delaware know that reposing special trust and confidence in your loyalty integrity and ability, we have assigned and appointed you . . . to be chief justice of our Supriem(sic) Court. Witness: John Penn, Esq, Governor and Commander in Chief of the counties above said 30 Oct 1773. A True Copy. (signed) John Penn. (V:p173)

235. 15 Nov 1773 Indenture between James Reed and Annalaney Craige both of Murtherkill Hund, Kent on Delaware, surviving heirs of Samuel Mann formerly of said place, decd and Willliam Rhodes same place, Esq. Consideration of one hundred forty pounds conveys parcel of land part of tract granted by warrant survey and patent to Samuel Mann and is residuary part not heretofore sold. Beginning on Banister's or Hudson's Branch . . . small distance from John Smith's grist mill . . . called Bishop's Branch . . . to Willcock's Branch . . . laid out for seventy seven and one quarter acres. Samuel McCall, Mark McCall apptd attys. Wit: Alxander Hudson, George Saxton. Ackn 24 Feb 1774. (V:p173)

236. 24 Feb 1774 Indenture between Waitman Booth of Mispillion Hund, Kent on Delaware and Lydia, his wife and John Edmondson, Francis Edmondson and Solomon Edmondson, yeomen. Consideration of eighty six pounds conveys parcel of land in hund and co afsd which by deed bearing 13 May 1768 was conveyed with other lands by Nathan Manlove to Waitman Booth containing eighty one acres and allowance (Book R, folio 261) but accurate survey made 13 Apr 1773 by Mark McCall is found ninety one acres and ninety three square perches now known as The Breeches. Beginning at cor of Drapersberry and Trinacria and land formerly of Daniel Brown . . . land of Elijah Sipple . . . in Dubrois's(Durborows?) Pond . . . James Purden's land . . . nr line of Jonathan Sipple's land formerly of Daniel and Pemberton Brown . . . land late claimed by Thomas Craige but now of Sampson Levi. Wit: William Gray, John Gray. Lydia Booth privately examined gave consent. Ackn 24 Feb 1774. (V:p174)

237. Draught of division of Richard Downham's Land. Plat shows allotted parts to Richard, Mary, Sarah, Elizabeth, Isaac, Rachal and Ruth. We, William Virdin, Gove Trippit, Joseph Downham, John Powell and William Powell send greeting that Richard Downham late of Kent on Delaware, decd, did bequeath to his several children: Isaac Downham; Ruth Downham; Mary, wife to John Beauchamp; Sarah Downham; Elizabeth Downham; Richard Downham and Rachal Downham all his lands equally divided except Richard is to have one hundred twenty acres of land

and swamp from land the decd bought of John Housman and decd authorized us the subscribers . . . to divide and lay off . . . amongst above named children . . . land was caused to be surveyed by John Powell (description and allotted parts given to each heir). 5th day 3rd mo 1774. (signed) John Powell, William Powell, William Virdin, Govey Trippet, Joseph Downham. A True Copy Test. (V:p175)

238. 9 July 1773 Bond: I, Ann King of Kent on Delaware, widow am firmly bound to Richard Tomlinson of same co, yeoman, in sum of two hundred forty pounds. Condition of the obligation is such that Ann King will convey and assume all charges for parcel of land including the plantation with appurtenances thereto belonging which Isaac King, Senr, husband to Ann, did by will 15 June 1771, devise to Ann part of tract called Angleton now in her tenure. Wit: William Merydith, Patrick Crain. Ackn 26 May 1774. (V:p176)

239. 12 Nov 1775 Bond: Know all men by these presents that we, John Cook, high sheriff of Kent on Delaware and James Raymond, William Cahoon, Junr, and Robert Rees, gents, are firmly bound unto our Sovereign Lord King . . . in just sum of fifteen hundred pounds. Condition being that John Cook, high sheriff shall and do well and truly seize and execute all the Kings writs and processes to him directed . . . and at all times in his continuance in said office of sheriff well and faithfully execute the said office. (signed) John Cook, Jas. Raymond, William Cahoon, Junr, Robert Rees. Wit: Samuel Chew, Clerk, Geo. Painter. (V:p177)

240. 6 Oct 1773 To all judges, justices, magistrates and other officers, freemen, and all other persons within Kent County, we have granted John Cook, Esq, the office of sheriff of said co . . . we do therefore by these presents require and command you and all and every of you . . . be aiding and assisting in all things that to the office of sheriff . . . may in anywise belong lawfully. In testimony whereof, we have caused the great seal of said province to be hereunto affixed. Witness: John Penn, Esq, Governor and Commander in Chief of counties afsd and province of Pennsylvania at Philadelphia. (V:p177)

241. 6 Oct 1773 Appointment: To Caleb Furbee of Kent on Delaware, gent, Greeting: Know that reposing special trust and confidence in your loyalty integrity and ability, we have nominated and appointed you to be coroner of said co. Witness: John Penn, Esq, Governor and Commander in Chief of counties afsd and province of Pennsylvania at Philadelphia. (V:p177)

242. 6 Oct 1773 Appointment: To John Cook, Esq of Kent on Delaware, Greeting. Know that reposing special trust and confidence in your loyalty integrity and ability, we have nominated and appointed you to be sheriff of said co. Witness:

John Penn, Esq, Governor and Commander in Chief of counties afsd and province of Pennsylvania at Philadelphia. (V:p177)

243. 17 Mar 1774 Indnture between Benjamin Benston and Elizabeth, his wife, of Kent on Delaware, yeoman and David Rowland of same place. Whereas William Rhodes, Esq, former high sheriff, by deed 14 May 1763 conveyed to Benson parcel of land in Mispillion Hund on Murtherkill Creek part of tract called Clayton containing one hundred acres. Description mentions . . . line of land formerly Joshua Wheelars now possessed by Kemuel Godwin. Deed recorded in Book Q, folio 158. Consideration of one hundred thirty five pounds conveys the land. Wit: David Hilford, John Alcock. Elizabeth Benston privately examined gave consent. Ackn 26 Masy 1774. (V:p177)

244. 10 May 1774 To all Christian People whereras by will of Robert Hall late decd of Kent on Delaware full power and authority was given to extx to sell and dispose of his real estate to pay testators debts . . . thought necessary to sell two hundred and twenty nine acres of fast land with seventeen and three quarters acres of branch cripple and fifty acres of marsh. Jerusha Hall, extx has married Thomas Cahoon and they sold the land at public vendue to Thomas Collins, being the highest bidder, for one thousand one hundred five pounds towards discharge of debts. Residue of Hall's real estate of about one hundred fifteen acres of fast land, sixty acres of branch cripple and two hundred acres of marsh . . . which was advertised and sold to Thomas Collins for five hundred sixty seven pounds. Thomas Cahoon and Jerusha, his wife, now convey afsd land situate in Little Creek Neck bounded by lands of John Frazer, Jonathan Caldwell, a branch of Duck Creek and sd Collins's land. Authorize Mr. French Battell and Samuel McCall to act as attys. Wit: Allen McLeane, Elizabeth Elliott. Ackn 11 May 1774. (V:p178)

245. 26 May 1774 Indenture between Valentine King of Murtherkill Hund, Kent on Delaware, yeoman, extr of Anne King, late of sd co and Richard Tomlinson of Mispillion Hund, same co, yeoman. Isaac King, father of Valentine, was seized of tract called Angleton orig surveyed for George Cullin, which part Isaac King purchased from Cornelius Dewese on 11 Feb 1746 (Book N, folio 122) said to contain one hundred ninety one acres. King made will 15 June 1749 devising half part of land and his dwelling plantation to his wife, Anne, and residue to son, Isaac, Junr. Andrew Doz of Philadelphia became seized in fee of the moiety devised to Isaac, Junr whereby a survey made by Mark McCall, surveyor, it was found to contain three hundred seventeen acres and eighty nine square perches and at same time was equally divided between Anne King and Andrew Doz in right of Isaac King, Junr to each one hundred fifty eight acres and one hundred twenty four and a half square perches and each releasing to the other a confirmation of the division.

Anne King by writing obligatory to Richard Tomlinson on 9 July 1773 to grant her moiety and having made her will on 30 July 1773 apptd her son, Valentine King, extr, who for consideration paid by Tomlinson of one hundred pounds now conveys the land. Wit: Mark McCall, William Hathorne. Ackn 6 May 1774. (V:p179)

246. 26 May 1774 Indenture between Sarah Greenwood, admx of Joseph Greenwood, late of Kent on Delaware, decd and Johnson Earickson of Mispillion Hund, same co, yeoman. Joseph Greenwood was seized in fee of tract of land in hund and co afsd and died intestate leaving insufficient personal estate to pay considerable debts. Sarah Greenwood, widow, petitioned court to sell real estate to pay his creditors, court considered and granted same. She sold the land to James Gordon for twenty shillings per acre and survey was made by Mark McCall, surveyor, and premises were found to contain one hundred twelve and a quarter acres of land. Beginning at cor of land of William Carpenter . . . land claimed by heirs of Benjamin Brown . . . land claimed by Sampson Levy of Philadelphia. James Gordon sold the land to Johnson Earickson who now requests deed for consideration of one hundred twelve pounds five shillings and Sarah Greenwood conveys same. Wit: Silas Snow, Mark McCall. Ackn 26 May 1774. (V:p179)

247. 7 May 1774 Indenture between Daniel Smith and Mary, his wife, of Kent on Delaware, yeoman and William Hatfield of forest of Murtherkill Hund, yeoman. Consideration of eighty pounds conveys tract of land in Little Neck laid out for ninety nine and three quarters of an acre and allowance of six percent . . . agst themselves, said Daniel Smith and Mary, his wife and agst Abraham Bush, Thomas Harper, Thomas Smith, John Hatfield, Benjamin Coomes and Isaac Lowber and any one of their heirs, shall and will warrant and forever defend by these presents. Wit: Solomon Wallace, Wm. Betts. Mary Smith privately examined gave consent. Ackn 11 May 1774. (V:p180)

248. 30 Mar 1774 Indenture between Philemon Dickinson of city of Philadelphia, gent and John Gordon of Kent on Delaware, farmer. Consideraton of one hundred fifty pounds conveys parcel of land containing fifty acres part of Lisbone on north side of Jone's Creek (on two hundred acres which Thomas French sometime before 14 Feb 1718 did live and died intestate . . . land descended to his children: Robert French, Catherine French since married Walter Dickinson, Mary French who married Benjamin Brown) in proportionate shares or one hundred acres or two fourths to Roberrt and one fourth or fifty acres to each dau. Robert, Katherine and Mary were so seized and Robert sometime later that year or beginning of 1718 died and fifty acres of his land descended to Walter Dickinson and wife, Katherine who on 14 Feb 1748 conveyed the land to Samuel Dickinson (Liber N, folio 256)

father of Philemon to whom it was devised by will. William Killen apptd atty. Wit: Mary Gorden, Joshua Gordon. Ackn 26 May 1774. (V:p181)

249. 26 May 1774 Indenture between William Hathorne of Newcastle on Delaware, impowered and authorized to act in place of Joseph Lee and Mary, his wife of South Carolina (she being one of children and heirs of Ebenezer Hathorne, late of Kent on Delaware) and Francis Jester, same co. Ebenezer Hathorne was seized in tract of land situate in Mispillion Hund nr Marshy Hope beginning . . . to tree of William Howgin's land . . . laid out for one hundred seventy nine acres. For consideration of ten pounds conveys the residue of above described land not sold, right of Mary Lee. Wit: Richard Brinkle, John Gullett, Junr. Ackn 26 May 1774. (V:p182)

250. 24 May 1774 Indenture between Henry Farson of Duck Creek Hund, Kent on Delaware, farmer and Jacob Lycan(?) same place. Consideration of three hundred pounds conveys two lotts or parcels of land within the limits of town of Salisbury. First was lott of David Marshall, innholder, decd, who died intestate and Reverend Hugh Neill was apptd admr and sold same to William Farson, Esq by deed 15 Aug 1753 (Book O, page 194) beginning at stake sixty six feet from mill dam . . . with Aaron Jorddon's lott . . . containing half an acre and eight perches. The other lott begins at the mill dam . . . to William Ball's lott . . . to line of Meeting House lott . . . containing three acres and a half . . . being part of lott Henry Farson bought of Dr. John Fothergill and others on 15 Oct 1770 (Book T, page 104). Wit: Morgan Blackshare, Thomas Steward. Ackn 25 May 1774. (V:p182)

251. 30 Mar 1774 Indenture between Caesar Rodney of Kent on Delaware, Esq and James Tilton same co, practitioner in physics. Consideration of five hundred fifty pounds conveys all that brick messuage or tenement and tenement on lot whereon same now stands on west side of court house square in town of Dover. Beginning at intersection of the square and court house alley . . . cor of messuage and lot late of Edmund Kearny now of Samuel MCcall. Also all that other lot adj containing one acre and thirty nine perces and forty five feet of land . . . excepting and always reserving out of this present grant to any person having title to same one half acre of the last lot to be laid off from the residue . . . all which premises heretofore belonging to and in possession of Edmund Badger, the elder, late of Dover, cordwainer, decd, who devised same to Edmund Badger, the younger, his son, who sold the land to John Baning in fee simple who conveyed the same to Caesar Rodney. Wit: William Killen, Thomas Rodney. Ackn 25 May 1774. (V:p183)

252. 25 May 1774 Indenture between Mary Catts of Kent on Delaware and Zadok Crapper same co. Consideration of thirteen pounds five shillings conveys parcel of

land part of tract called Stockfield situate in forest of Mispillion Hund lately purchased by Thomas Fitzsimmons, late of co afsd of John Cade of Sussex co on 6 Feb 1753 (Book O, folio 191) and Fitzsimmons died intestate leaving Mary Catts one of his children who now conveys her share. Beginning at cor of Fitzsimmon's land and cor of land William Tharp bought of heirs of William Downs . . . laid out for eight acres and one hundred thirty five perches. Wit: William Cahoon, James Sterling. Ackn 25 May 1774. (V:p184)

253. 24 May 1774 Indenture between Joseph David, Junr of forest of Little Creek Hund, Kent on Delaware, yeoman and Joseph David, Senr, same place, yeoman. Joel Lewis of city of Philadelphia, hatmaker, by deed dated 1771 made over to Thomas Murphy who deeded his undivided share to Joseph David, Junr in a tract of land orig surveyed for John Hillyard known as The Exchange. Share being one eighth part of two hundred acres which tract was conveyed by Charles Hillyard to Evan Lewis, decd, who was uncle to Joel Lewis. Consideration of seventy five pounds conveys twenty five acre part of tract called The Exchange. Wit: James Moore, James Jones. Ackn 25 May 1774. (V:p184)

254. 11 Apr 1774 Indenture between Isaac Tumblin, blacksmith and Jacob Tumblin, cordwainer, of Kent on Delaware and Covil Tumblin of same co, yeoman. Whereas William Manlove by deed on 25 Nov 1721 granted to Nathaniel Tumblin (Book H, folio 117) a parcel of land in Mispillion Hund . Beginning on Virgins Branch . . . laid out for one hundred fifty acres part of tract granted by patent on 5th day 5th mo 1684 to Edward Piner. Tumblin devised by will dated 27 Jan 1755 to Isaac and Jacob Tumblin who now convey same for consideration of one hundred pounds. John Banning and Thomas Peterkin apptd attys. Wit: Joseph Brown, Caleb Sparks. Ackn 10 May 1774. (V:p185)

255. 6 Apr 1774 Indenture betweern Robert Palmetry, Allen Palmetry, James Severson and Elizabeth, his wife, sister to afsd Robert and Allen, all being children of Robrt Palmetry the second who was son of Robert Palmetry, alias, Robert Palmatary, the elder, patentee of tract called Robert's Chance, and also Samuel Murphy, William Murphy, Thomas Harwood and Susannah, his wife, Thomas Jones and Hannah his wife, said Susannah and Hannah sisters to Samuel and William, all four grandchildren to Eleoner Dawson, dau to Robert Palmetry, the patentee, and also Anthony Snow and Rachel his wife, she being dau to Robert Dawson, son of Eleoner Dawson, all of Duck Creek Hund, Kent on Delaware, all of one part and Arnold Hawkins same co, yeoman. A survey was made for Robert, the patentee, on 6 Jan 1679/80 called Robert's Chance in hund afsd on Palmetry's Branch of five hundred acres parts of which have been sold and a parcel is possessed by Arnold Hawkins and it is alleged that sales made to John Hawkins,

father of Arnold, did not extend to head of whole tract and the above named heirs of Robert Palmetry, patentee, are about to make a deed of confirmation for said land in consideration of one hundred pounds. William Killen apptd atty. Wit: Allen McLeane, William Cahoon. Elizabeth Severson, Susannah Harwood and Rachel Snow privately examined gave their consent. Ackn 10 May 1774. (V:p186)

256. 26 May 1774 Indenture between William Hathorne, single person of Newcastle on Delaware being lawful authority to act in place of Joseph Lee and Mary his wife of South Carolina, she being an heir of Ebenezer Hathorne late of Kent on Delaware and John Gullett same co. Whereas Ebenezer was seized in tract situate nr Marshapope(sic) beginning at cor of Joseph Bradley's land . . . laid out for two hundred twenty nine acres . . . William Hathorne in consideration of eleven pounds three shillings nine pence received conveys the right, title and interest of Joseph Lee and Mary his wife to the residue of above described land to John Gullett. Wit: Richard Brinkle, Francis Jester. Ackn 26 May 1774. (V:p187)

257. 4 May 1774 Indenture between William Anderson of Kent on Delaware and Margaret his wife and Joseph Morris same co. William Anderson by good conveyance from William Langarel for parcel of land in forest of Mispillion Hund and also one other tract adj surveyed for George Langarel, decd, by warrant 24th day August 1752 why by will devised same to William Langarel. Description mentions Isaac Marrel's land . . . laid out for one hundred forty one and one quarter acres and the other tract . . . oak by Richard Jester's fence . . . cor of William Jester's line . . . laid out for one hundred thirty six acres. Consideration of two hundred four pounds conveys above described lands. Wit: John Clark, Ann Clark. Margaret Langarel privately examined gave consent. Ackn 12 May 1774. (V:p187)

258. 11 May 1774 Indenture between William Manlove of Kent on Delaware, merchant and Elizabeth his wife and John Mastin same place, yeoman. Whereas William Rhodes, Esq of same place by deed on 16 Apr 1771 (Book T, folio 143) granted to William Manlove all right, title, etc. to a dividend of land bought by Caleb Tucker of Benjamin McNatt, part of tract called Long Green situate in Mispillion Hund. James Caldwell, high sheriff, by deed 16 May 1771 did grant all right, title, etc. which Benjamin McNatt had to William Manlove (Book T, folio 82) by whioh deeds he became lawfully seized of two tracts he now conveys for consideration of sixty pounds. Description mentions land of Elijah Morris . . . road by Marmaduke Morgan's . . . cor of Thomas Cain's land . . . containing one hundred forty four acres. Wit: Richd. Lockwood, Elizabeth Paton. Elizabeth Manlove privately examined gave her consent. Ackn 11 May 1774. (V:p188)

259. 27 Apr 1774 Indenture between John Gordon of Dover Hund, Kent on

Delaware, cabinet maker and John Ware same place, blacksmith. Whereas Philemon Dickinson by deed 30 Mar last past granted to John Gordon a parcel of fifty acres, part of tract called Lisborn in Dover Hund in which deed is set forth that two hundred acres part of Lisbon was formerly property of Thomas French and afterwards property of his children, and by conveyance from Walter Dickinson and Katherine, his wife, she being a child of French, the fifty acres became property of Samuel Dickinson who devised same to Philemon Dickinson. Consideration of two hundred six pounds conveys the property. Description mentions land late of Abraham Barber, decd . . . land of John Ware . . . containing fifty three acres of upland besides the cod of creek cripple (acreage unknown). Noted that John Gordon conveys only his private right or title to body of the cripple contained in the cod between the upland and the creek and doth only warrant it from himself and Gordon and agst the heirs of Benjamin Brown claiming under above named Thomas French. Wit: James Robinson, Mark McCall. 26 May 1774. (V:p189)

260 11 May 1774 Indenture between Mary Sipple of Murtherkill Hund, Kent on Delaware, spinstress, one of children of Caleb Sipple, same place, mariner, decd and Caleb Sipple, her brother of same place, yeoman. Whereas Joseph Brincklee and John Brincklee, sons of John Brincklee, decd, granted unto legal heirs of Caleb Sipple, two hundred twenty acres on north side of Murther Creek and on west side of Kings Road. By order of court a third was laid off to Sarah, widow of Caleb Sipple and now, Mary is conveying her share of twenty seven and half acres of land and marsh to her brother, Caleb, a part of the one third which must remain until decease of their mother. For consideration of ninety pounds Mary now conveys all her right, title, interest, property claim and demand to all of the land. Wit: Mark McCall, Samuel McCall. Ackn 11 May 1774. (V:p189)

261. 25 May 1774 Indenture between William Betts of Kent on Delaware, yeoman and Elizabeth his wife and Robert Minors same place, yeoman. Whereas Betts is seized of parcel of land and marsh situate on north side of Mispillion Creek in Mispillion Hund. Description mentions Caleb Luff's land . . . said tract containing two hundred five and a half acres of upland and one hundred three acres and one hundred thirty seven perches of marsh exclusive of cripple and marsh on the said branch, all of which is part of land . . . Mount Pleasant and sixty three acres and one hundred and thirty seven perches of marsh being residue of the whole, part of residue is part of survey made for William Betts and Curtis Brinckle, both of said co, decd and part is part of parcel of marsh surveyed for Matthew Manlove and purchased by John Bessex of George Manlove and bartered with Betts by Bessex. Consideration of three hundred four pounds conveys above described parcels containing in the whole three hundred nine acres and fifty seven perches of land.

Wit: Edward Fisher, Avary Draper. Elizabeth Betts privately examined gave consent. Ackn 25 May 1774. (V:p190)

262. 12 May 1774 Indenture between John Smith and Sarah, his wife of Kent on Delaware and Thomas Davis of same place. Witnesseth that John Smith and Sarah his wife are seized in parcel of land in forest of Murtherkill Hund which by warrant was surveyed to Thomas Smith, father of John, heir to tract. Consideration of twenty pounds conveys land beginning in line of John Davis's land ... in William Morris's line ... land belonging to Martha, wife of William Morris, tanner ... laid off for twenty acres of land. Wit: James Clark, John Gray. Sarah Smith privately examined gave consent. Ackn 12 May 1774. (V:p191)

263. 20 May 1774 Indenture tripartite between John Casson of Kent on Delaware, hatter, and Elizabeth, his wife and Thomas Parke of Kent Co, province of Maryland, student in physics and son of Elizabeth Casson and William Killen, atty at law. Witnesseth that as well for consideration of five shillings paid by Thomas Parke and like sum paid by William Killen convey all those three parcels of land and marsh, being parcel in Dover Hund beginning at cor poplar of land of William Rodney ... with land of John Irons ... line of land called Burton's Delight ... land late of Robert Gerald ... containing one hundred seven acres and seventy five square perches. Also a moiety or equal half part of and in two hundred acres of marsh situate nr place called Hay Point or Long Point and also all that other parcel part of tract called Lisbon situate in Dover Hund beginning at a walnut tree of land called Troy ... land late of Griffith Gordon ... containing one hundred twenty nine acres. All properties late est of John Edingfield of Kent Co, yeoman, who died intestate and lands descended to Elizabeth Casson, his dau, and others ... and as to the one hundred twenty nine acres unto the proper use and behoof of said John Casson during his natural life without impeachment or manner of waste, and after his death to proper use and behoof of Elizabeth Casson and after her death the same for Thomas Parke. Wit: John Chew, Myres Casson. Elizabeth Casson privately examined gave consent. Ackn 27 May 1774. (V:p192)

264. 9 Dec 1773 Power of Attorney: South Carolina, I, Hugh Durborow late of Kent on Delaware, son to John Durborow of same co, decd, for divers good causes and considerations appoint David Durborow and James Moore both of Kent Co my true and lawful attys for me and in my name and stead, and to my use, to ask, demand, sue for, levy, recover and receive all such sum and sums of money, etc. (signed) Hugh Durborow. Wit: Benjamin Jones, Thomas Murphey. Ackn 11 May 1774. (V:p193)

265. 10 Aug 1774 Bond: I, Andrew Saxton of Kent on Delaware am firmly bound

to Thomas Edmondson of Dorchester Co, province of Maryland, in full sum of five hundred twenty pounds. Condition of above obligation being that Andrew Saxton convey parcel of land where John Holston now lives formerly same of William Morgan which Saxton purchased from Ruben Walters. (signed) Andrew Saxton. Wit: Powell Cox, John Edmondson.

    I, Thomas Edmondson of Dorchester Co in province of Maryland do hereby sign over all my right, title and interest of this within bond agst Andrew Saxton to Benjamin Coombe of Murtherkill Hund, Kent on Delaware. 6th Oct 1773. (signed) Thomas Edmondson. Wit: Nimrod Maxwell, Sarah Maxwell. Ackn 12 Aug 1774. (V:p194)

266. 4 June 1774 Indenture between Matthew Jarrard of Murtherkill Hund, Kent on Delaware, yeoman (eldest son of Matthew Jarrard, same place, decd) and Willson Jarrard same place, tanner, (younger son of Matthew Jarrard) both of one part and James Jarrard same place, tanner (bro to Matthew and William). Whereas Matthew Jarrard, father to above parties was seized in sundry tracts of land and by will made 14 Dec 1768 devised to son, Matthew, the dwelling plantation with adjacent woodland to make quantity of three hundred acres and also devised remaining part equally to his other sons, James and Willson. A survey was made on the whole between 6th and 12th Dec 1769 by Mark McCall, surveyor, and found tract to contain seven hundred and ninty eight and a quarter acres of land and swamp and at same time found three hundred acres including the mansion plantation was laid off for Matthew Jarrard. Willson and James were agreeable to division of the remainder which was made and now confirm and establish the division among them. Matthew and Willson in consideration of James release to them, now release to him all their right, title and interest in part allotted to him with the sum of five shillings paid. Beginning at marked oak of land formerly claimed by John Rhodes . . . said land being conveyed contains two hundred forty three acres. Mark McCall apptd atty. Wit: F. Battell, Absalom Morris. Ackn 12 Aug 1774. (V:p194)

267. 4 Feb 1774 Indenture between Benjamin Downing of Duck Creek Hund, Kent on Delaware, yeoman and Joseph Downing of same place, yeoman. Whereas Ezekiel Downing, now decd, was seized of parcel of land part of tract called Coventry orig surveyed for John Hilliard, and made his will devising same equally to sons, Benjamin and Joseph and Ezekiel's personal estate was insufficient to satisfy debts an order was granted for sale of one hundred acres which was sold to John Moore Junr and the residue of one hundred fifty eight and a half acres is now equally divided between Benajamin and Joseph who have attained age of twenty one years by releasing each to the other a certain part. Benjamin in consideration of Joseph releasing the other moiety to him and for sum of five shillings paid by

Joseph, Benjamin now releases all that part of land beginning at a stone a cor of John Moore's land . . . with land now of Joseph Hill . . . laid out for seventy two and a half acres. Wit: Thomas Collins, Matthew Manlove. Ackn 11 Aug 1774. (V:p196)

268. 9 Aug 1774 Indenture between Chilion Miller of Kent on Delaware, yeoman and Conrad Miller same co, yeoman. Whereas John Miller late of same co, yeoman, was seized in tract of land called Maidstone on north side of branch of Dover River called Maidstone's Branch and on Mill Branch in Murtherkill Hund, containing seven hundred seventy seven acres. Chilion Miller contracted with Conrad for conveyance of small part beginning at a cor stake between allotment of Chilion and Adam Miller . . . Chilions dividend of whole tract late of John Wood now decd . . . containing five acres for consideration of nine pounds. Wit: Saml. McCall, Mark McCall. Ackn 9 Aug 1774. (V:p196)

269. 4 Aug 1774 Indenture between Fenwick Fisher, Esq. of Kent on Delaware and Mary his wife and David Kennady same place, merchant. Consideration of seventy five pounds convey all that lott nr the crossroads on south east side of Landing Road a part of land purchased from extrs of John Vining, Esq. decd. Fisher has divided the land into lotts and conveys lott No. 4 on the draught made by Mark McCall, surveyor begins at cor of No. 3 in line of piece of ground laid out by Fisher for use of a public market place . . . with No. 3 now in tenure of Joseph Holliday . . . to southeast cor of No. 5 now in tenure of John Walker . . . laid out for one hundred thirty one and a quarter square perches. Thomas Rodney apptd atty. Wit: Thos. Tilton, E. Needham. Mary Fisher privately examined gave consent. Ackn 12 Aug 1774. (V:p197)

270. 1 June 1774 Indenture between Thomas Green of Duck Creek Hund, Kent on Delaware and Mary, his wife and Thomas Skillington of the Crossroads said hund, inn holder. Whereas Thomas Green, Senr in his will of 14 May 1766 devised to dau, Mercy Buckingham, three acres situate between county road and landing road adj lott of James Morris, Esq. and she is now decd without issue and right of inheritance descends to her brothers and sisters and Thomas Green now conveys to Skillington all his undivided one fifth part in consideration of fifty pounds. Mark McCall apptd atty. Wit: Martin Evans, Allen McLeane. Mary Green privately examined gave consent. Ackn 10 Aug 1774. (V:p198)

271. 12 Aug 1774 Indenture between Henry Elbert of Caroline county, province of Maryland, doctor and Thomas Proctor same co, yeoman and Isaac Hastings of afsd co. Consideration of one hundred twelve pounds ten shillings convey parcel of land surveyed to them the 1st, 2nd and 3rd of Feb 1770 by virtue of assignment from

Waitman Sipple which he secured by warrant 30 Aug 1740 for land called Long Chaise situate nr Tappahannah, Kent on Delaware. Begins with line of William Hodge's land . . . at intersection of Jone's lott and land called Dannels Fancy . . . land surveyed for Samuel Walters . . . cor of land of Morris McBride . . . laid out for one hundred fifty one and a half acres and allowance of six per cent for highway and roads. William Lynch apptd atty. Wit: Wm. Hodges, Daniel Kinnard. Ackn 12 Aug 1774. (V:p199)

272. 12 Aug 1774 Indenture between Henry Elbert of Caroline county, province of Maryland, doctor and Thomas Proctor same co, yeoman and William Hodges of afsd co. Consideration of one hundred twelve pounds ten shillings convey parcel of land surveyed to them the 1st, 2nd and 3rd of Feb 1770 by virtue of assignment from Waitman Sipple which he secured by warrant 30 Aug 1740 for land called Long Chaise situate nr Tappahannah, Kent on Delaware. Begins at a cor of Tappahannah and the Spicy Grove . . . with land called Fancy's Addition . . . land called Jones's Lott . . . laid out for one hundred fifty one and a half acres with allowance of six per cent for highways and roads. William Lynch apptd atty. Wit: Isaac Hastings, Daniel Kinnard. Ackn 12 Aug 1774. (V:p199)

273. 11 Aug 1774 Indenture between James Moore of Murtherkill Hund, Kent on Delaware, yeoman and Letitia, his wife and Thomas Marsh of Kingstown in Queen Ann's County, province of Maryland, gent. Consideration of one hundred seventy five pounds en shillings convey parcel of land situate in forrest of Duck Creek Hund part of Moore's Purchase surveyed for James Moore between 11th and 20th Jan 1773 by virtue of warrant granted to Daniel Durborow on 3 Dec 1734 who assigned same to James Moore. Begins at cor of Matthew Hazlet's land . . . to cor of William Rolph's part of said tract . . . to line of tract surveyed under Maryland for Cornelius Comegys called Timber Fork now belonging to Matthew Tilghman . . . to James Scotten's part . . . cor of tract surveyed under Maryland for John McLain called McLain's Addition now belonging to Thomas Marsh . . . line of land surveyed for Thomas Ebtharp now of John Numbers . . . part of Moore's Purchase laid off for Edmund Lynch . . . Hazlet's part where he now lives . . . laid off for one hundred sixty five acres and fourteen square perches. Wit: John Draughton, Mark McCall. Letitia Moore privatedly examined gave consent. Ackn 11 Aug 1774. (V:p200)

274. 11 Aug 1774 Indenture between James Moore of forrest of Murtherkill Hund, Kent on Delaware, yeoman and Letitia, his wife and Matthew Hazlet of Duck Creek Hund, brick layer. Consideration of forty nine pounds eleven shillings six pence conveys parcel of land in afsd hund called Moore's Purchase surveyed for James Moore between 11th and 20th Jan 1773 by virtue of warrant granted to

Daniel Durborow, son of Hugh Durborow of Kent Co, on 3 Dec 1734 who assigned same to James Moore. Begins at cor of Matthew Hazlet's other land formerly surveyed for Thomas Blackshare . . . land formerly surveyed for John McLain now Edmund Lynch . . . to part conveyed to Captain Thomas Marsh . . . laid off for forty four acres and ten and a half square perches. Wit: John Draughton, Mark McCall. Letitia Moore privately examined gave consent. Ackn 11 Aug 1774. (V:p201)

275. 19 July 1774 Indenture between Caleb Webb of forrest of Murtherkill Hund, Kent on Delaware, yeoman and Robert Bohannan same place, yeoman. Consideration of one hundred twenty five pounds for land conveyed by Owen Seney on 8 May 1771 to Webb during his minority, said tract surveyed for Seney on 6 Sept 1753 by warrant granted 2 June 1746. Begins at cor of tract called Wedmore late of James Bedwell . . . land late of Matthew Wallace, decd . . . land in possession of Timothy Jenkins . . . land of Cowpling and Company, late of Henry Wells . . . land of Samuel Howell late of John Housman, Esq . . . laid off for one hundred acres of land and swamp. Samuel McCall and Mark McCall apptd attys. Wit: George Goforth, George McCall. Ackn 10 Aug 1774. (V:p202)

276. 20 July 1774 Indenture between William Manlove of forrest of Murtherkill Hund, Kent on Delaware, sheep (shop?) keeper and Robert Bohannon same place, yeoman. Consideration of five pounds conveys parcel of land in afsd hund part of Sicamore Plains which was surveyed to John Housman by virtue of warrant on 25 June 1735(?) part of deeded on 17 Feb 1748 (Book N, folio 251) to Samuel Howell who conveyed the part to William Manlove on 12 Feb 1754 (Book O, folio 211) and part conveyed by Manlove to Thomas Cain, part here conveyed is residue of twenty acres and twenty five square perches. Samuel McCall apptd atty. Wit: Levy Munch, Mark McCall. Ackn 10 Aug 1774. (V:p203)

277. 10 Aug 1774 Indenture between James Moore of forrest of Murtherkill Hund, Kent on Delaware and Letitia, his wife and Nicholas Lynch of forrest of Duck Creek Hund, yeoman. By virtue of warrant granted to Daniel Durborow on 3 Dec 1764 and assigned to James Moore 18 Jan 1770, survey was made between 1st and 20th Jan 1773 for tract called Moore's Purchase. Consideration of seventeen pounds fourteen shillings two pence convey beginning at cor of land surveyed for Thomas Blackshare now of Matthew Hazlet and of land surveyed for John McLain now of Edmund Lynch . . . with land of John Numbers . . . laid off for fifteen acres and one hundred eighteen and a half perches. Wit: John Draughton, Mark McCall. Letitia Moore privately examined gave consent. Ackn 11 Aug 1774. (V:p203)

278. 1 July 1774 Indenture between David Gordon of Duck Creek Hund, Kent on

Delaware, house carpenter and Ruth, his wife and James Townsend of same place, coach maker. Consideration of thirty five pounds conveys a lot of land being part of lot which Gordon bought of William and Samuel Ball (Book T, folio 84) lying on a new street called Ball's Street nr cross roads. Begins in line of lot of Thomas Skillington . . . John McDonough's lot . . . Thomas Jordan's lot . . . containing thirty four and two tenths square perches. Wit: Jno. McDonough, William Rees. Ruth Gordon privately examined gave consent. Ackn 10 Aug 1774. (V:p204)

279. 22 June 1774 Indenture between Robert Maxwell of Duck Creek Hund, Kent on Delaware, yeoman and one of sons of James Maxwell late of same place, decd and John Spruance, same place, yeoman. Whereas heirs of Peter Galloway, Esq, decd, granted to James Maxwell parcel of land containing one hundred fifty two and a half acres part of tract called Mannor of Frieth situate in forrest of Duck Creek Hund who by will devised same equally to sons, Robert and James Maxwell now having reached age of 21 no division has yet been made. In consideration of three hundred pounds, Robert Maxwell conveys his full undivided moiety or half part of the land. Samuel McCall apptd atty. Wit: John Draughton, John Bllen. Ackn 10 Aug 1774. (V:p205)

280. 10 Aug 1774 Indenture between Zachariah Goforth of Kent on Delaware, yeoman and John Dill same place, inn holder. Goforth for and in consideration as well as rents and covenants hereinafter mentioned to be paid and performed and the sum of five shillings conveys all that lot of ground and marsh situate at Johny Cake Landing on Murtherkill Creek containing two thousand two hundred fifty square feet provided yearly and every year forever on 29th Sept next the sum of thirty shillings rent be paid. Wit: Geo. Painter, John Rhodes, James White, Francis Muncy. Ackn 10 Aug 1774. (V:p205)

281. 13 Apr 1774 Indenture between William Ball of city of Philadelphia, goldsmith and Elizabeth, his wife, and Thomas Cahoon of Duck Creek Hund, Kent on Delaware, farmer, Consideration of forty five pounds conveys piece of ground part of larger tract called Gravesend. Begins cor of Alexander Worknotts lott . . . containing one and a quarter acres and four perches. Impower John Cook, Esq., high sheriff of Kent Co to be their lawful atty. Wit:Thomas Skillington, Wm. Jordan, Wm. Barker. Ackn 11 Aug 1774. (V:p206)

282. 10 Aug 1774 Indenture between Reynear Williams and Avary Draper of Kent on Delaware admrs d.b.n. of est of Thomas Arrowsmith late of said co, decd and Joshua Spencer of Sussex on Delaware, yeoman. Whereas Reynear Williams and Avary Draper on 24 Feb 1774 obtained an order from orphan's court for sale of lands of Arrowsmith for payment of debts, conveyance for part of tract called

Middle Town situate in Mispillion Hund which was sold at public auction to Joshua Spencer, he being highest bidder. Tract was purchased by Arrowsmith from the Pennsylvania Land Company of London on 10 Sept 1762 (Book Q, folio 226). Consideration of two hundred twenty one pounds convey tract beginning at cor of Cornelius Dewees's land . . . by tract called Ceedar Neck . . . containing one hundred fifty acres. Wit: Simon W. Willson, Cornelius Comegys. Ackn 10 Aug 1774. (V:p207)

283. 27 June 1774 Indenture between Jonathan Rees, yeoman and Prisila, his wife of Springhill Township, Westmoreland Co in Pennsylvania and John Russel, tanner of Kent on Delaware. Consideraton of one hundred fifty pounds conveys parcel of land in Duck Creek Hund being land granted to Daniel Shannan by virtue of warrant and assigned by Shannan to John and Stephen Barns who died without issue and said tract was claimed by John Barns who by will 6 Jan 1767 devised the land to dau, Prisila, wife of Jonathan Rees. Begins at a cor of lands of Perry Leatherbury and Edmond Lynch . . . to land surveyed for William Smith . containing one hundred seventy two acres. Wit: Cuthburt Green, Morgan Blacksher. John Smith of Little Creek Hund apptd as atty. Prisila Rees privately examined gave consent. Ackn 10 Aug 1774. (V:p207)

284. 22 July 1774 Indenture between Timothy Caldwell of Murtherkill Hund, Kent on Delaware, stoorkeeper(sic) and James Hutchings, Junr of Kent Island, Queen Ann's Co, Maryland, merchant and gent. Consideration of thirty seven pounds ten shillings conveys parcel of land in forrest of Murtherkill Hund situate on Tanner's Branch, part of real est of Benja. Jones who by will to devised the land equally to sons, Nicholas Jones and James Jones. Nicholas Jones moiety was sold by James Caldwell, late sheriff, to Timothy Caldwell on 27 May 1662 by virtue of writ of John Banning and others. The deed sets forth the quantity of about one hundred four acres which remains undivided and sheriff's deed sets forth recitals of the whole tract. A former sheriff conveyed the land in two parts, one to Benja. Jones, the other to James Smith to which deed is referred for a description thereof. Samuel McCall and Mark McCall apptd attys. Wit: William Merydith, Peter Torbert. Ackn 11 Aug 1774. (V:p208)

285. 4 Feb 1774 Indenture between Joseph Downing of Duck Creek Hund, Kent on Delaware, yeoman and Benjamin Downing same place, yeoman. Whereas Ezekiel Downing, father of Joseph and Benjamin, was seized in parcel of land part of tract called Coventy (orig surveyed for John Hilliard) and devised same equally to his two sons. Ezekiel's personal estate was insufficient to pay debts and an order was secured from the court to sell one hundred acres which was sold to John Moore, Junr. There remains one huindred fifty eight and a half acres which Joseph

and Benjamin having reached age of 21 years are about to divide between them releasing each to the other a part thereof. Joseph Downing in consideration of Benjamin releasing the moiety or half part to him, the said Joseph, and also for sum of five shillings, Joseph now releases and conveys all that part beginning at a cor of Joseph Hill's land . . . laid off for eighty six acres. Wit: Thomas Collins, Matthew Manlove. Ackn 11 Aug 1774. (V:p209)

286. 11 Aug 1774 Indenture between Samuel Gooden of town of Dover, Kent on Delaware, black smith and Andrew Butler of Murtherkill Hund, taylor. A tract of land in forrest of afsd hund on north side of Isaac Webb's Brranch called Long Reach of which the parents of Samuel Gooden was legally seized of a part which was conveyed by extrs of Henry Bedwell to John Robeman, by survey made by Mark McCall 29 July 1771. Begins in line of Greenwich and Long Reach . . . cor for heirs of James Gardner . . . part called Ezekiel Needham's land . . . land of Mark Condrat . . . heirs of Daniel Condrat . . . containing one hundred nineteen acres and four perches. Samuel Gooden and his sister, Elizabeth, in right of their father, Samuel sometime decd are entitled to one half of the whole survey being the north end thereof marked "A" containing fifty nine acres and eighty two square perches and Samuel is now conveying his undivided right in consideration of one hundred pounds. Wit: Abraham Vanhoy, Junr., Saml. McCall. Ackn 12 Aug 1774. (V:p209)

287. 9 Aug 1774 Indenture between Joseph Standley of Kent on Delaware and Mary, his wife and Richard Accles of Talbot County, province of Maryland. Consideration of one hundred eighty nine pounds conveys parcel of land in forrest of Mispillion Hund nr Marshahope called Good Luck being plantation that Daniel Bozman bought of John Marret and another tract adj taken up by Daniel Bozman called Bozman's Addition. The tract Good Luck begins on south side of Holly Branch . . . at Mark Marret's line . . . laid out for one hundred thirty seven and a quarter acres exclusive of eleven and three quarter acres deeded to Francis Jester by Daniel Bozman. Bozman's Addition begins at cor of William Howgin's land . . . laid out for one hundred thirty three and seventeen tenths acres. Wit: John Dickinson, Junr., Jona. Neall. Mary Standley privately examined gave consent. Ackn 9 Aug 1774. (V:p210)

288. 16 June 1774 Know all men by these presents that I, Benjamin Durborow, late of Kent on Delaware for divers good causes and considerations have appointed Mr. James Moore of same co my true and lawful attorney . . . Witness whereof I have here unto set my hand and seal . (signed) B. Durborow. Wit: James Hayson, Adam Taylor, Luke Mason. Ackn 10 Aug 1774. (V:p211)

289. 7 June 1774 Indenture between John Fothergill, London, doctor in physick; Daniel Zackary, London, goldsmith; Jacob Hagan, Silvanus Grove and William Heron of London, merchants, surviving trustees of a proprietorship commonly called Pennsylvania Land Company of London by Jacob Cooper, Samuel Shoemaker and Joshua Howell of Philadelphia, merchants and their attys, of the one part and James Craige of town of Dover, taylor. By virtue of an act passed by Parliament entitled an Act for vesting certain estates in Pennsylvania, New Jersey and Maryland belonging to proprietors of partnership in London called Pennsylvania Land Company to be sold and several lands, tenements and herediments vested in Thomas Hyam, Thomas Reynolds and Thomas How, surviving trustees of said partnership were settled and vested in John Fothergill, Daniel Zachary, Thomas How, Devereaux Bowley, Luke Hind, Richard How, Jacob Hagan, Silvanus Grove and William How to appoint persons to convey lands and estates. Whereas the messuage, tenement, etc. herein after described is inended to be granted being in Mispillion Hund was sold at public auction in city of Philadelphia to Mark McCall who assigned and set over his right to James Craige. Consideration of forty six pounds fifteen shillings nine pence convey part of tract called Longford, orig surveyed to John Rawlings, said part marked No. 8 - beginning at cor of part sold to William Carpenter . . . land now possessed by Mark Clampit . . . part sold to Nathan Goodin . . . laid out for one hundred twenty three acres and sixty five square perches. Samuel McCall apptd atty. Wit:Hugh Roberts, Robert McYarment. Ackn 11 Aug 1774. (V:p210)

290. 7 June 1774 Indenture between John Fothergill, London, doctor in physick; Daniel Zackary, London, goldsmith; Jacob Hagan, Silvanus Grove and William Heron of London, merchants, surviving trustees of a proprietorship commonly called Pennsylvania Land Company of London by Jacob Cooper, Samuel Shoemaker and Joshua Howell of Philadelphia, merchants and their attys, of the one part and Nathan Goddin of Mispillion Hund, Kent on Delaware, yeoman. By virtue of an act passed by Parliament entitled an Act for vesting certain estates in Pennsylvania, New Jersey and Maryland belonging to proprietors of partnership in London called Pennsylvania Land Company to be sold and several lands, tenements and herediments vested in Thomas Hyam, Thomas Reynolds and Thomas How, surviving trustees of said partnership were settled and vested in John Fothergill, Daniel Zachary, Thomas How, Devereaux Bowley, Luke Hind, Richard How, Jacob Hagan, Silvanus Grove and William How to appoint persons to convey lands and estates. Land to be granted is part of tract situate in Mispillion Hund sold at public auction in Philadelphia to Nathan Goddin, he being highest bidder for seventy three pounds nineteen shillings three pence. Tract is constituted of parts of three tracts, Carbron orig surveyed for Henry Stevens, Long Acre orig survey for Nicholas Bartlett, and Longford orig surveyed for John Rawlings shown

on draught made by Samuel McCall, surveyor, and marked No. 9. Beginning at cor of Carbron part conveyed to John Dillen . . . land of Moses Clampit . . . land surveyed for Alec Peak called Pathalia Plains . . . land conveyed to Turbeth Cottinham . . . laid out for one hundred twenty two acres of land. Wit: Hugh Roberts, Robert McYarment. Samuel McCall apptd atty. Ackn 11 Aug 1774. (V:p212)

291. 25 Aug 1774 Indenture between John Cook, Esq, sheriff of Kent on Delaware and Peter Wikoff of city and co of Philadelphia, merchant. By virtue of writ from court of Common Pleas dated 14 May in fourteenth year of his Majesty's reign, directed to late sheriff, Thomas Collins that of goods, chattles, lands and tenements of James Gorrell, merchant, he should cause to be levied certain debt of seventeen hundred sixty pounds which Peter Wikoff recovered agst him and also forty one shillings three pence like money in damages. Thomas Collins seized and placed in execution two hundred acres of land in Murtherkill Hund nr Jones Creek, one hundred five acres in Murtherkill forrest and one hundred three acres adj the last afsd parcel. John Bell, Junr and Asa Manlove appraised said land to see if rents and profits within seven years would sastisfy the debt and damages stated above and also one Thomas Smith his debt and damages. Bell and Manlove stated that the land would not and Thomas Collins exposed the land to public vendue, selling same to Peter Wikoff for four hundred nine pounds. John Cook, present sheriff now conveys said three parcels of land being two hundred acres part of Cypress Neck, one hundred five acres called Owen's Folly conveyed by Hollingsworth Vanderford to James Gorrell, and one hundred three acres beginning nr plantation sometime belonging to John Freeland . . . said tract sold by Thomas Green to James Gorrell, the elder, late father of said James first mentioned by deed 16 Feb 1744. Wit: Jno. Smithers, George Saxton. Ackn 25 Aug 1774. (V:p214)

292. 25 Aug 1774 Indenture between John Cook, Esq, sheriff of Kent on Delaware and John Baning same co, merchant. By virtue of writ from court of Common Pleas dated 15 May in Thirteenth year of his Majesty's reign directed to James Caldwell, then sheriff that of goods, chattles, lands and tenements of Francis Harris, late of Kent co, he should cause to be levied certain debt of thirty six pounds four shillings five pence which James Caldwell recovered agst him for damages as well as for non performance of promises and assumptions to said James Caldwell, John Cook for want of goods and chattles to satisfy the debt seized and placed in execution three parcels of land, one in Little Creek Hund adj land of John Ham containing one hundred thirty acres. One tract situate in forrest of Murtherkill Hund adj land of William Morris. One other parcel of five acres in same place adj land of Elizabeth Rowe. Samuel McCall and French Battell appraised the land to see if rents and profits for seven years would be sufficient to

satisfy and on their oath, said they would not. John Cook exposed the land to public vendue selling same to John Baning for two hundred fifty one pounds. Description mentions land of Benjamin Brook . . . land of Peter Shankmire . . . land formerly of Elizabeth Hines . . . tract called Content . . . part of tract called Springfield . . . said two tracts were conveyed by James Colgun to Francis Harris 5 Aug 1763. The five acres begins nr late dwelling of James Rowe, decd. Wit: Jno. Smithers, George Saxton. Ackn 25 Aug 1774. (V:p215)

293. 2 Nov 1774 Indenture between John Killen of Mispillion Hund, Kent on Delaware, joiner and Martthew, his wife and Henry Killen same place, yeoman. Consideration of sixteen pounds conveys all their claim, sheare, right, title and interest in parcel of land Robert Killen, Esq. bought of Philamon Dickinson of city of Philadelphia, situate in forrest of Dover Hund part of tract confirmed by patent for George Stevenson and conveyed to Edmond Badger on 8 July 1768 (Liber P, folio 80(?) afterwards conveyed to Jordan Coburn by Samuel McCall, extr of Badger on 17 May 1765(?) recorded (Liber R, folio 95) beginning at cor of James Corbian's land . . . by John Housman's land . . . in Randal Blackshear's line . . . by John Jones's . . . John Stanton's land . . . laid out for three hundred twelve acres and allowance. Wit: Mark Killen, Benjamin Downs. Samuel McCall and Mark McCall apptd attys. Ackn 25 Aug 1774. (V:p216)

294. 1 July 1774 Indenture between Robert McYarmant of town of Dover, Kent on Delaware, store keeper admr of est of Isaac Cox late of said co and Peter Lowber, Junr of Murtherkill Hund same co, gent. Whereas Benjamin Chipman, decd, by deed on 2 May 1772 conveyed to Isaac Cox a parcel of land part of Bishop's Choice situate in afsd hund on east side of Popler Branch and south side of Bishop's Branch. Begins at cor of Mill Land . . . containing fourteen acres of land. Caesar Rodney and Thomas Nixon, gents, trustees of General Loan Office by deed on 1 June last past conveyed to Robert McYarmant as admr of Isaac Cox an order to sell two separate parcels of land, mills and mill houses build by George Goforth who had mortgaged same. Peter Lowber purchased same for five hundred pounds and Robert McYarmant now conveys the land and premises. Wit: Saml. McCall, Isaac Lowber. Ackn 26 Aug 1774. (V:p217)

295. 25 Aug 1774 Indenture between Henry Killen of Mispillion Hund, Kent on Delaware and Susannah, his wife and Richard Smith, Esq. of St. Jone's Hund and James Moore, yeoman of Murtherkill Hund, both same co. A tract of land in St. Jone's forrest alias Dover forrest called Peloponne formerly surveyed for George Stevenson, John Housman and Thomas Blackshare in three parts, one part was lately purchased by Robert Killen, Esq., decd, from Mr. Philamon Dickinson and Robert Killen neglected a devise of the land and left several children and

grandchildren, to wit: Adam, his eldest son; Henry, William, John, Mark, Robert and heirs of Anne who married Robert Buchanan, and Henry having contracted for purchase of shares from his four brothers whereby he holds five shares out of eight, being seven heirs as eldest son holds two. Henry by articles of agreement 2 Mar last past, sold the five eighths to Richard Smith and James Moore in partnership. In order to secure proper lines a survey was made by Mark McCall by order of Samuel McCall, surveyor on 24 May last past and corrected bounds are as follows. Begins at a small branch of Dover River separating this land from that of Richard Smith, Esq. called Little Neck . . . cor of land late of James Carbine . . . as shown by Thomas Murphy . . . land late of Maslin Clarke now of Daniel Wright . . . cor oak of Newnam's land . . . land of Robert Blackshare . . . land surveyed for James Moore in right of Peter Stout now of James Jones . . . containing four hundred nine acres and ninety three perches . . . the five eighths part contains two hundred fifty six acres being sold at fifteen shillings per acre amounts to one hundred ninety two pounds and Henry Killen and his wife, Susannah, now convey the said undivided parts for consideration given. Wit: Saml. McCall, Robert Killen. Ackn 25 Aug 1774. (V:p218)

296. 1 June 1774 Indenture between Caesar Rodney, Esq. and Thomas Nixon, gents, trustees of the General Loan Office of Kent on Delaware and Robert McYarmant of town of Dover, admr of est of Isaac Cox. Whereas George Goforth by deed 12 May 1748 purchased a lot from James Taylor with grist mill and saw mill thereon situate on part of Bishop's Choice, said lot laid off for two and three quarter acres and George Goforth secured a legal condemnation of five acres on the north side of Bishop's Branch and on 11 Oct 1749 entered two tracts of land in General Loan Office and thereby conveyed same to John Brinckle, Esq. and Thomas Green, trustees thereof and by another deed, Goforth on 11 July 1750 conveyed the two lots to Daniel Robinson who contracted for conveyance to Paris Chipman and in like manner to Robert Miller and he to Benjamin Chipman and he to William Rhodes who sold same to Isaac Cox with no deed from Daniel Robinson so no sales could be confirmed and by writ directed to the sheriff for payment of mortgaged lands, sheriff could convey the land to the purchaser. Most of the purchase money is still due and several of parties are deceased and as the deed before Robinson was to the trustees of General Loan Office, they now convey same to Robert McYarment, admr of Isaac Cox. William Killen apptd atty. Wit: Isaac Lowber, Jonathan Molleston. Ackn 25 Aug 1774. (V:p219)

297. 25 Apr 1774 Indenture between Jesse Beauchamp of Murtherkill Hund, Kent on Delaware, yeoman and Leah, his wife and Benjamin Coombe of same place, yeoman. Robert Beauchamp by deed 13 Feb 1771 (Book T, folio 31) conveyed to son, Jesse, part of tract called Saint Column orig surveyed for Benoni Bishop said

grant included neck of land called Hang Man's Neck whose courses are as follows. Begins at orig cor of Saint Column and Bishop's Choice . . . land of William Thompson . . . laid off for two hundred acres. Consideration of four hundred pounds paid by Benjamin Coombe. Saml. McCall and Mark McCall apptd attys. Wit: Saml. McCall, Richard Bishop. Leah Beauchamp privately examined gave consent. Ackn 23 Aug 1774. (V:p220)

298. 23 Aug 1774 Indenture between Annalane Craig, widow, of Kent on Delaware and George Saxton, yeoman. Consideration of one hundred fifteen pounds fifteen shillings conveys parcel of land on south side of Hudson's Branch adj tract called Gilford patented to Samuel Mann who devised same to his sister, Annalane Craig. Beginning at a cor new made in the mill pond . . . laid out for seventy three acres and twenty two perches. Wit (cut off). Ackn 25 Aug 1774. (V:p220)

299. 17 Aug 1774 Indenture between James Scotton, Junr, house carpenter of Kent on Delaware and James Scotton, Senr of Little Creek Hund, same co, tanner. Consideration of five pounds and other valuable considerations conveys all that messuage or tenement situate in afsd hund being one moiety or half part of tract called James Park which was sold by James Scotton, Senr to James Scotton, Junr on 14 May 1772 laid out for two hundred acres. Wit: Jno. Smithers, James Moore. Ackn 25 Aug 1774. (V:p221)

300. 1 May 1774 Indenture between Mark Killen and Robert Killen, both of Mispillion Hund, Kent on Delaware and Henry Killen same place, yeoman. Where Robert Killen, Esq, late decd, father to above parties purchased tract of land from Philemon Dickinson situate in forrest of St. Jones's Hund (alias Dover Hund) part of tract called Peloponnesees and made no mention in his will thereof thus he died intestate to the parcel of land. Mark and Robert Killen for consideration of seventy seven pounds convey their undividied share to their brother, Henry. Wit: Saml. McCall, Silas Snow. Ackn 25 Aug 1774. (V:p221)

301. 26 Aug 1774 Indenture between Thomas Nock, Junr of Murtherkill Hund, Kent on Delaware, extr of Ezekiel Nock same place, decd and Oliver Caulk of Cecil Co in province of Maryland, gent. Whereas Robert Rowland formerly of said place conveyed to Ezekiel Nock a parcel of land on south side of Dover River on Tidbury Branch part of tract called The Grove, and by alienation writing of 5 Feb 1765 did oblige himself to convey the parcel to John Brown who intermarried with Sarah one of daus of Ezekiel and John Brown died before paying the consideraton money and John Morris having married Sarah, the widow, obtained court order for sale of the land. Ezekiel Nock died before any deed was passed to John Brown and

now Thomas Nock, extr of his father, petitioned the court praying for authority to make such deeds and obtained a survey of the one hundred twenty five acres, now for consideration of two hundred fifty pounds paid to Ezekiel Nock conveys the land. Wit: John Gordon, Saml. McCall. Ackn 26 Aug 1774. (V:p221)

302. 23 Aug 1774 Indenture between John Cox and his wife, Marthew of Mispillion Hund, Kent on Delaware, yeoman and George Turner same place, yeoman. Consideration of one hundred twenty five pounds conveys all that land and swamp and plants from that, formerly belonged to Alexander Hamilton and conveyed to John Cox on 1 May 1765 situate in forrest of Mispillion Hund on both sides of road from Dover by house of Robert Killen to Marshy Hope bridge. Begins at cor of land of James McKnatt and Alexander Fleming . . . to land late of Robert Knox(Knocks) . . . lands surveyed for William Fleming, Senr . . . orig surveyed for Alexander Hamilton on 7 May 1737 by John Willson, sureyor and by warrant of resurvey granted to John Cox 19 Sept 1766 and by survey adding vacancies of twenty eight acres and allowance, found the orig tract to contain one hunded thirty eight and one quarter acres and allowance, the old and new to contain one hundred sixty six acres. Wit: Zadok Crapper, Richard McWait. Martha (Marthew) Cox privately examined gave consent. Ackn 25 Aug 1774. (V:p222)

303. 12 June 1774 Indenture between John Draughton of Duck Creek Hund, Kent on Delaware gent and Margaret, his wife and William Savin, Senr of Cecil Co, province of Maryland, gent. Consideration of four hundred pounds convey parcel of land in hund afsd adj to the west side of Joseph Moore's Branch being parts of two tracts, one patented to Robert Draughton and other to Nathan Standbury. Description mentions line of Northampton . . . cor of Nathan Standbury's patent . . . containing one hundred fifty acres of land. Samuel McCall apptd atty. Wit: Rachel Crozier, Jacob Stout. Margaret Draughton aged twenty three years privately examined gave consent. Ackn 23 Aug 1774. (V:p222)

304. 3 May 1774 Know all men by these presents that I, Major Evens of Kent on Delaware for consideration of twelve pounds do bargain and sell to James Hatfield one bay horse caught by him of James Thisselwood about three years old . . . and Major Evens will warrant and forever defend the afsd horse from the lawful claim or demands of any person. In witness whereof I have hereunto set my hand and seal. (signed) Majar Evens. Wit: Daniel Steuert, Willim Hall. (V:p224)

305. 28 Oct 1774 Know all men by these presents that I, William Tarring, late of Kent on Delaware, weaver, am firmly bound to Elias Bayly of Sussex Co in full and just sum of one hundred pounds. The condition being to convey by deed of sale parcel of land purchased by Tarring from John Reynold containing two hundred acres of land. Wit: Ned Lockerman, Hugh Durborow, Junior. (signed) William

Tarring. I, Nathan Bailey, son of Elias Bayly, decd, do sign over all my right and title to within bond to Richard Lockwood and John Voshell. (signed) Nathan Bailey. Wit: William Marriner, Sarah Lockwood. Ackn by Vincent Loockerman 25 Aug 1774. (V:p224)

306. 15 Aug 1774 Plat of land of Daniel Shannon surveyed 12 June 1750 by William Killen, then surveyor but not by him returned but now of John Russell for one hundred fifty three and a half acres and allowance. (shows adj lands). Whereas a warrant was granted to Daniel Shannon on 4 Feb 1742 for two hundred acres of land on Duck Creek . . . and another warrant on 1 May 1750 for three hundred acres was also granted to adjoin which warrants were assigned to John and Stephen Barns by Shannon on 23 Jan 1756 and John Barns by survivorship is entitled to the whole and devised said land to one of his daus, Priscilla who married Jonathan Rees who by deed 17 June last past conveyed same to John Russell . . . and having surveyed the lines thereof on 12 Mar 1773, I therefore make return of survey to Russell this 15 Aug 1774. (signed) Samuel McCall, Depty Surveyor. Certified a true copy for John Lukens, Esq by Robert Dill. (V:p225)

307. 9 Aug 1774 Know all men by these presents that I, Alexander Jamison of Duck Creek Hund, Kent on Delaware, yeoman, am firmly bound unto William Cahoon in sum of five hundred pounds. Condition of the obligation being that Jamison stand to obey, abide, observe and in and by all things perform by determination of judgment of Richard Smith, Esq, James Wells, James Raymond, Silas Snow and Abraham Tantroy(?), Junr, arbitrators, on behalf of Alexander Jamison and William Cahoon . . . concerning lines of tract of land called Pairman's Choice situate in Duck Creek Hund of which William Cahoon has part from land of Alexander Jamison. Wit: Saml. McCall, Mark McCall. (signed) Alexander Jamison. (V:p225)

308. 1 Oct 1774 We, Richard Smith, James Wells, James Raymond, Silas Snow all of Kent on Delaware, send greeting, whereas controversy has arisen between William Cahoon and Alexander Jamison concerning the lines of Pairman's Plains of which Cahoon has a part and Jamison has a part whereon he lives, and for the settling and final end, they have become bonded to each other in sum of five hunded pounds to obey the arbitration thereof. Beginning at cor of land claimed by heirs of William Cahoon, decd, part of Christiana . . . line of John Joy's land . . . and Alexander Jamison shall hence forward quit claim to all parts of said tract found on northern side of above said branch. A true copy, test. (V:p225)

309. 4 Oct 1774 Appointments: To James Hamilton, Joseph Turner, William Logan, Richard Peters, Benjamin Chew, Thomas Cadwalader, Richard Penn,

James Tilghman, Andrew Allen and Edward Shippen, Junr, Esqrs, members of the Proprietary and Governor's Council and to Charles Ridgely, James Sykes, William Rhodes, John Clark, Jacob Stout, Finwick Fisher, Thomas Tilton, James Boyer, Thomas Hanson, Jonathan Emerson, John Chew, Richard Smith, Richard Lockwood, Zadok Crapper, Thomas Rodney and Thomas White of the county of Kent . . . Esqrs, greetings . . . Reposing special trust and confidence in your loyalty integrity and ability, know ye that we have assigned you jointly and severally our justices our peace in the counties afsd. Witness: John Penn, Esq, Governor and Commander in Chief of the counties afsd and of province of Pennsylvania. A true copy, test. (V:p226)

310. 24 Oct 1774 Appointments: To Caesar Rodney and Samuel Chew, Esqrs, of Kent on Delaware, greeting. Reposing special trust and confidence in your loyalty and integrity, I have authorized and impowered you to administer to all judges, justices and sheriffs concerns and all other offices, civil and military and all other person and persons . . . as well the oaths of office as also the oaths of allegiance and supremacy and other the usual declarations., etc. (signed) John Penn. A true copy, test. (V:p226)

311. 20 Oct 1774 Appointment: To Jacob Moore of county of Sussex in our government of counties of Newcastle, Kent and Sussex, Esq. Reposing special trust and confidence in your loyalty fidelity learning and ability, we have nominated and appoint you to be Attorney General. Witness: John Penn. A true copy, test. (V:p227)

312. 13 Nov 1773 Whereas my honored father by will directed that a line drawn north and by east from a white oak standing by side of a marsh nr a little branch running into a creek unto the land called Burton's Delight should be the perpetual boundary between my brother, Philemon Dickinson's land and mine situate in Dover Hund and whereas the line would strike Burton's Delight a considerable distance to westward of cor of field called _____ Field and land of late John Smith and whereas my honored mother informs me that it was my father's intention that the boundary line should strike Burton's Delight at cor afsd and agreeable to the line ought to be drawn from the white oak to the cor and shall forever be boundary between my brother's land and mine. (signed) John Dickinson. A true copy, test. (V:p227)

313. 26 Aug 1774 Indenture between Thomas Nock of Murtherkill Hund, Kent on Delaware, extr of will of Ezekiel Nock, decd and John and Thomas Brown, heirs and representatives of John Brown, decd. Whereas Ezekiel Nock on 5 Feb 1765 by his alienation bond did obligate himself to convey a parcel of land to John Brown,

the elder, which Ezekiel purchased from Robert Rowland situate on Tidbury Branch of the Dover River and John Brown died before conveyance was made or consideration money was paid. John Morris married Sarah, John Brown's widow, and by order of the Orphans Court issued for sale of one hundred twenty five acres to discharge debts, said part was sold to Oliver Caulk and Ezekiel Nock died before a deed was made to Caulk and the residue to the heirs of John Brown. Thomas Nock executed a deed to Caulk and now conveys the residue to the said Brown heirs. Wit: John Gordon, Saml. McCall. Ackn 26 Aug 1774. (V:p227)

314. 5 Feb 1765 Know all men by these presents that I, Ezekial Nock of Kent on Delaware unto John Brown, millwright of same place in full sum of seven hundred pounds. Condition of the obligation being the conveyance of a tract of land purchased of Robert Rowland whereon John Brown now lives. (signed) Ezekiel Nock. Wit: Thomas Nock, J. Nock. Ackn 26 Aug 1774. (V:228)

315. 12 Aug 1774 Indenture between William Brown and Nancy, his wife, admrs of estate of Andrew Saxton, late of Mispillion Hund, Kent on Delaware and Jesse Beauchamp of Murtherkill Hund, yeoman. Whereas Thomas Hatfield conveyed to William Morgan a small parcel of land in forrest of said hund who obtained warrant for adj vacant land on 27 Apr 1761 and survey made 10th and 11th June following and survey was made of the old part which old and new contained two hundred sixty acres neat measure. Beginning at cor of land late of Curtis Evans . . . cor of land sometime surveyed for George Pratt . . . land of Isaac Lowber . . . and Morgan then conveyed all to Henry Corkerin and Pierce Jones who conveyed same to Rubin Wallace who conveyed the land to Andrew Saxton who on 19 Aug 1771 by alienation bond on condition of conveyance to Thomas Edmondson who contracted with Benjamin Coombs who contracted for conveyance to Jesse Beauchamp and all parties agree that William Brown and Nancy, his wife, as admrs of Andrew Saxton for consideration of two hundred twenty pounds paid by Jesse Beauchamp now convey the land. Wit: Coe Gordon, Nancy Cowel. Ackn 20 Aug 1774. (V:p228)

316. 19 Aug 1771. Know all men by these presents that I, Andrew Saxton of Kent on Delaware am firmly bound to Thomas Edmondson of Dorchester County, province of Maryland, planter, in sum of five hundred twenty pounds. Condition being the conveyance of tract whereon John Wolston now lives formerly lands of William Morgan which Saxton purchased of Rubin Wallace. (signed) Andrew Saxton. Wit: Powell Cox, John Edmondson. Ackn 12 Aug 1774. Thomas Edmondson signed over his right, title and interest of above bond to Benjamin Coombs of Murtherkill hund. 16 Oct 1773. Wit: Nimrod Maxwell, Sarah Maxwell. Ackn 23 Aug 1774. Benjamin Coombs signed over his right, title and interest to

above bond to Jesse Beauchamp. Ackn 23 Aug 1774 (V:p229)

317. 23 May 1774 Know all men by these presents that I, Mary Gardner, widow and relict of James Gardner late of Kent on Delaware, hath made ordained authorized and constituted and appointed William Rees of same co, blacksmith, my true and lawful atty. (signed) Mary Gardner. Wit: Rebecah Hartshorn, James Vandyke. Ackn 22 Nov 1774. (V:p230)

318. 10 Nov 1774 Indenture between Vincent Dehorty, Samuel Harrington and Sarah, his wife, George Anderson and Mary, his wife, all of Murtherkill Hund, Kent on Delaware and George Dehorty of same place. Whereas Absalom Dehorty of Dorchester County, Maryland, died ceased(sic) of tract of land in forrest of hund and co afsd containing two hundred sixty four acres surveyed for him by virtue of warrant. He died intestate leaving a widow and four children: Vincent, George, Sarah and Mary. Widow now wife of Francis Clamer and Sarah has married Samuel Harrington and Mary has married George Anderson and aforesaid heirs have agreed to sell their shares to George Dehorty for sum of forty pounds. Wit: Saml. McCall, Sarah McCall. Sarah Harrington and Mary Anderson privately examined gave their consent. Ackn 10 Nov 1774. (V:230)

319. 9 Nov 1774 Indenture between Samuel Morris of Appoquinamink Hund, Newcastle on Delaware, farmer and Joseph Smith of Kent on Delaware, blacksmith. Consideration of twenty pounds conveys lott situate on north side of road from Duck Creek Hund to Holliday's land. Description mentions dwelling of _____ Pope . . . said lot containing two thousand feet of ground. Wit Mary Pugh, Rach. Offley. Ackn 11 Nov 1774. (V:p231)

320. 7 Oct 1774 Indenture between John Chambers of Calvert County, province of Maryland, carpenter and William Chambers, alias Allen of Kent on Delaware. Consideraton of five pounds conveys tract or parcel of land in Kent Co part of tract known as Gravesend situate in or nr the fork of the roads where they divide, one to William Farson's, the other toward the head of Chester . . . place where Thomas Green and William Chambers, decd, staked out one acre of land, on part of land purchased by Chambers of Green by bond dated 17 Apr 1759. Chambers died and land descended to his eldest bro, John Chambers, who now conveys the land. Wit: Mary Allen, James Heighe. Ackn 8 Nov 1774. (V:p231)

321. 3 June 1774 Indenture between William Carpenter, Senr and Elizabeth, his wife of Murtherkill Hund, Kent on Delaware, yeoman and William Betts of same co, yeoman. Consideration of five shillings and for true love and affection that they owe William Betts, they now convey all their right, title and claim to two hundred

acres of upland and forty acres of marsh part of larger tract called Mount Pleasant in Mispillion Hund and also all their right, title and claim to a piece of marsh that William Betts and Curtis Brinkle, both decd, took up in partnership. Wit: Richd. Lockwood, Mary Right. Elizabeth Carpenter privately examined gave consent. Ackn 9 Nov 1774. (V:p232)

322. 16 Oct 1765 Indenture between Immanuel Stout of Little Creek Hund, Kent on Delaware, yeoman and William Cook same place, merchant. Consideration of thirteen pounds parcel of land situate in afsd hund whereon Immanuel Stout now lives part of tract called Kingsale. Beginning at cor of Daniel Johnson's lott . . . to Daniel Dingee's lott . . . containing one quarter of an acre and one perch of land. Wit: David Johnson, Thos. Parry. Ackn 9 Nov 1774. (V:p232)

323. 8 Nov 1774 Indenture between Daniel Dingee of Sussex on Delaware, yeoman and William Cook of Kent on Delaware, merchant. Whereas Dingee by virtue of a indenture of bargain by Immanuel Stout of 9 Nov 1763 and recorded (Book Q, folio 203) became seized of parcel of land in Little Creek Hund, Kent Co containing three quarters of an acre and twelve square perches. Consideration of twenty one pounds thirteen shillings four pence conveys two thirds part of above lott of land on southwest branch of Duck Creek known as Little Duck at a place called the Fast Landing. Beginning at cor of lott formerly belonging to Samuel Hand now to William Cook . . . said part containing one half of an acre and eight square perches. Wit: Nathan Hart, Thos. Perry. Ackn 9 Nov 1774. (V:p233)

324. 24 Dec 1766 Indenture between David Johnson of Dover but late of Little Creek Hund, Kent on Delaware, blacksmith and William Cook of Kent on Delaware, merchant. Consideration of fifteen pounds conveys a lott of land situate in Little Creek Hund part of tract called Kingsale containing one quarter of an acre and one perch of land. Wit: Iml. Stourt, Charles Johnson. Ackn 10 Nov 1774. (V:p233)

325. 16 Oct 1765 Indenture between Immanuel Stout of Little Creek Hund, Kent on Delaware, yeoman and David Johnson same place, blacksmith. Consideration of thirteen pounds conveys parcel of land in afsd hund being part of lands whereon Immanuel Stout now dwelleth known as Kingsale. Begins on south side of Little Duck Creek containing one quarter of an acre and one perch of land. Wit: William Cook, Thomas Parry. Ackn 10 Nov 1774. (V:p234)

326. 1 Nov 1773 Indenture between Vincent Loockerman the elder of Kent on Delaware, gent and Vincent Loockerman the younger, his son of same place. Consideration of natural love and affection and sum of five shillings conveys all

those his secveral parcels of land situate in Dover Hund. Wit: Mary Rush, Will. Killen. Ackn 9 Nov 1774. (V:p234)

327. 10 Sept 1774 Indenture between John Baning of Kent on Delaware, merchant and William Pollard of city and co of Philadelphia, merchant. Consideration of two hundred fifty pounds conveys parcel of land part of tract called Content in Little Creek Hund. Description mentions land late of Benjamin Brooks . . . land late of Peter Shankmire . . . land late of Elizabeth Hines . . . containing one hundred thirty acres. Wit: William Killen, Vincent Loockerman, Junr. Ackn 9 Nov 1774. (V:p235)

328. 8 Nov 1774 Indenture between Daniel Dingee of Sussex on Delaware, yeoman and Immanuel Stout of Kent on Delaware, yeoman. Whereas Daniel Dingee under an agreement of bargain and sale under the hand and seal of Immanuel Stout dated 9 Nov 1763 recorded in (Liber Q, folio 203), he became seized in lott of land in Little Duck Creek containing three quarters of an acre and twelve square perches. Dingee now for sum of ten pounds sixteen shillings eight pence conveys above lott of land beginning at cor of a lot being conveyed by Dingee to William Cook . . . containing one quarter of an acre and four square perches. Wit: Nathan Hart, Thos. Parry. Ackn 9 Nov 1774 (V:p235)

329. 2 Nov 1774 Indenture between Isaac Lowber and Mary his wife of Kent on Delaware and Jonathan Emerson and Ruth his wife of same place and Rachel Bowers of co afsd of one part and Zadok Crapper of same place of other part. Consideration of two hundred twenty one pounds seventeen shillings six pence convey all that parcel of land and plantation in Mispillion Hund which was surveyed to Alexander Whitely late of said co, decd, by warranty dated 31 Jan 1744 who sold same to John Bowers, decd. Beginning at a former cor of land of John Catt and Timothy Long, decd, but now a cor of heirs of John Catts and Benjamin Clark's land . . . oak of late Abraham Bing Whitely . . . of Thomas Summer's land . . . heirs of William Down's land . . . cor of Wm. Steven's land . . . laid out for one hundred seventy seven and a half acres. Wit: John Clarke, John Steuart. Mary Lowber and Ruth Emerson privately examined gave their consent. Ackn 11 Nov 1774. (V:p236)

330. 4 June 1774 Indenture between James Jarrard of Murtherkill Hund, Kent on Delaware, tanner and Willson Jarrard of same place, tanner (they being two of sons of Matthew Jarrard, decd, and Matthew Jarrard, his son, of other part. Whereas Matthew Jarrard, decd, in his lifetime was seized of sundry tracts of land and in his will 19 Oct 1768 devised to son, Matthew, his dwelling plantation and enough adj land to make up three hundred acres, also devising the remainder to sons, James

and Willson Jarrard. A survey was made between 6th and 12th Dec 1769 by Mark McCall, surveyor and the whole premises were found to contain seven hundred ninety eight and a quarter acres and at same time, the three hundred acres with mansion house was laid off to Matthew, the son. Willson Jarrard has attained age twenty one and is desirous to have division made with his brother, James, of the remainder. So they in consideration of Matthew Jarrard releasing to them his interest and title and for sum of five shillings convey all that part of real estate beginning at land formerly claimed by John Rhodes . . . land late claimed by Robert Cummins . . . land surveyed for Robert New(?) now of William Harper . . . land surveyed for David Barnhill(?) now of Matthew Jarrard . . . laid off for three hundred acres. Mark McCall apptd atty. Wit: F. Battell, Absolom Morris. Ackn 22 Nov 1774. (V:p236)

331. 4 June 1774 Indenture between Matthew Jarrard of Murtherkill Hund, Kent on Delaware, yeoman and James Jarrard of same place, tanner and Willson Jarrard same place, tanner, all sons of Matthew Jarrard, decd. Whereas Matthew Jarrard, decd, in his lifetime was seized of sundry tracts of land and in his will 19 Oct 1768 devised to son, Matthew, his dwelling plantation and enough adj land to make up three hundred acres, also devising the remainder to sons, James and Willson Jarrard. A survey was made between 6th and 12th Dec 1769 by Mark McCall, surveyor and the whole premises were found to contain seven hundred ninety eight and a quarter acres and at same time, the three hundred acres with mansion house was laid off to Matthew, the son. Willson Jarrard has attained age twenty one and is desirous to have division made with his brother, James, of the remainder , a survey made 1st June this instant agreeable to all parties. Matthew and James Jarrard in consideration of Willson Jarrard releasing all his right and title to their respective two parts and sum of five shillings, grant to him the following land. Description mentions land formerly claimed by Robert Cummins . . . land of Joseph Campbell . . . heirs of Samuel Johns, Esq . . . laid off for two hundred fifty five and a quarter acres. Wit: F. Battell, Absolom Morris. Mark McCall apptd atty. Ackn 22 Nov 1774. (V:p237)

332. 1 Nov 1774 Whereas John Fothergill of London, doctor in physick, Daniel Zachary of London, gent, Jacob Hagan, Silvanus Grove and William Heron of London, merchants and surviving trustees to Proprietorship of Pennsylvania Land Company of London by Jacob Cooper, Samuel Shoemaker and Joshua Howel of Philadelphia, merchants and attys of one part and Waitman Booth of Mispillion Hund, Kent on Delaware, yeoman. By an act of Parliament vesting certain estates in province of Pennsylvania, New Jersey and Maryland belonging to the Pennsylvania Land Company to be sold and lands vested in Thomas Hyram, Thomas Reynolds and Thomas How, surviving trustees, were vested in John

Fothergill, Daniel Zachary, Thomas How, Devereaux Bowly, Luke Hind, Richard How, Jacob Hagan, Silvanus Grove and William Heron and could from time to time sell the land by public auction. Whereas on 10 June 1773, was sold to Joseph Brown, he being highest bidder who transferred his right to Waitman Booth who for consideration of eighty seven pounds eight shillings six pence paid receives deed for part of tract called Proprietorship in the possession of Benjamin Brown, decd, marked No. 5. Description mentions land of Christopher Sipple . . . land orig surveyed for John Newell called A----ster . . . part in possession of William Carpenter . . . to Dividend No. 6 in possession of Edward Cox . . . land orig surveyed for John Rawlins called Rawlins Lott . . . laid out for one hundred fifteen acres and one hundred forty seven square perches. Samuel McCall apptd atty. Wit: John Parke, Mark McCall. Ackn 9 Nov 1774. (V:p238)

333. 1 Oct 1774 Indenture between Job Willoby of Murtherkill Hund, Kent on Delaware, cordwainer and Elizabeth, his wife, George Herring same place and Mary, his wife, Curtis Herring same place, yeoman, Daniel Carter same place, yeoman and Mary, his wife, all of one part (they said Elizabeth Willoby, Mary Carter, George Herring and Curtis Herring, heirs of James Herring, same place decd) of one part and Thomas White same co, yeoman. Consideration of one hundred sixteen pounds convey parcel of land in hund and co afsd containing two hundred six acres and usual allowance for highways, etc. surveyed 1 Nov 1752 unto James Herring by William Killen, surveyor. Beginning at cor of land of Thomas Cox . . . line of Richard White's land . . . land claimed by Absolom Stradley . . . John Reed's land . . . heirs of Samuel Ross . . . laid out for two hundred thirty two acres and four square perches. Mark McCall apptd atty. Elizabeth Willowby and Mary Carter privately examined gave their consent. Wit: John Gray, Joseph Campbell. NOTE: The signatures are spelled by the clerk as "Willoughby" and "Harring". Ackn 9 Nov 1774. (V:p239)

334. 7 Oct 1774 Maryland. Know all men by these presents that I, John Chambers of Calvert County and province afsd, carpenter, constitute and appoint Mr. Matthew Hutchingson of Kent on Delaware, gent, my true and lawful attorney to acknowledge in court at Dover deed between me and William Chambers alias Allen of Kent Co of other part for conveyance of one acre of land part of Gravesend. (signed) John Chambers. Wit: Mary Allen, James Highe. Ackn 8 Nov 1774. (V:p240)

335. 23 Nov 1774 Indenture between Caesar Rodney of Kent on Delaware, Esq and Thomas Nixon same co, gent, trustees of General Loan Office and Elias Wood same co, husbandman. Whereas Edmond Hardin late of Kent Co, husbandman, decd by deed of mortgage dated 1 June 1759 did sell unto John Brinckle and John

Vining, Esqrs, then trustees of General Loan Office, for consideration of thirty five pounds parcel of land on north side of Dover River containing two hundred acres. Hardin failed to make payments and the land was exposed at public vendue and sold to Elias Wood for two hundred ten pounds. Wit: Charles Ridgely, John Wood. Ackn 23 Nov 1774. (V:p240)

336. 24 Nov. 1774 Indenture between William Pegg and Rachel his wife of Kent on Delaware and Johnson Eareckson same place. Consideration of eight pounds conveys parcel of land in forrest of Mispillion Hund whereon William Pegg lives being part of fifty acres that he purchased from _____. Beginning in an angle of Patrick Hugg's land . . . cor of Brown's field . . . containing six and one quarter acres and thirty two perches. Rachel Pegg privately examined gave consent. Wit: F. Battell, James Tilton. Ackn 24 Nov 1774. (V:p241)

337. 22 Nov 1774 Indenture between James Hamilton of Mispillion Hund, Kent on Delaware, yeoman and Joseph Fleming same place, taylor. By virtue of warrant granted to Alexander Hamilton, father of James, on 31 May 1745 and by survey a parcel of land was laid out in same hund and co. Beginning at a cor of land called Underwood Forest . . . land now of John Cox . . . land of Robert Knox . . . laid out for one hundred twelve and a quarter acres with the usual allowance for highways, etc. Whereas Alexander Hamilton and James Hamilton by written agreement dated 6 Feb 1767 contracted with James that Alexander could possess the land during his natural life and after his death should become property of James, agreement witnessed by Robert Killen and Richard Dallinar. Alexander Hamilton is now decd and James Hamilton conveys the land for consideraton of forty pounds to Joseph Fleming. Wit: Sarah McCall, Mark McCall. Ackn 22 Nov 1774. (V:p242)

338. 10 Jan 1774 Indenture between Elizabeth Fleming one of heirs and minors of Archibald Fleming, decd of Kent on Delaware and James Boyer same co, yeoman. Consideration of thirty pounds conveys one third part of parcel of land known as Brown's Chance situate in Murtherkill Hund. Description mentions land of Ezekiel Knock . . . line of Hargrove's land . . . containing one hundred acres. Tract granted to John Brown by warrant 15 Oct 1735 who by deed on 10 Feb 1741 conveyed same to John Coohn who conveyed same to Archibald Fleming on 9 Nov 1748, now Elizabeth Fleming, heir and minor of said Fleming conveys the land. Wit: J. Walker, Daniel Boyer. Ackn 23 Nov. 1774. (V:p242)

339. 12 May 1769 Indenture between Samuel Chew, John Clayton and John Chew all of Philadelphia, province of Pennsylvania, merchants and copartners in trade and Joseph Turner, same city, Esq. atty duly constituted of David Barclay & Sons, merchants in London and Amos Strettell of Philadelphia, Esq. the atty duly

constituted of John Strettell merchant in London, said David Barclay & Sons and John Stuttell being creditors of Samuel Chew, John Clayton and John Chew, who in consideration of certain debts and sums of money owed to David Barclay & Sons and John Stretell and others, and for consideration of ten shillings sterling money turn over to Joseph Turner and Amos Strettell monies, goods, wares, merchandise, ships, vessels, chattells, moveables, plate, effects and estate real, personal or mixed whatsoever of them and each of them . . . in the province of Pennsylvania or elsewhere in the world Wit: Th. Ringgold, M. Earle. Ackn 24 Nov 1774. (V:p243)

340. 11 June 1774 Indenture between Joseph Turner and Amos Strettell of city of Philadelphia, Pennsylvania, Esqrs and Samuel Hanson of Kent on Delaware, gent. Whereas Samuel Chew, John Clayton and John Chew, all late of city and province afsd, merchants in copartnership by deed 12 May 1769 for consideration therein mentioned conveyed to Turner and Strettell as attys for David Barclay & Sons, merchants in London and John Strettell, merchant same place, creditors of Samuel Chew, John Clayton and John Chew, among other things, messuages plantations tracts pieces or parcels of land and now Turner and Strettell for sum of four hundred thirty eight pounds five shillings convey part of the White Oak Swamp which in division of estate of _____ decd was devised to Samuel and John Chew situate in St. Jone's Hund. Beginning at stone of Porter's Lodge and Berry's Range . . . part belonging to Benjamin Chew . . . land of Samuel Hanson . . . containing one hundred nine acres and thirty seven perches. Wit: John Chew, Joseph N_____. Ackn 24 Nov 1774. (V:p244)

341. 11 Nov 1774 Indenture between Lamuel Burriss of Kent on Delaware, weaver and Mary, his wife and David Moore same place, yeoman. Whereas a parcel of land situate in forrest of Murderkill Hund beginning at cor of Hugh Durborow's land . . . to post in line of Gravesend . . . cor of Nathaniel Smither's land . . . containing seventy acres of land . . . subject to Loan Office of Kent Co and Clayton Levick and Hannah, his wife, by virtue of a court order in 1765 conveyed the land to Peter Vanburcolo (Book B, folio 11) who with wife, Sarah, by indenture of release on 22 Feb 1768 sold the land to Thomas Burriss (Book R, folio 250). Consideration of one hundred five pounds, Lamuel Burriss now conveys afsd tract to David Moore. Wit: Jno. Smithers, Daniel Newnam. Mary Burriss privately examined gave consent. Ackn 11 Nov 1774. (V:p244)

342. 24 Nov 1774 Indenture between Samuel Hanson of Kent on Delaware, gent and Ezekiel Needham same co, practitioner in physic and Jonathan Needham same co, yeoman. Consideration of two hundred ninety pounds sixteen shillings conveys parcel of land on Morgan's Branch in Dover Hund. Description mentions Samuel

and Thomas Hanson's land . . . Berry's Range . . . Porter's Lodge . . . said parcel contains seventy two acres and one hundred thirteen square perches part of larger tract together with other tracts were conveyed by Samuel Chew, John Clayton and John Chew to Joseph Turner and Amos Strettell of Philadelphia, Esqrs on 12 May 1769 and sold by them on 11 June last past to Samuel Hanson. Wit: Thomas Nixon, Junr, John Dill. Ackn 24 Nov 1774. (V:p245)

343. 11 June 1774 Indenture between Elizabeth Wynn of Little Creek Neck and Hund, Kent on Delaware, widow and Abraham Vanhoy, Junr. same place, yeoman. Whereas on a division of land of Simon Hirons late of same place being part of land called London a part in Nov 1764 was laid off jointly to Elizabeth (then wife of Benjamin Wynn) and her sister, Mary Hirons, containing thirty three acres and one hundred thirty eight perches. Mary Hirons conveyed her undivided moiety to Elizabeth and one third at time of the division was laid off to Persis Edingfield, the widow of Simon Hirons. Description mentions Simon Hirons, oldest son . . . said widow's part contains four and a half acres whereby Elizabeth is vested in thirty eight acres and fifty eight perches of land part of est of her father only some part thereof is detained by Timothy Jenkins and by heirs of James Blundell, not yet settled. Elizabeth for consideration of fifty pounds conveys all above mentioned and in some part described parcels, part of London whereon she dwells. Samuel McCall and Mark McCall apptd attys. Wit: John Edingfield, Mary Hirons, Hosea Wilson. Ackn 17 Feb 1775. (V:p245)

344. 2 Aug 1760 Know all men by these presents that I, Thomas Hanson of Kent on Delaware, yeoman and Joshua Grigg of Chester County, Pennsylvania, millrite(sic) are firmly bound to James Clayton of Kent Co, miller, in just and full sum of one thousand pounds. Condition being that Hanson and Grigg pay the sum of five hundred pounds on 1st Oct next with lawful interest. Wit: John Clayton, Jno. Sutton. Received 2 Oct 1760 from Thomas Hanson and Joshua Grigg one hundred eighty seven pounds four shillings nine pence (signed) James Clayton. Received 20 Oct ____ from (same) one hundred eighty seven pounds fifteen shillings three pence. (signed) James Clayton. Received 14 Jan 1761 from Thomas Hanson sixty six pounds seven shillings half pence half penny part of within bond being one half of what is due. (signed) James Clayton. Received 11 Feb 1761 from Joshua Grigg sixty six pounds fourteen shillings in for ballance of the within bond. (signed) James Clayton. Note the above bond was canselld before it was recorded and at the request of Joshua Grigg, I recorded it. (V:p246)

345. 5 Sept 1774 Indenture between Bartholomew Eggmen of Burlington Co, Chester Township in western division of province of West Jersey, farmer and Daniel Billiture of Dover Hund, Kent on Delaware, wheel wright. Whereas

Emmanuel Stout of Kent Co, yeoman, by deed dated 14 Feb 1750 conveyed to Bartholomew Eggmen parcel of land in St. Jone's Hund on a branch of Dover River being westernmost moiety of one hundred acres laid out for Thomas Lucas, since conveyed to Nicholas Powell and then to Samuel Thorp, then to Jonathan Davis, and then to Cornelius Eggmen who by will devised same to son, Christopher Eggmen who conveyed same to Emmanuel Stout and Bartholomew Eggmen is about to convey his right and title to the moiety to Daniel Billiture for sum of fifty pounds. Wit: Simon W. Willson, John Rhodes. French Battel and Charles Ridgely apptd attys. Ackn 15 Feb 1775. (V:p246)

346. 15 Feb 1775 Indenture between Ezekiel Cowgill and Mary, his wife, of Little Creek Hund, Kent on Delaware and Vincent Emerson of Mutherkill Hund same co, yeoman. Mary Cowgill being extx of will of Christopher Sipple who was seized of sundry lands and devised his extrs to sell land adj that of Mark Manlove purchsed from Samuel Hews and also the land of Blaids(?) and the money distributed one third to widow and remainder equally between his four daus: Mary Ann Jenkins, Mary, Elizabeth and Alice Sipple and apptd wife, Mary, (now wife of Ezekiel Cowgill) as extrx; his bro, John Sipple, since decd, and friend, Mark Manlove as co-extrs. (Liber K, folio 52). Mary, surviving extx, now conveys for consideration of twenty two pounds nine shillings and a penny a parcel of land beginning and extending with land of Robert Beauchamp formerly Samuel Hews . . . land of Matthew Manlove . . . land of William Thompson formerly Biards(?) . . . laid out for seventeen acres and one hundred fifty four square perches. Wit: John Dill, Isaac Dawson. Ackn 15 Feb 1775. (V:p247)

347. 16 Feb 1775 Indenture between Joseph Parsons of Mispillion Hund, Kent on Delaware, yeoman and Margaret, his wife and James Hattfield same co, innkeeper. Whereas Thomas Collins, gent by deed dated 9 Nov 1773 conveyed parcel of land in co and hund afsd to Joseph Parsons adj land now possessed by James Hattfield. Description mentions Fairfield . . . land late of John Falconer, decd . . . containing one hundred and a half acres and allowance (Book C, folio 162). Land conveyed for sum of one hundred twenty five pounds. Margaret Parsons privately examined gave consent. Wit: Simon W. Willson, Cors. Comegys. Ackn 16 Feb 1775. (V:p247)

348. 20 Oct 1774 Indenture between Paris Chipman of Kent on Delaware, husbandman and Margaret, his wife and Charles Emory of Queen Ann's Co, province of Maryland, yeoman. Consideration of four hundreed fifty three pounds two shillings six pence paid now convey parcel of land on north side of Tidbury Branch in Murtherkill Hund. Beginning at cor of Reuben Gilder's land . . . said tract contains one hundred forty five acres, part of larger tract called Road's Fores

orig granted to John Roads by patent 10th day 5th mo 1684 and by force and virtue of sundry conveyances duly made is now vested in Paris Chipman. Wit: Abel Janney, William French. Margaret Chipman privately examined gave consent. John Baning apptd atty. Ackn 17 Feb 1775. (V:p248)

349. 5 Nov 1774 Indenture between Joshua Clayton late of Murtherkill Hund, Kent on Delaware, practitioner in physic and John Clayton, bro of above Joshua, now of same place, yeoman. Consideration of five hundred seventeen pounds conveys parcel of land on north side of Dover River on Isaac Webb's Branch part of larger tract called Smyrna being piece cut off of head thereof and part of real est of James Clayton, decd, and valued by Orphan's Court, Joshua Clayton now conveys to bro, John Clayton. Beginning at the land now of Benjamin Vining . . . cor of land conveyed by heirs of Benjamin Shurmer to Isaiah Worton . . . laid out for two hundred fifty eight and a half acres. Samuel McCall apptd atty. Wit: F. Battell, Matthew Manlove. Ackn 15 Feb 1775. (V:p249)

350. 12 Jan 1775 Indenture between Caleb Luff, Nathaniel Luff, Hannah Paradee, widow, Deborah Pleasonton, widow, all of Kent on Delaware and Phillip Rasin of Kent Co, province of Maryland, heirs and representatives of Nathaniel Luff, late of Kent Co, decd and William Tharp of same place, yeoman. Whereas a survey was made for Nathaniel Luff, decd, in right of Edward McKemmey situated in Brown's Neck, Mispillion Hund. Beginning at cor red oak of land at the time of survey, on 10 Dec 1750 in possession of Edward Melvin . . . land in possession of William Harper . . . land of Solomon Eagle . . . William Jacob's land . . . in McClen's(?) line . . . laid off for one hundred fifteen acres and one hundred perches. Luff died intestate and land was undivided among his heirs when other real estate was divided and now his children above named and grandson, Phillip Rasin, now convey the tract for sum of two hundred two pounds ten shillings paid by William Tharp. Samuel McCall and Mark McCall apptd attys. Wit: George McCall, Thomas Nixon, Junr. Ackn 15 Feb 1775. (V:p249)

351. 16 Jan 1775 Indenture between John Draughton of Duck Creek Hund, Kent on Delaware, yeoman and Jacob Jones of Kent Co, province of Maryland, yeoman. Consideration of eight hundred ninety pounds conveys tract situate in hund and co afsd. Beginning on Joseph Moore's Gutt . . . land of William Savin . . . laid off for three hundred ten acres. Samuel McCall and Mark McCall appt attys. Wit: Thomas Nixon, Junr, Sarah McCall. Ackn 15 Feb 1775. (V:p250)

352. 8 Nov 1774 Indenture between Peter King of Kent on Delaware, yeoman and Anne his wife and John Beauchamp of Murtherkill Hund, yeoman. Whereas Peter King on 26 Aug 1773 executed an alienation bond to William Handy for

conveyance of tract in afsd hund formerly surveyed for Curtis Evans on 20 June 1758 by warrant 2 June 1746 by William Killen, surveyor. Beginning at cor oak of land of Thomas Parke and land late of Curtis Evans . . . laid out for one hundred eleven and a half acres and allowance. William Handy on 16 May 1774 by his assignment on said bond, transferred his right to John Beauchamp, Junr who having paid Peter King the consideration money, now King is about to make a conveyance to John for sum of thirty five pounds. Samuel McCall and Mark McCall apptd attys. Wit: John Clark, John Williams. Ann King privately examined gave consent. Ackn 14 Feb 1775. (V:p250)

353. 23 June 1774 Indenture between John Cook, high sheriff of Kent on Delaware and Andrew Jamison, Isaac Carty, Edward Rees and John White all of said co. For sum of five shillings good and lawful money of the government paid by above named and divers other good causes . . . releases a small lott or piece of ground part of larger tract called Permaine Price in Duck Creek Hund adj east side of Gravelly Branch . Beginning on east side of Peterson's Mill Pond . . . nr south side of Presbyterian Meeting House and Burying Ground . . . cor of land belonging to heirs of Andrew Peterson . . . laid out for half an acre of ground . . . in trust nevertheless to and for benifit and behoof of the members of the Presbyterian Church or Congregation residing and hereafter residing in Duck Creek Hund. Wit: Mark McCall, Jonah Thomas. Ackn 16 Feb 1775. (V:p251)

354. 1 June 1774 Indenture between Mary Hirons of Little Creek Neck & Hund, Kent on Delaware, spinstress and Elizabeth Wynn same place, widow. Whereas by division of lands of Simon Hirons, father of Mary and Elizabeth, in Nov 1761, following land was laid off to Elizabeth and husband, Benjamin Wynn, who had purchased Mary's part. The two parts begin at stake of land laid off for Robert Hirons, one of the heirs, in line of land of James Blundel . . . to one third part laid off to Persis Edingfield, widow of Simon Hirons . . . to part laid off for Simon Hirons, eldest son . . . to land claimed by Timothy Jenkins . . . laid off for thirty three acres and one hundred thirty eight square perches, part of which is detained by Timothy Jenkins and another part detained by heirs of James Blundel. Mary Hirons now conveys her one undivided half part of described land to her sister, Elizabeth Wynn, as bargain between Mary and Benjamin Wynn was never completed. Consideration of four pounds per acre to amount of sixty seven pounds fourteen shillings six pence received of Elizabeth Wynn. Samuel McCall and Mark McCall apptd attys. Wit: John Edenfield, Hosea Wilson. Ackn 17 Feb 1775. (V:p251)

355. 15 Feb 1775 Indenture between John Pattison of Duck Creek Hund, Kent on Delaware, farmer and Joseph Moore same place, black smith. Witnesseth that John

Pattison is seized of parcel of land part of Manor of Frieth in his demesne as of fee by sundry conveyances and assurances in the law . . . by deed 21 Sept 1772 duly executed by Matthew Griffin, Saml. Griffin and Mary, his wife, Joseph Mereith and Elizabeth, his wife, and also Isaac Griffin, reps of Saml. Griffith, farmer, decd. John Pattison in consideration of three hundred seventy pounds conveys one hundred five acres of described land to Joseph Moore. Wit: Silas Snow, James Vandyke. Ackn 16 Feb 1775. (V:p252)

356. 9th day 9th mo 1774 Indenture between Jonathan Emerson of Murtherkill Hund, Kent on Delaware, Esq and John Fisher same place, yeoman. Emerson for consideration, rents and covenants hereinafter mentioned and sum of five shillings . . . conveys two lotts in Federica at head of Murtherkill marked in town plat as No. 23 and No. 24 beginning at upper cor of No. 25 . . . binding on First Street . . . lower cor of No. 22 . . . side of each street to be posted and reserved for a foot passage . . . paying yearly and every year thereafter on 29th day of 9th mo the sum of three pounds . . . first payment to be made 29 Sept next. Wit: George Lambden, Pene O. Mekinn (her mark). Ackn 15 Feb 1775. (V:p252)

357. 23 Aug 1774 Indenture between Benjamin Chew of Philadelphia, atty at law, Charles Ridgely of Kent on Delaware, physician and Benjamin Wynkoop of Philadelphia, merchant, and extrs of John Vining of Kent Co, decd and William Rees of Duck Creek Hund, same co. John Vining was seized in his demesne as of fee in sundry lands in Kent Co and elsewhere together with lotts situate at the Cross Roads and in his will of 13 Nov 1770 authorized his extrs to sell all his land for best prices obtainable. Now they convey a lott part of tract called Gravesend which was by deed from William Green and James Green, extrs of Thomas Green, decd, by deed 12 Feb 1768 (Book R, folio 123) conveyed to John Vining beginning at cor of James McMullin's lott . . . road by Fenwick Fisher's plantation . . . stake in Robert Holliday's line . . . laid off for two acres. Consideration of three hundred pounds paid by William Rees. Wit: Josims(?), Mark McCall, Edward Dyer, Israel Allston. Ackn 16 Feb 1775. (V:p253)

358. 12 Jan 1775 Indenture between William Wallace, Junr of Kent on Delaware, husbandman and Vincent Loockerman the elder of same place, merchant. In consideration of one thousand seven hundred pounds conveys all that plantation part of tract called Greenwich situate on southwest side of branch of Dover River called Metetones Branch in Murtherkill Hund. Beginning at a cor of tract late of John Vining, Esq, decd . . . line of Greenwich . . . tract called Long Reach . . . part belonging to Charles Ridgely, Esq. . . . part in possession of Matthew Manlove . . . containing four hundred one acres and three tenths part of an acre and allowance of 6% for roads and highways. Greenwich was granted to Norton Claypole in fee by

James Claypole and Robert Turner, two of the late proprietary commissioners and by patent bearing date 27th day 11th mo 1684 and by sundry conveyances, the property became vested in James Armitage late of Newcastle Co, Esq, decd and part of Greenwich now being conveyed was by Thomas Dunn, surviving extr of James Armitage entered into contract with William Wallace, the elder, father of afsd William Wallace on 4 Feb 1769 and after the death of William Wallace, the elder who died intestate, and for consideration mentioned, granted and conveyed to Katharine Wallace, widow, and Robert Wallace, eldest son. By division of the estate made by the Orphans Court, William Wallace, party hereto, was allotted the part now being conveyed. Wit: William Killen, Thomas Nixon, Junr. Ackn 17 Feb 1775. (V:p254)

359. 15 Feb 1775 Indenture between Jonathan Emerson of Murtherkill Hund, Kent on Delaware and John Gibson same place, carpenter. Consideration as well as rents and covenants hereinafter mentioned and sum of five shillings conveys two lotts of ground in town of Frederica marked in plat of town as No. 18 and No. 19 . . . yielding and paying therefore to Jonathan Emerson the sum of three pounds . . . yearly and every year forever beginning on the 29th Sept next. Wit: John Dill, John Fisher. Ackn 15 Feb 1775. (V:p254)

360. 6th day 2nd mo 1775 Indenture between Jonathan Emerson of Murtherkill Hund, Kent on Delaware, yeoman and Solomon Emerson same place, shop joiner. For consideration as well as rents and covenants hereinafter mentioned and sum of five shillings conveys two lotts of ground in town of Frederica marked in plat of town as No. 8 and No. 22. Description mentions lott of Zachariah Goforth and David Lucke's land . . . yielding and paying therefore to Jonathan Emerson the sum of three pounds yearly and every year forever beginning on 29th Sept next. Wit: John Dill, John Fisher. Ackn 15 Feb 1775. (V:p255)

361. 20 Sept 1772 Indenture between Samuel Goodwin, blacksmith, Elizabeth Goodwin, his sister, now Elizabeth Forsith, lately Elizabeth Evans, late wife of Henry Evans and Nathaniel Forsith, husband of Elizabeth, heirs and representatives of Samuel Goodwin and Elizabeth, his wife, late of Kent on Delaware, decd and Andrew Butler same co, taylor. Consideration of one hundred pounds conveys the moiety or half part of tract called Long Reach in forrest of Murtherkill Hund orig surveyed for Henry Bedwell, Thomas Bedwell, Robert Bedwell, Junr and Adam Fisher being the same land conveyed by extrs of Henry Bedwell to John Robinson. Beginning at part belonging to James Gardner . . . part purchased from Thomas Pennrose . . . land adj of Mark and Daniel Coudratt . . . Greenwich . . . land orig surveyed for Norton Claypole . . . laid off for fifty nine acres and eighty two perches of land surveyed by Mark McCall on 29 July 1771.

Wit: Thomas Gordon, John Smith, Mark McCall. William Killen apptd atty or Joshua Clayton, practitioner in physics. Elizabeth Forsith being of full age and examined privately gave consent. Ackn 1 March 1775. (V:p255)

362. 2 Mar 1775 Indenture between Robert Rees of Duck Creek Hund, Kent on Delaware, yeoman and Barthia Hazel, relict and widow of Isaac Hazel late of same place, decd. Whereas said parties at present are possessed of lands, branch and cripple situate in hund and co afsd separated by a small run of a water course . . . of Gravelly Run or Branch and parties hereto have agreed to swap some parts of the branch cripple for converting same into meadow grounds . . . and Robert Rees now conveys two parcels of branch cripple lying on his side of the run to Barthia Hazel for like conveyance made to him by Barthia Hazel of two parcels of like branch cripple on her side of the run and sum of five shillings. Description mentions lands of William and Robert Rees . . . his part laid off for sixty seven and a half acres . . . and another part laid off for one acre one hundred forty one and a quarter square perches of land and branch cripple. Wit: George McCall, Henry Farson. Ackn 2 Mar 1775. (V:p255)

363. 9 Feb 1775 Indenture between Rachel Streep, relict and widow of William Streep (alias Street) late of Murtherkill Hund, Ken on Delaware, decd of one part and Uriah, Robert, Jane, William and Auther Streep, children and heirs of William Streep. Whereas James Bedwell late of same co, decd, by writing alienation obligatory became bound to William Streep in sum of seventy pounds condition being conveyance of parcel of land in hund and co afsd on north side of and adj Isaac Webb's Branch being part of Long Reach between part formerly of Ezekiel Needham and the branch and William Streep gave his obligation to James Bedwell for conveyance and died before deed was made. Letters of admin were given to the widow, Rachel Streep, and James Bedwell having died, his son, Robert Bedwell, was apptd admin of his father's estate. Rachel Streep paid the residue of the consideration money and Robert Bedwell made deed on 15 May 1774 to Rachel Streep (Book T, folio 91) who has since married Thomas Milner who hath appeared to be a married man having at least one wife to whom he was formerly married, Rachel freed of the bonds of matrimony desires to convey the land to the heirs of her husband, William Streep. She now for natural love and affection and sum of five shillings conveys parcel of land described except before excepted to his children. Wit: Saml. McCall, Sarah McCall. Ackn 14 Feb 1775. (V:p256)

364. 2 Mar 1775 Indenture between Barthia Hazel, relict and widow of Isaac Hazel late of Duck Creek Hund, Kent on Delaware and Robert Rees same hund and co. Whereas these parties are possessed of lands and branch cripple situate in same hund and co afsd, separated from each other by a water course of Rees

Branch and said parties have agreed to swap parts of the branch cripple for use of converting same into meadow ground. Barthia Hazel now conveys her part of the same on her side of the branch to Robert Rees and for like conveyance made to her and sum of five shillings releases two parcels of the cripple. One part laid off for one acre and forty and a half square perches and the other part laid off for two acres and thirty eight square perches. Wit: George McCall, Henry Farson. Ackn 2 Mar 1775. (V:p257)

365. 2 Mar 1775 Indenture between James Raymond of Duck Creek Hund, Kent on Delaware, yeoman and Angelica, his wife and Thomas Stewart of forrest of Little Creek Hund, yeoman. Consideration of nine hundred twenty pounds conveys two parcels of land in afsd hund and co, one being part of tract formerly surveyed for James Steel and became property of James Morris who conveyed it to Presley Raymond, father of James. Beginning at cor white oak at mouth of Allstone Branch . . . with line of land commonly called Travillers Delight . . . tract of land called Wappin . . . formerly surveyed for John Willis . . . land claimed by Hugh Suiter . . . land claimed by John Ham . . . laid out for two hundred twenty four acres and forty seven square perches. Other parcel is part of two ancient tracts, Travillers Delight, the other called Little TowerHill. Description mentions Jordon Robinson's lott in Charles Robinson's line . . . heirs of John Robinson, decd . . . laid out for seventy eight acres and thirty two square perches. Wit: Nehemiah Tilton, Richd. Smith. Angelica Raymond privately examined gave consent. Ackn 2 Mar 1775. (V:p258)

366. 2 Mar 1775 Indenture between William Rees of Duck Creek Hund, Kent on Delaware, blacksmith and Barthia Hazel, widow of Isaac Hazel. Whereas parties hereto possess land, meadows, and branch cripple in afsd hund separated from each other by Gravelly Branch and have agreed to divide the said branch cripple. William Rees now conveys a small parcel in consideration of Barthia Hazel making a like deed and for sum of five shillings. Description mentions line between lands of William and his brother, Robert Rees . . . tract laid out for one acre sixty five and a quarter perches. Wit: George McCall, Henry Farson. Ackn 2 Mar 1775. (V:p258)

367. 2 Mar 1775 Indenture betwee Barthia Hazel, widow of Isaac Hazel, of Duck Creek Hund, late decd and William Rees same place, blacksmith. Whereas Barthia Hazel has become vested in land of her former husband which was exposed to sale by the Orphan's Court and purchased by Henry Farson who reconveyed same to Barthia Hazel. Tract situated on Gravelly Branch sometime called Rees Branch, part of tract called Branford and land called Fox Hall and is separated from land of William Rees and his bro, Robert Rees and said parties have agreed to swap each other part of the meadows and branch cripple. Barthia Hazel now conveys small

part of same for a conveyance of even date from William Rees and sum of five shillings . . . laid out for one acre and one hundred nine square perches. Wit: George McCall, Henry Farson. Ackn 2 Mar 1775. (V:p259)

368. 28 Feb 1775 Indenture between Garrat Sipple of Murtherkill Hund, Kent on Delaware, gent and William Jones, same co. Consideration of sixty pounds conveys all the estate, right, title and interest, etc. to parcel called Sipple's Lott. Beginning at a cor of James Water's land . . . in William Robert's line . . . land formerly belonging to Andrew Caldwell . . . laid out for one hundred fifty three acres. Wit: Thomas Rodney, George Saxton. Ackn 28 Feb 1775. (V:p259)

369. 2 Mar 1775 Indenture between Joseph Mason of Kent on Delaware and Isaac Mason same place Whereas David Row of said co devised to his wife, Susannah, a parcel of land situate in Mispillion Hund called Fairfield and she died intestate leaving issue two sons, above parties who agree to divide said land releasing each to the other parts of said tract. Joseph Mason now conveys a part laid out for one hundred forty three acres being the full third part of the described land and full share belonging to Isaac Mason, he being the younger heir. Wit: Saml. McCall, James Anderson. Ackn 2 Mar 1775. (V:p259)

370. 2 Mar 1775 Indenture betwee Isaac Mason of Kent on Delaware and Joseph Mason of same place. Whereas David Row of said co devised to his wife, Susannah, a parcel of land in Mispillion Hund called Fairfield and she having died intestate, leaving two sons, above parties to this deed, who agree to divide said land releasing each to the other parts of said tract. Isaac Mason now conveys a part laid out for two hundred eighty six acres being two thirds of above mentioned land and a full share belonging to Joseph Mason, he being the elder heir. Wit: Saml. McCall, James Anderson. Ackn 2 Mar 1775. (V:p260)

371. 27 Feb 1775 Indenture between Hezekiah Downs and Levin Downs, two of the children of William Downs late of Mispillion Hund, Kent on Delaware and William Tharp, city of Philadelphia, merchant. William Downs was seized in fee in his lifetime in lands in hund and co afsd and William Tharp is now possessed of part of said lands and Downs devised his land to his children, dividion never being made and some have conveyed their undivided part to Tharp, now Hezekiah and Levin Downs convey their interest to him for sum of one hundred pounds. Samuel McCall apptd atty. Wit: Thos. Sheriff, Thos. Morgan. Ackn 2 Mar 1775. (V:p260)

372. 2 Mar 1775 Indenture between James FitzJarrold of Kent on Delaware and Eleazer FitzJarrold and Sarah, his wife, same place. Consideraton of one hundred pounds conveys part of his dwelling plantation called Poplar Cove in forrest of

Murtherkill Hund beginning at a cor of Joseph Powell's land . . . land of Bryan Seena . . . containing one hundred acres of land. Wit: Martha Powell, William Powell. Ackn 2 Mar 1775. (V:p261)

373. 2 Mar 1775 Indenture between Eleazer FitzJarrold and Sarah, his wife of Kent on Delaware and Isaac Downham and Ruth, his wife same place. Whereas Richard Downham was seized in fee of several tracts of land and by his will devised that his land should be divided among his children, but he lived sometime after making the will and during the time purchased of William Grey small parcel called Long Day containing sixty two acres fifty two perches and Eleazer FitzJarrold marrying one of Richard Downham's daus became entitled to part of the intestate land and also a part of the decd's other lands. Now for consideration of one hundred pounds paid by Isaac Downham and Ruth, his wife, he conveys his right, title, estate and interest in a tract beginning in line of Joseph Downham's land . . . cor of John Beauchamp, Jr and Mary, his wife . . . tract being conveyed containing forty six acres. And also all right, title, estate and interest to tract called Long Day. Wit: Martha Powell, William Powell. Sarah FitzJarrold examined privately gave consent. Ackn 2 Mar 1775. (V:p261)

374. 12 Nov 1772 Indenture between Robert Rees of Duck Creek Hund, Kent on Delaware and William Rees same place, blacksmith. Consideraton of three hundred forty six pounds conveys parcel of land in Duck Creek Hund part of tract conveyed by Samuel Smith and Tamsey, his wife, to Robert Rees on date preceeding this present indenture. Beginning at cor of land of heirs of Daniel Smith, decd . . . land in possession of heirs of Isaac Hazel . . . laid out for one hundred fifteen acres and fifty four square perches. Wit: John Cook, Saml. McCall. Ackn 16 Feb 1775. (V:p262)

375. 22 Feb 1775 Indenture between Jonathan Rees of Westmoreland Co and Springhill Township, province of Pennsylvania, farmer, by Joseph David, Senr of Little Creek Hund, Kent on Delaware, yeoman and Joseph David, Junr of last mentioned place. Whereas Timothy Irons formerly of forrest of Little Creek Hund was seized in parcel of land in hund afsd and died intestate leaving two male children: Timothy and William Irons and Timothy as oldest son was legally heir. William Rees, father of Jonathan, had no other child by the mother of Jonathan who following death of William Rees married Timothy Irons thus Jonathan Rees became half bro to Timothy and William Irons. Timothy, Junr died before lawful age and Jonathan Rees and William Irons became heirs to his part and Jonathan Rees sold his part to Joseph David, Junr and did not make deed but by power of atty constitute and appoint Joseph David, Senr, his power of atty who for consideration of one hundred pounds conveys said land. Wit: Morgan Blackshere,

James Moore. Ackn 1 Mar 1775. (V:p262)

376. 11 July 1774 Know all men by these presents that I, Jonathan Rees, farmer of Westmoreland County, Springhill Township, province of Pennsylvania, authorize and appoint Joseph David, Senr. my true and lawful attorney to make over to Joseph David, Junr all my right, title and interest and claim to a tract of land late the property of Timothy Irons, minor, decd to the estate of Timothy Irons, decd, of county of Kent on Delaware, Litle Creek Hund. (signed) Jonathan Rees. Wit: Daniel Vernum, Wm. Burns. Ackn 1 Mar 1775. (V:p263)

377. 27 Feb 1775 Indenture between Caleb Hunn of Little Creek Hund, Kent on Delaware, house carpenter and Mary Hunn, same place, relict and widow of David Hunn, late decd, they being extr and extx nominated by said David Hunn, and John Bell same hund and co, shallopman. Whereas David Hunn was seized in certain tracts of land in right of his father, John Hunn, sometime since decd. otherwise consisting of part of Simpson's Choice and tract called Shrewsberry also a marsh adj on Little Creek . . . coupled with said Creek and land of John Clifford . . . Garrat Sipple's land . . . land late of Silas Crispin . . . and other marshes adj . . . in consequence of warrant granted to Timothy Hanson on 27 Nov 1730 for two hundred acres marsh and by Hanson transferred to John Hunn on 3 Feb 1749. David Hunn so seized died with will dated 24 June 1775 devising that Caleb Hunn (his brother) and his wife, Mary, make over and sell his land. Said land was sold at public auction to John Bell for sum of one thousand pounds and is now conveyed. Wit: James Wells, Junr., George McCall. Ackn 2 Mar 1775. (V:p263)

378. 1 Mar 1775 Indenture between John Bell of Little Creek Neck and Hund, Kent on Delaware, shallopman and Caleb Hunn same place, carpenter. Consideration of one thousand pounds conveys all the lands, marshes, swamps and branches, and whereas David Hunn, bro of Caleb Hunn, late of same place, now decd, was in his lifetime seized of lands situate in hund and co afsd or elsewhere . . . ordered in his last will all lands to be sold by his extr and extx and they were sold by Caleb and Mary Hunn the relict and widow, for sum of one thousand pounds to John Bell. Said lands bounded (see above deed for description). Wit: James Wells, Junr., George McCall. Ackn 2 Mar 1775. (V:p263)

379. 16 Feb 1775 Indenture between Thomas Jamison, farmer, of Duck Creek Hund, Kent on Delaware and Catharine, his wife and David Kennedy same place, merchant. Consideraton of three hundred fifty pounds conveys lott or small piece of ground nr the crossroads. Beginning at cor of Howel Buckingham's lott in right of Mary, his wife, devisee under will of Thos Green, Junr, decd . . . containing thirty two square perches of land. Wit: Allen McLane, William Rees. Catharine

Jamison privately examined gave consent. Ackn 16 Feb 1775. (V:p264)

380. 9 Mar 1775 Indenture between Elizabeth Raymond, relict and widow of John Raymond of Duck Creek Hund, Kent on Delaware and Silas Snow same place, joint admtrs of estate of John Raymond and James Raymond of hund and co afsd. Administrators by petition to Orphan's Court 25 Nov 1773 stated they had administered away all personal part of estate save fifteen pounds and estate was still indebted to amount of fiteen or sixteen hundred pounds and prayed for permission to sell enough of Raymond's land which was granted and court ordered that one hundred fifty acres of upland including the mansion brick dwelling place be sold and all the salt marsh thereto belonging and survey was made by Mark McCall. Beginning nr head of a branch dividing this land from land of Joseph Hillyard, decd . . . beginning course of patent of Thomas Sharp for whole premises . . . to cor of patent to James Still and Thomas Sharp . . . for line of Whitwell's Chance . . . laid off for one hundred fifty acres of land . . . marsh and branch cripple laid off for fifty six acres and one hundred twenty four square perches. Said land was sold to Thomas Collins, gent, for nineteen hundred and fifty pounds who assigned his right of purchase to James Raymond. Now Elizabeth Raymond, widow and Silas Snow, admtrs, convey the said land. Samuel McCall and Mark McCall apptd attys. Wit: Abrhm. Allee, Eliz. Nancy. Ackn 20 Mar 1775. (V:p264)

381. 15 Feb 1775 Petition of William Clark of Newcastle on the Delaware, yeoman most humbly sheweth that the sheriff of Kent on Delaware was commanded of the goods, chattles, lands and tenements of David Clark, then late of Kent Co, yeoman, decd in hands of Nicholas Vandike, Annalina Clark and William Clark, extrs of will of David Clark, he should be made and levied the sum of one hundred pounds fourteen shillings two pence which Elizabeth Ebtharp and John Numbers extrs of Thomas Ebtharp, decd, then lately recovered. James Wells, Esq., then sheriff took into execution and sold seventy four acres of David Clark's land called Partnership now Calf Pasture and land late of John Barne, Esq., decd, in forrest of Duck Creek Hund and sold same to your petitioner for sum of fifty nine pounds four shillings and deed has not been made. Your petitioner humbly prays that an order be made for John Cook, present sheriff, to do so. Petition being read order was granted. (signed) William Clark. (V:p265)

382. 6 July 1775 Indenture between John Wethered of Kent County, province of Maryland, gent and Mary, his wife, and John Farquarson of Charles Town, South Carolina. John Wethered and Mary, his wife, for the conveying and settling of such lands hereinafter mentioned and the sum of ten shillings sterling money of Great Britain by virtue of an indenture of bargain and sale made by John Wethered for one full moiety or half part of those two messuages and parcels of land formerly

known as Great and Small Tinheads Corte(sic) situate on south side of main branch of Little Creek in Dover Hund, Kent on Delaware. Description mentions old Tynhead Corte . . . along line of John Nickerson's land . . . Little Tynhead Corte tract . . . tract called Edington . . . cor of Little Pipe Elm . . . containing seven hundred acres. Also a full moiety of tract of four hundred acres in Dover Hund formerly belonging to William Perry . . . containing one hundred seventy five acres of upland and fifty acres of marsh. Also one full moiety or half part of tract called Kingston Upon Hull situate in Dover Hund containing fifty acres. Also a full moiety or half part of tract situate in Kent Co beginning at cor of land of John Staten, decd . . . containing fifty acres. Being the lands in Kent Co where Robert French by his will devised to his eldest dau, Catherine who married John Shannon and left two daus only: Mary who married James Sykes and left her only child, Mary, wife of John Wethered, and Ann, wife of John Maxwell, now living. Conveyed with limitation for use of John Wethered during his lifetime and John Farquharson shall permitt and suffer John Wethered to take the rents, issues and profite thereof and after his death, to use of Mary Wethered and after her death to the use of their first son and to the heirs of the body of the first son and for default of such issue, then to use of second son and in default of issue to third son, fourth son, fifth, sixth, seventh, eighth, ninth and tenth and all and every other the sons of John Withered on the body of Mary begotten severally and successfuly one after another in order and course as they shall be in seniority of and in priority of birth. (signed) John Wethered, Mary Wethered, John Farquharson. Wit: Edm. Quincy, Mary Dunn, Jas. VanDyke, Dorcas Montgomery. Mary Wethered in presence of Edmund Quincy, Justice of the Peace for county of Suffolk in the province of Massachusetts in New England privately examined declared she did acknowledge the within instrument freely. Ackn 6 July 1774 in province of Massachusetts Bay.. Sworn to in Kent on Delaware 10 May, 1775 by witness Mary Dunn. (V:p265)

383. 5 July 1774 Indenture between John Wethered of Kent County in province of Maryland, gent and John Farquharson of Charles Town, South Carolina. Witnesseth that John Wethered in consideration of sum of five shillings sterling money of Great Britain conveys one full and equal moiety of and in all those two messauge and parcells of land formerly known as Great and Small Tynheads Corte situate on main branch of Little Creek in Dover Hund, Kent on Delaware. Description mentions Great Tynhead Corte . . . John Nickerson's line . . . Little Tynhead Corte . . . tract called Edington . . . tract called Little Pipe Elm . . . containing seven hundred acres. And one full moiety of plantation situate in Dover Hund said parcel containing four hundred acres formerly belonging to William Berry . . . containing one hundred thirty acres upland and fifty acres of marsh and one full and equal part of tract known as Kingston Upon Hull situate in Dover Hund containing fifty acres and also one full equal moiety of tract situate in Kent

Co beginning at a stake in line of land formerly John Auters, decd, . . . containing fifty acres of land, being the lands within the said county of Kent where Robert French by will devised to his eldest dau, Catherine, who married John Shannon and left two daus: Mary who married James Sykes and left issue, Mary (wife of John Wethered, her only child) and Ann the wife of John Maxwell, now living. To have and to hold . . . unto the said John Farquharson, his extrs, administrators and assigns from the day next after the day of the date hereof for and during the term of one whole year from thence next ensuing and fully to be his compleatly, yielding and paying the rent of one ear of Indian corn on the Feast of St. Michael the Archangel. Wit: Mary Dunn, Dorcas Montgomery, Jas. VanDyke. Ackn 5 July 1774 by Edmund Quincy. Ackn (in Kent Co) 10 May 1775. (V:p267)

384. 11 May 1775 Indenture between Samuel Robinson of Murtherkill Hund, Kent on Delaware and George Manlove, Junr same place. Whereas Daniel Robinson, father of Samuel and grandfather to George Manlove by his last will devised to Samuel a parcel of land whereon Samuel now lives and also gave land in Mispillion Hund to George Manlove which land was sold by the sheriff to discharge debts of the disceased estate and George is now entitled to an equity in Daniel Robinson's estate. . Description mentions part sold to John Caten . . . line of Samuel Hanson's land . . . with S---- Jackson's land . . . containing one hundred acres. Wit: Wm. Manlove, John Gildersleve. Ackn 11 May 1775. (V:p268)

385. 4 Mar 1775 Indenture between Enoch Jones of Duck Creek Hund, Kent on Delaware, farmer, Moses Hudson, (alias Hutson) same place, yeoman. Whereas Moses Hudson hath lately intermarried with Penelope, only surviving heir and dau of Doctor Peter Storey late of Duck Creek Town or Salisbury Town in hund and co afsd who is devisee by will of William Mullet, Junr, formerly of said place, of and in a lot of ground and brick house thereon situate in Salisbury Town but subject to time of natural life of Penelope Mullet, mother of Penelope Hudson, but her natural life interest was taken and sold to Enoch Jones and conveyed to him by James Caldwell, late sheriff on 15 May 1772 (Book T, folio 230). Now Enoch Jones is conveying the lot and premises for consideration of one hundred twenty five pounds back to Moses Hudson and family. Wit: Saml West, James McMullen. Ackn 11 May 1775. (V:p268)

386. 16 Feb 1775 Indenture between Enoch Jones of Duck Creek Hund, Kent on Delaware, gent of one part and Samuel West, Daniel Davis, Moleston Curry and Benjamin Hazel, Junr, gent of other part. Whereas a school house is late built on land of Enoch Jones and nr the road from Salisbury Town or old Duck Creek Town in hund and co afsd to and over the Province Bridge so called and the place known by that name. Whereas West, Davis, Curry and Hazel, gents, all living nr the

school house are now chosen guardians and trustees for and in behalf of said school and Enoch Jones willing for the encouragement of the school and for the education of your be continued in that place by the inhabitants round about it and all others who may be willing to assist therein . . . trustees and their successors shall have use of said ground as long as a school house and school shall be supported . . . should school be removed then the ground shall become legal property of Enoch Jones . . . who for one pepper corn yearly to be paid by the trustees . . . doth give grant and confirm unto the Trustees said ground. Wit: John Cook, James McMullen, John Banning. Ackn 11 May 1775. (V:p268)

387. 10 Dec 1774 Indenture between Preston Berry of Kent on Delaware, gent and Ruth Lewis of same co, widow and relict of Joseph Lewis, decd. Whereas Preston Berry in consideration of a marraige intended (by God's permission) shortly to be had and solemmized(sic) between he and Ruth Lewis and sum of two hundred pounds received by Preston Berry as a marriage portion from Ruth Lewis and for that, a conpetent jointure may be had made and provided for Ruth Lewis (in case the said marriage shall take effect) and for the settling and assuring of the said messuage and lands and tenements hereditaments herein after mentioned, to and for the use intents and purposes hereinafter limited and declared pursuant to the agreement made upon the contract of intended marriage, he the said Preston Berry grants and confirms to Ruth Lewis all that messuage stable kitchen and dwelling house whereon Timothy Caldwell now keeps store and lot of ground with one brick well , etc. Beginning on line of Francis Edmondson's land . . . a lot Preston Berry bought of Ezekiel Thompson . . . land called Bald Eagle. Wit: Danl. Duhadway, Catherine Duhadway. Ackn 10 May 1775. (V:p269)

388. 1 Nov 1773 Indenture between John Banning of town of Dover, Kent on Delaware, sadler and Moses Jackson of Murtherkill Hund, yeoman. Consideration of one hundred seventy nine pounds conveys parcel of land in hund and co afsd which John Banning purchased from John Rash, Junr conveyed by deed dated 7 Aug last past (Book V, folio 102). Beginning on line of an old tract Dundee and Howell's Lott . . . land of William Pearse . . . corner between John and Henry Rash . . . estate of Samuel Rash . . . laid off for eighty nine and a half acres. Wit: Henry Clampitt, William Dunning. Ackn 10 May 1775. (V:p269)

389. 6 May 1775 Indenture between Noah Cox and Mary, his wife of Kent on Delaware, farmer and Benjamin Coomb same co, husbandman. By warrant and survey laid out to William Dill, husbandman, late of said co in his lifetime, a parcel of land situate in forrest of Murtherkill Hund. Beginning at a cor white oak and by land late in possession of John Dill, Junr . . . stake in John Baynard's line . . . land late in possession of John Sap . . . land late of Job Willoughby . . . containing one

hundred sixty four and three quarter acres and allowance of six percent for roads and highways. William Dill died intestate leaving only son, Nathan Dill, and three daus: Mary Dill, party hereto, Elizabeth Dill and Jemimah Dill. Nathan Dill died intestate without issue his share descended to his sisters. Mary Dill has married Noah Cox who for consideration of eighteen pounds convey one full equal third part, the whole containing ine hundred sixty four and three quarter acres, and also one third interest in the parcel of land . Wit: Cox Gordon, George Lambdin. Ackn 29 May 1775. (V:p270)

390. 1 Nov 1775 Indenture between John Banning of town of Dover, Kent on Delaware, sadler and John Voshal and Elizabeth his wife and Ezekiel Jackson and Elizabeth his wife all of Murtherkill Hund of one part and Moses Jackson of same hund and co, yeoman. Whereas Richard Jackson, decd, was seized of sundry lands and died leaving widow, Elizabeth, and issue of sundry children of which Moses and Ezekiel are part. His widow's third was allotted from an ancient tract called ____ containing one hundred fifty acres. Elizabeth the widow has married John Voshal who with Ezekiel Jackson conveyed all their right, title and interest to the undivided property to John Banning by deed 8 July 1771 (Book T, folio 153) and John Banning is about to convey same to Moses Jackson and John Voshal and Ezekiel Jackson willing to join in the conveyance only for the opportunity of their wives to join in likewise now they convey for consideration of forty pounds their right, title, interest and claim to the one hundred fifty acres of land. Wit: William Dewese, Samuel Nicholas. Elizabeth Voshal and Elizabeth Jackson privately examined gave their consent. Ackn 10 May 1775. (V:p270)

391. 24 May 1775 Indenture between Francis Edmondson of Kent on Delaware, farmer and Preston Berry, Junr of same co, blacksmith. Consideration of nine pounds thirteen shillings eight pence conveys parcel of land herein circumscribed. Description mentions land of John Greers . . . Chopt Ank(sic) road . . . William Berry's lott . . . said parcel containing two acres and ninety perches. Wit: William Berry, John Rhodes. Ackn 24 May 1775. (V:p271)

392. 17 Sept 1774 Indenture between William Pollar of city and co of Philadelphia, merchant and Vincent Loockerman, Junr of Kent on Delaware, gent. Consideration of three hundred pounds conveys parcel of land part of called Content in Little Creek Hund situate on Muddy Branch. Description mentions line of land late of Benjamin Brooks . . . land late of Peter Shankmire . . . land late of Elizabeth Hines . . . containing one hundred thirty acres including one hundred acres sold to James Colgan by above named Benjamin Brooks and also thirty acres conveyed by Frederick Hines and Mary, his wife, to James Colgan who sold same to Francis Harris 5 Aug 1763 and sold by John Cook, Esq, by writ of venditioni

exponas on 25 Aug last past to John Banning who on 10 Sept last past conveyed same to William Pollard. Wit: Andrew Butler, Martha Green. Ackn 10 May 1775. (V:p271)

393. 28 Nov 1770 Indenture between Edward Evans of city of Philadelphia, province of Pennsylvania, cordwainer and Rebecca, his wife and Elizabeth Clarke of same place, spinster (said Rebecca and Elizabeth being daus and surviving issue of William Clarke, late of same city, decd, gent by Rebecca his wife which William Clarke was only heir of William Clarke sometime of city of Dublin in the Kingdom of Ireland late of the county Sussex on Delaware by Honor his wife, also decd) of one part and John Parker of last named co. Consideration of fifty pounds release and convey all parcel of land on north side of Mispillion Creek, Kent on Delaware. Description mentions the London Company . . . Saw Mill Range patent . . . containing one hundred ninety five acres part of Saw Mill Range granted to Henry Bowman who died seized thereof intestate and his estate was committed to William Clark the grandfather then of Sussex on Delaware who by order of Orphans Court obtained the tract for sum of two hundred pounds paid to settle and discharge Henry Bowman's debts and the tract descended to Edward Evans and Rebecca, his wife, in her right and Elizabeth Clarke in her right. Daniel Nunez and Boaz Manlove, Esq apptd attys. Wit: Purnal Johnson, Mark Killen. Ackn 10 Aug 1775. (V:p272)

394. 4 Aug 1775 Indenture between William Jester of Mispillion Hund, Kent on Delaware, yeoman and Delilah, his wife and Joshua Willis of same place. Consideration of twenty five pounds convey parcel of land in afsd hund being part of land described in will of William Jester, yeoman, to his son, afsd William, being a third of Jesters Plaine. Beginning at cor of William Jester's dwelling plantation . . . cor of Richard McNatt's land . . . containingf forty eight and three quarter acres. Wit: John Clarke, William Cullen. Delilah Jester privately examined gave consent. Ackn 10 Aug 1775. (V:p273)

395. 7 Aug 1775 Indenture between William Rees of Duck Creek Hund, Kent on Delaware, blacksmith and Martha, his wife and John Derrach, shop keeper. Whereas a small piece of ground situate at the Crossroads was lately conveyed by extrs of John Vining to William Rees containing two acres who by alienation bond has contracted with John Derrach for the lott which he now conveys for consideration of two hundred pounds. Description mentions orig line of Green's tract . . . cor of Charles Pope's lot . . . with James McMullan's line. Wit: James Townsend, Simon Vanwinkle. Martha Rees privately examined gave consent. Ackn 10 Aug 1775. (V:p273)

396. 10 Mar 1775 Indenture between Joshua Underwood and Mary his wife of Kent on Delaware and John Cook same place. Consideraton of one hundred sixteen pounds convey parcel of land in Mispillion Hund known as Underwood's Forest by orig survey made 1 May 1739 in what number of acres it may appear and all that moiety or undivided half part of land and swamp in afsd hund in original metes and bounds given in survey made 1 Nov 1749 containing two hundred two and a half acres. Wit: John Clark, Richard McNatt. Mary Underwood privately examined gave consent. Ackn 9 Aug 1775. (V:p274)

397. 10 Apr 1774 Indenture between Richard McNatt of Kent on Delaware and Solomon Kimmey. Consideration of eleven pounds conveys part of tract called Pea Hill situate in forest of Mispillion Hund. Beginning at a cor of William Kimmey's land . . . containing eleven acres of land with six percent for roads and highways. Wit: Robert Brodie(?), Francis Tesestor. Ackn 9 Aug 1775. (V:p275)

398. 8 Aug 1775 Indenture between William Freeman and Ann, his wife of Kent on Delaware and John Beauchamp same place. Whereas there was surveyed unto Robert Maxwell late of afsd co by virtue of warrant 10 May 1759 and survey by Willilam Killen, depty surveyor on 27 June 1759 tract situate in forest of Murtherkill Hund called Maxwell's Adventure containing one hundred eighty seven and a half acres with usual allowance and by his will bequeathed said land to two sons, David and James and David Maxwell caused the land to be divided and conveyed his moiety to Ann Wooderson (Book V, folio 101). Consideration of sum of thirty seven pounds ten shillings, William Freeman and wife, Ann, convey their moiety beginning at a cor of Richard Downham's land . . . John Chamber's land . . . containing ninety three and three quarter acres. Wit: Henry Wells, John Bullen. Ann Freeman privately examined gave consent. Ackn 9 Aug 1775. (V:p275)

399. 2 Aug 1775 Indenture between Joanna Clarke of Caroline co in province of Maryland and John Alcocks of Kent on Delaware. Whereas Alexander Wheatley had surveyed on 12 Oct 1747 a tract of land in the forest of Mispillion Hund. Beginning at intersection of land called Hayfield . . . with George Stevenson's land . . . Alexander Wheatley and Stephen Catt's land . . . cor of two tracts called Hunting Quarter and Hayfield . . . containing one hundred twelve acres and one other tract adj containing one hundred five and a quarter acres. For consideration of one hundred pounds, Joanna Clarke conveys the land and whereas seventy pounds is to be paid to Samuel Alcocks, son of Joanna Clarke and the other thirty pounds to be paid to Burtonwood Alcocks, son of Burtonwood Alcock, when he arrives at full age of twenty one. John Banning apptd atty. Wit: James Harrington, Thomas Hughs. Ackn 10 Aug 1775. (V:p275)

400. 9 May 1775 Indenture between Benjamin Needham of Little Creek Hund, Kent on Delaware, yeoman and Ezekiel Cowgill same hund, yeoman. Whereas Benjamin Needham and Ezekiel Cowgill by their bond of obligation bearing equal date herewith to Jonathan Needham of same hund, yeoman, in penal sum of four hundred thirty four pounds with condition of payment of two hundred seventeen pounds with interest on or before 10th day of 2nd mo 1780. This indenture witnesseth that Benjamin Needham in consideration of Ezekiel Cowgill entering with him as his security and to secure Ezekiel Cowgill agst all damages that may arise. Benjamin Needham hath granted, bargained . . . and confirm unto Ezekiel Cowgill all his allotment of land out of his father's estate. Beginning at a cor stake of Joshua Clayton's land . . . to land called Chipping Norten . . . containing one hundred four acres of land and also another parcel of ground . . . cor of Highams _____ . . . containing eighty four acres and one hundred forty one perches. Wit: William Levick, Ebenezer Manlove. Ackn 10 Aug 1775. (V:p276)

401. 23 Aug 1775 Indenture between James Sykes of Kent on Delaware and Agnes, his wife and Samuel Magaw os same co. Consideration of five shillings sterling money of Great Britain convey parcel of land known as Skipton according to the metes and bounds as mentioned in orig warrant of survey being a tract orig taken up and laid out for three hundred acres. Wit: Katharine Kelly, John Chew. Agnes Sykes privately examined gave consent. Ackn 23 Aug 1775. (V:p277)

402. 8 Aug 1775 Indenture between Abraham Allee and Elizabeth, his wife; John Allee and Rachel, his wife of Duck Creek Hund, Kent on Delaware, yeomen and Presley Allee. Whereas Abraham and John Allee by virtue of their father, John Allee's will in which he stated the remainder of said tract should be divided among his three sons, Abraham, Peter and John, share and share alike of which they became seized as well as the part of their brother, Peter, decd, into a parcel of land called The Grove otherwise called Hilliards Adventure. Description mentions Charles Ridgely's line . . . containing one hundred one acres which now for sum of one hundred fifty pounds they convey. Wit: Thos Parry, Thos Tilton. Elizabeth Allee and Rachel Allee privately examined gave their consent. Ackn 9 Aug 1775. (V:p277)

403. 1 Aug 1775 Indenture between Abraham Allee and Elizabeth, his wife, John Allee and Rachel, his wife of Duck Creek Hund, Kent on Delaware and Presley Allee, all of same place, extrs and heirs at law of Peter Allee, decd of one part and William Cook of Little Creek Hund, merchant. Whereas Abraham Allee, Senr by virtue of indenture of bargain and sale executed by James Hamilton, city of Philadelphia was seized in tract called The Grove as by record (Book O, folio 222) and by will of 8 May 1770 devised the same by name of Hilliard's Adventure

to his eldest son, John, who by will of 8 Aug 1771 devised same to his eldest son, Peter Allee with a description of the division lines. Peter Allee by will 7 May 1773 ordered his dwelling plantation devised to him by his father, to be sold for purposes mentioned and apptd his bros, Abraham and John, extrs, who on 15 June 1775 put land up for sale and sold same to William Cook, highest bidder, for sum of twelve hundred pounds. The heirs herein stated convey the tract of land above described. Wit: Thos. Tilton, Thos Parry. Elizabeth Allee and Rachel Allee privately examined gave their consent. Ackn 9 Aug 1775. (V:p278)

404. 8 Aug 1775 Indenture between John Allee and Rachel, his wife of Duck Creek Hund, Kent on Delaware, yeoman and Abraham Allee of same place. Whereas John Allee by virtue of his father's will made 8 Aug 1771 wherein he devised land lying to the southward of said land and to westward of said line (excepting as therein excepted) to son, John, and further devised all marsh belonging to the plantation (stated as plantation bought from Widow Steel) be equally divided between sons, Abraham and John. In consideration of nine hundred nine pounds, John and Rachel, his wife, convey plantation formerly belonging to Rebecca Steel to Abraham Allee. Wit: Thos. Tilton, Thomas Parry. Rachel Allee privately examined gave consent. Ackn 9 Aug 1775. (V:p278)

405. 8 Aug 1775 Indenture between William Cook and Hannah, his wife, of Little Creek Hund, Kent on Delaware, merchant and John Allee of Duck Creek Hund, yeoman. Whereas William Cook and Hannah, his wife, by virtue of deed of bargain and sale under seal of Abraham and John Allee, extrs of Peter Allee, decd, dated 1 Aug 1775 became seized of tract called The Grove otherwise Hilliard's Adventue lately belonging to Peter Allee devised to him by his father, said tract lying on north side of Iron's Branch containing one hundred seventy five acres. William Cook and Hannah, his wife, in consideration of twelve hundred fifty pounds convey all that tract of land formerly belonging to Peter Allee. Wit: Thos. Tilton, Thos. Parry. Hannah Cook privately examined gave consent. Ackn 9 Aug 1775. (V:p279)

> This ends Book V containing Two Hundred and Seventy Nine folios ended the Thirteenth day of September Seventeen Hundred and Seventy Five 1775. p. Caesar Rodney, recorder.

INDEX

-A-

A---STER, 118
AARON, Michael Carey, 54; Michael Cary, 39
ABBOT, ---, 3; Catharine, 3; Sylvester, 3; William, 3
ABBOT'S GIFT, 3
ACCLES, Richard, 104
ADAMS, ---, 4; Levin, 4; Nathan, 4, 88
ALCOCK, Burtonwood, 138; John, 91
ALCOCKS, Burtonwood, 138; John, 138; Samuel, 138
ALFORD, Joseph, 32
ALLEE, Abraham, 132, 139, 140; Elizabeth, 139, 140; John, 139, 140; Peter, 139, 140; Presley, 139; Rachel, 139, 140; Rchel, 139
ALLEN, Andrew, 9, 112; Mary, 114, 118; William, 114, 118
ALLSTON, Israel, 125
ALSTON, Authur, 12; Israel, 62; Martha, 12; Randel, 62, 63; Randle, 12; Thomas, 12
ANCASTER, 56
ANDERSON, ---, 24, 71, 83; David, 11; Ezekiel, 27, 83; George, 114; James, 24, 52, 65, 129; John, 4; Major, 34; Margaret, 71, 95; Mary, 114; William, 15, 24, 34, 71, 95
ANDREWS, Sir Edmond, 39
ANGHTON, 18
ANGLEFORD, 58
ANGLETON, 21, 22, 41, 42, 71, 90, 91
ARMITAGE, James, 23, 126
ARNETT, John, 5
ARROWSMITH, ---, 102, 103; Thomas, 102
ATKINSON, William, 22
AULER, John, 29

AUTERS, John, 134

-B-

BADGER, ---, 107; Edmond, 107; Edmund, 27, 93; Eleazar, 27; Eliazar, 27
BAILEY, Nathan, 111
BAKER, William, 30, 76
BALD EAGLE, 1, 135
BALL, Elizabeth, 30, 75, 76, 102; Samuel, 13, 14, 15, 30, 42, 43, 78, 102; William, 30, 43, 75, 76, 93, 102
BALLANTINE, Hamilton, 13
BANDY, Richard, 64
BANING, John, 45, 78, 79, 80, 93, 106, 107, 116, 123; Phinehas, 81
BANNING, John, 2, 3, 15, 57, 62, 65, 94, 103, 135, 136, 137, 138; Phinehas, 36; Richard, 65
BARBER, Abraham, 96; Francis, 33, 45; John, 23
BARCLAY, David, 119
BARDON, Mark, 54
BARDONS, Mark, 23
BARE GARDIN, 1
BARKER, Thomas, 77, 81; William, 36, 102
BARKSTEAD, Joshua, 32, 75, 77
BARNE, John, 132
BARNETT, Moses, 19
BARNHILL, David, 117
BARNS, John, 103, 111; Priscilla, 111; Prisila, 103; Stephen, 103, 111; William, 44
BARN'S CHANCE, 1, 36
BARRAT, Andrew, 16
BARRATT, Phillip, 21, 55, 59
BARREN POINT, 12, 13, 18
BARRET, ---, 25; Miriam, 25; Philip, 25
BARRY'S RACE GROUND, 29
BARTLET, Nicholas, 77

BARTLET'S LOT, 38
BARTLETT, Nicholas, 105
BARTLETTS POINT, 63, 64
BASSETT, Richard, 32, 43, 65, 76, 83
BATTEL, French, 8, 61, 62, 122
BATTELL, ---, 8; F., 17, 83, 98, 117, 119, 123; French, 1, 7, 8, 14, 28, 42, 91, 106
BAYLY, Elias, 110, 111
BAYNARD, ---, 9; John, 9, 12, 69, 135; Mary, 9
BEADWELL, ---, 5; Thomas, 5
BEALEY, Simon, 16
BEAR SWAMP, 29
BEAUCHAMP, Grace, 11; Isaac, 10, 11, 35; Jesse, 108, 113, 114; Jessey, 34; John, 10, 11, 89, 123, 124, 130, 138; Leah, 108, 109; Marcey, 10, 11; Mary, 78, 89, 130; Robert, 24, 108, 122
BEDWELL, ---, 6; Elijah, 6; Henry, 104, 126; James, 6, 51, 101, 127; Robert, 126, 127; Thomas, 41, 126
BELL, ---, 106; Hayly, 78; Henry, 28; John, 3, 28, 30, 32, 34, 53, 62, 85, 86, 87, 106, 131; Letitia, 53
BELLACH, ---, 53; Hannah, 53; John, 53, 54; Robert, 53
BENEFIELD, 33
BENN, James, 18
BENSON, ---, 91; Daniel, 52
BENSTEN, Daniel, 26; Sarah, 26
BENSTON, Benjamin, 79, 91; Elizabeth, 91
BERRES, William, 28
BERRY, Elijah, 66, 80; Grace, 66; Joseph, 25; Preston, 39, 40, 55, 56, 135, 136; William, 20, 29, 32, 33, 49, 63, 64, 68, 79, 133, 136
BERRY'S RACE GROUND, 29
BERRY'S RANGE, 120, 121
BESSEX, ---, 96; John, 96

BETTS, ---, 96; Elizabeth, 96, 97; John, 45; William, 21, 92, 96, 114, 115
BETTS ENDEAVOR, 53
BETT'S PURCHASE, 48
BETTY'S FOLLY, 1, 36
BETTY'S PURCHASE, 14
BIARDS, ---, 122
BIAYS, Matthew, 31
BIDDLE, Augustine, 76
BIGGS, William, 16
BILLITURE, Daniel, 121, 122
BISHOP, Benoni, 20, 24, 81, 108; Richard, 109
BISHOP'S CHOICE, 20, 24, 80, 81, 107, 108, 109
BLACK SWAMP, 69, 88
BLACKISTON, ---, 7; George, 7, 8, 61
BLACKSHARE, Morgan, 93; Randal, 15; Robert, 67, 108; Thomas, 50, 68, 101, 107
BALCKSHEAR, Randal, 107
BLACKSHER, Morgan, 103
BLACKSHERE, Morgan, 130
BLAIDS, ---, 122
BLLEN, John, 102
BLUNDEL, James, 124
BLUNDELL, James, 121
BOAZMAN, ---, 34; Daniel, 34; Sinah, 34; Sinna, 34
BOGG, Joseph, 46; William, 46
BOGGS, John, 54; Mathew, 68
BOHANAN, Robert, 8
BOHANNAN, Robert, 101
BOHANNON, Robert, 8, 101
BOHANON, Robert, 61
BOND, Thomas, 29, 30
BOOTH, Joseph, 87; Lydia, 89; Waitman, 89, 117, 118
BOSTICK, Robert, 4, 44, 66, 67, 69; Shadrack, 63, 64
BOWERS, John, 116; Rachel, 116
BOWLEY, Devereaux, 105

BOWLY, Devereaux, 78, 118; Devereux, 28, 77
BOWMAN, ---, 83; Henry, 83, 137; Thomas, 4, 16, 17, 45, 54, 56, 58
BOYER, Daniel, 119; James, 9, 38, 112, 119
BOZEMAN, ---, 48; Daniel, 48; Sinah, 48
BOZMAN, Daniel, 104; Sinah, 48
BOZMAN'S ADDITION, 104
BRADLEY, Isaiah, 82; Joseph, 95; William, 82
BRANFORD, 128
BREAK NOCK, 6
BRECNOCK, 47
BREECHES, THE, 45, 89
BRICE, Benedict, 87
BRIDGE TOWN, 55, 58
BRIGGS, John, 39
BRIGHT, Abraham, 24
BRIGHT'S GLADE, 52
BRINCKLE, Curtis, 96; John, 51, 74, 76, 85, 108, 118; Pheebe, 27; Richard, 27, 51
BRINCKLEE, Amelia, 51; John, 51, 96; Joseph, 96; Sarah, 51; Southy, 51
BRINCKLE'S RANGE, 46
BRINCKLOE, John, 48; Southy, 50
BRINKLE, Curtis, 115; Richard, 93, 95
BRINKLEE, ---, 58; John, 58
BRINKLEES ISLAND, 58
BRODIE, Robert, 138
BROOK, Benjamin, 107
BROOKS, Benjamin, 116, 136; Samuel, 25
BROOK'S BAY, 53
BROOKSBAY, 53
BROTHER'S PORTION, 37
BROWN, ---, 75, 113, 119; Benjamin, 32, 92, 96, 118; Daniel, 59, 60, 67, 89; Elizabeth, 4, 49, 59, 60, 62, 75; Hester, 2; John, 49, 75, 87, 109, 112, 113, 119; Joseph, 94, 118; Mary, 49, 75, 92; Nancy, 113; Pemberton, 59, 60, 89; Rachal, 75; Rachel, 49; Sarah, 109, 113; Stephen, 78; Thomas, 2, 15, 19, 31, 43, 112; William, 64, 65, 82, 113
BROWNE, John, 14
BROWN'S CHANCE, 119
BROWN'S NECK, 4, 78, 123
BRUBSHAW, 53
BRUNETT, Paul, 22
BRYAN, John, 54
BUCHANAN, Anne, 108; Robert, 108
BUCKINGHAM, Howel, 131; Howell, 30, 31, 75, 76; Marcey, 31; Marcy, 30; Mary, 76, 131; Mercy, 99
BUCKMASTER, 43; ---, 43; Thomas, 25, 40, 43
BUCKWELL, William, 46
BULLEN, John, 138
BURBERRY'S BERRY, 11
BURNS, William, 131
BURRISS, Lamuel, 120; Mary, 120; Thomas, 120
BURROUGHS, William, 79
BURRY, Preston, 1
BURTON'S DELIGHT, 97, 112
BUSH, Abraham, 71, 92
BUSHBERRY, 71
BUTINTON, 80
BUTLER, Andrew, 104, 126, 137
BYEFIELD, 87

-C-

CADE, John, 68, 94
CADWALADER, Thomas, 9, 111
CAHOON, ---, 111; Charles, 42; Jerusha, 42, 91; Thomas, 42, 91, 102; William, 13, 24, 56, 90, 94, 95, 111
CAIN, ---, 62; James, 62, 65; Manassah, 65; Manasseh, 62; Owen, 62, 65; Thomas, 95, 101

CALDWELL, ---, 30, 43, 85; Andrew, 9, 10, 23, 44, 75, 85, 86, 88, 129; David, 35, 52, 58, 62, 85, 86; James, 6, 21, 22, 26, 30, 43, 49, 65, 75, 86, 88, 95, 103, 106, 134; Jonathan, 31, 70, 87, 91; Joseph, 78; Margaret, 87; Timothy, 10, 39, 88, 103, 135; Train, 46, 47, 50
CALF PASTURE, 132
CALLOWAY, Elizabeth, 27; James, 27; Joseph, 77; Peter, 57; Thomas, 27, 59, 60
CAMBRIDGE, 66
CAMPBELL, Joseph, 9, 11, 12, 15, 117, 118
CAMPBLE, Joseph, 11
CANDBY, Thomas, 52
CANDY, Cashena, 54; Susanna, 54
CANTERBURY, 23
CARBINE, James, 108; Jane, 41; Seames, 15
CARBRON, 105, 106
CARDEEN, Elizabeth, 11; William, 11
CARLISLE, John, 59, 60
CAROON MANOR, 83
CARPENTER, Allivia, 30, 31; Elizabeth, 114, 115; Jasper, 30, 31; Joshua, 30, 31; Mary, 30, 31, 40, 41; Molley, 41; Samuel, 31, 67; William, 40, 41, 82, 92, 105, 114, 118
CARTER, Daniel, 118; Henry, 9, 12, 64; John, 27; Mary, 118; Suchak, 27
CARTY, Isaac, 8, 61, 64
CASBRON, 78
CASSON, Elizabeth, 97; John, 97; Myres, 97
CATEN, John, 134
CATT, John, 116; Stephen, 138
CATTS, John, 68, 116; Mary, 68, 93, 94; Stephen, 68; William, 81, 82
CAULK, ---, 113; Oliver, 109, 113
CAVE, THE, 11, 48

CAVENDER, Daniel, 3
CEDAR NECK, 103
CHADWICK, ---, 79; John, 10, 27; Joseph, 79
CHAMBER, John, 44, 138
CHAMBERS, ---, 114; John, 69, 114, 118; Nathaniel, 5; William, 114, 118
CHANCE, Elijah, 12, 74, 76
CHARLES, Levin, 66, 79; Mary, 66, 79
CHEFFINS, James, 8
CHESTER, 12, 62
CHEW, Anna Maria, 29; Benjamin, 2, 6, 9, 31, 40, 47, 52, 64, 74, 111, 120, 125; Elizabeth, 40; John, 9, 10, 17, 20, 25, 32, 33, 48, 60, 97, 112, 119, 120, 121, 139; Samuel, 9, 10, 19, 20, 22, 30, 32, 39, 40, 43, 57, 60, 62, 70, 81, 83, 84, 85, 86, 88, 90, 112, 119, 120, 121
CHICKEN, John, 26
CHIFFINS, James, 8
CHIPMAN, Benjamin, 24, 107, 108; Margaret, 122, 123; Paris, 47, 108, 122, 123
CHIPPING NORTEN, 139
CHIPPON NORTON, 53
CHRISTIANA, 56, 111
CHRISTOPHER, Sarah, 76
CITTINBOURN, 40
CLAMER, Francis, 114
CLAMPIT, ---, 80, 81; Ebenezer, 13, 80; Gove, 80; John, 66, 80; Mark, 105; Mary, 66; Moses, 106; William, 80, 81
CLAMPITT, Henry, 24, 66, 135
CLAPHAM, 83
CLARK, ---, 25; Ann, 95; Annalina, 132; Benjamin, 116; David, 132; Elizabeth, 82, 83, 137; Honor, 82; James, 97; John, 16, 18, 55, 58, 95, 112, 124, 138; Jonathan, 23; Joshua, 51, 55, 57, 58; Mary, 57,

58; Masculine, 15; Rebecca, 82; William, 25, 26, 82, 83, 132, 137
CLARKE, Ann, 18; Benjamin, 41; David, 41; Elizabeth, 5, 137; Honor, 137; Joanna, 138; John, 3, 4, 5, 9, 57, 73, 86, 116, 137; Joshua, 51; Mary, 51; Masculine, 41; Maslin, 108; Rebecca, 137; Thomas, 41; William, 137
CLAYON, Joshua, 5
CLAYPOLE, James, 126; Norton, 125, 126
CLAYTEN, 79
CLAYTON, 13, 33, 91; James, 121, 123; John, 23, 65, 83, 84, 119, 120, 121, 123; Joshua, 32, 123, 127, 139; Rachel, 32
CLERK, Robert, 31
CLIFFORD, John, 131
CLIFFORTH, Thomas, 17
CLIFORD, Thomas, 28
CLIFTON, John, 83
CLOTHIER, John, 1
COBURN, Jordan, 107
COLE, Amelia, 51, 58; Dr., 57; Mary, 51, 58; Penelope, 51; Sarah, 51, 58; Spencer, 51, 57, 58
COLGAN, James, 136
COLGUN, James, 62, 107
COLLINGS, ---, 12, 18; Jonathan, 18; Mary, 12; Thomas, 12
COLLINS, ---, 38, 81, 91; Jonathan, 15, 16; Thomas, 12, 37, 38, 42, 51, 62, 63, 79, 81, 82, 83, 84, 85, 86, 91, 99, 104, 106, 122, 132
COMEGYS, Cornelius, 100, 103; Cors., 122; John, 34, 49
CONDRAT, Daniel, 104; Mark, 104
CONEY, Samuel, 30; William, 30
CONNER, Dennis, 87
CONTENT, 67, 107, 116, 136
COOHN, John, 119
COOK, Hannah, 140; John, 9, 16, 18, 20, 22, 30, 38, 50, 53, 54, 62, 65, 74, 76, 78, 83, 84, 85, 86, 88, 89, 90, 102, 106, 107, 124, 130, 132, 135, 136, 138; William, 115, 116, 139, 140
COOLE, Benjamin, 28; Richyate, 28
COOMB, Benjamin, 135
COOMBE, ---, 11; Benjamin, 11, 25, 98, 108, 109; Elizabeth, 25
COOMBS, Benjamin, 113
COOMES, Benjamin, 92
COOPER, Jacob, 28, 29, 30, 77, 105, 117
CORBIAN, James, 107
CORKERIN, Henry, 113
CORREY, Molleston, 64
COTTENHAM, 78; Charles, 12, 87
COTTINGHAM, Charles, 15; Jonathan, 15; Lydia, 15
COTTINGHAM'S OUTLET, 15
COTTINHAM, Lady, 15; Turbeth, 106
COTTONBOROUGH, 26
COTTONHAM, Jonathan, 26
COUDRATT, Daniel, 126; Mark, 126
COURSEY, William, 12
COVENTRY, 98, 103
COW BREATH MARSH, 71
COWDRATT, Mark, 54
COWEL, Nancy, 113
COWGILL, Ezekiel, 5, 22, 122, 139; Ezel., 37; Henry, 27; John, 27; Mary, 122
COWILL, Ezekiel, 27
COWPAN, 76
COWPEIN, 76
COWPLAND, Jonathan, 29; Mary, 29
COX, ---, 24; Daniel, 25; Edward, 118; Isaac, 19, 20, 24, 107, 108; John, 17, 69, 86, 88, 110, 119; Martha, 110; Marthew, 110; Mary, 135, 136; Noah, 135, 136; Powel, 40; Powell, 20, 65, 98, 113; Susannah, 20, 24; Thomas, 37, 118

CRAIG, Annalane, 109; George, 47; Isabel, 44; James, 35; John, 67
CRAIGE, ---, 4; Annalaney, 89; James, 18, 86, 87, 105; Thomas, 89
CRAIN, Patrick, 90
CRAPPER, ---, 54; Levin, 82, 87, 88; Zadock, 3, 4, 9, 16, 17, 48, 54, 55, 66; Zadok, 84, 86, 93, 110, 112, 116
CRAWFORD, Letitia, 48; Mary, 48
CREIGHTON, William, 30, 76
CREMEEN, Jacob, 76
CRISPIN, Elizabeth, 38; Joseph, 38; Mary, 38; Sarah, 38; Silas, 38, 131; Tabitha, 38
CROMPTON, John, 13
CROSIER, ---, 26; Matthew, 26
CROSS ROADS, 78
CROSSROADS, 75
CROZIER, Rachel, 110
CRUMPTON, ---, 59; John, 58, 79
CUBBAGE, Philemon, 37
CULLEN, ---, 54; Anne, 54; Jonathan, 54; William, 16, 137
CULLIN, ---, 35; George, 21, 35, 41, 91; Georged, 21; John, 35; Jonathan, 35; William, 35
CUMINGS, Robert, 75
CUMMINS, Robert, 117
CURRY, ---, 134; Archibald, 36; Moleston, 134; Molleston, 49, 50; Sarah, 36
CYPRESS NECK, 106

-D-

DALLENER, Richard, 33
DALLINAR, Richard, 119
DANNELS FANCY, 100
DARRACH, James, 43; John, 43
DAVID, Daniel, 49; Joseph, 44, 67, 71, 94, 130, 131
DAVIS, ---, 12, 17, 18, 134; Caleb, 12, 18; Daniel, 17, 134; Jehu, 17; John, 74, 97; Jonathan, 122; Mathias, 35; Matthias, 55; Rhoda, 17, 18; Robert, 16, 18; Thomas, 97
DAVISON, ---, 15, 16, 18; Thomas, 15, 16, 18
DAWSON, Eleoner, 94; Isaac, 59, 63, 65, 122; John, 56; Rachel, 94; Robert, 94
DEAN, Mary, 67
DEHORTY, Absalom, 114; George, 114; Mary, 114; Sarah, 114; Vincent, 114
DELANER, Richard, 15
DENBIGH, 2, 37
DENNEY, Christopher, 33; Elizabeth, 33; Francis, 33; Joseph, 33; Margret, 33; Mary, 33; Philip, 33; Rebecca, 33
DENNY, Joseph, 33
DERRACH, John, 137
DEWEES, Cornelius, 41, 42, 103
DEWEESE, Cornelius, 21, 22; Esther, 21; Joshua, 5; Lewis, 41
DEWESE, Cornelius, 21, 91; Esther, 21; Jonathan, 39; William, 136
DICKINSON, ---, 8, 63, 64; Catherine, 92; John, 8, 17, 61, 63, 64, 67, 104, 112; Katherine, 92, 96; Mary, 61; Philamon, 107; Philemon, 8, 17, 61, 92, 93, 96, 109, 112; Samuel, 92, 96; Walter, 92, 96
DICKISON, Philamon, 15
DILL, ---, 65; Edward, 64, 65, 66; Elizabeth, 69, 136; James, 34; Jemima, 69; Jemimah, 136; John, 9, 12, 51, 59, 69, 102, 121, 122, 126, 135; Mary, 66, 69, 136; Nathan, 69, 136; Robert, 111; William, 12, 34, 35, 66, 69, 135, 136
DILLEN, John, 77, 78, 106
DINGEE, ---, 115, 116; Daniel, 115, 116
DIVIDEND NO. 6, 118

DONN, William, 28
DONNABELS, Perkins, 75
DORRACH, John, 25
DOWN, William, 116
DOWNHAM, ---, 11; Ann, 11;
  Elizabeth, 11, 89; Isaac, 89, 130;
  Joseph, 44, 89, 90, 130; Mary, 89;
  Rachal, 89; Richard, 11, 44, 89,
  130, 138; Ruth, 89, 130; Sarah,
  89
DOWNING, Benjamin, 98, 99, 103,
  104; Ezekiel, 98, 103; Joseph, 98,
  99, 103, 104
DOWNS, ---, 129; Benjamin, 107;
  Hezekiah, 129; Levin, 129;
  William, 33, 68, 82, 94, 129
DOWNS, THE, 49, 75
DOZ, ---, 42; Andrew, 21, 41, 42, 71,
  91
DRAPER, Avary, 97, 102
DRAPERSBERRY, 59, 89
DRAUGHTEN, John, 1
DRAUGHTON, John, 100, 101, 102,
  110, 123; Margaret, 110; Robert,
  110
DUBROIS, ---, 89
DUBROISE, John, 41
DUHADWAY, Catherine, 135;
  Daniel, 135
DUKE OF YORK'S MANNER, 11
DUKE OF YORK'S MANNOR, 41
DUNDEE, 46, 135
DUNGAN, Levi, 17
DUNN, Mary, 133, 134; Thomas,
  126
DUNNING, ---, 44; William, 44, 135
DURBOROUGH, Hugh, 85
DURBOROW, ---, 89; B., 104;
  Benjamin, 104; Daniel, 23, 100,
  101; David, 97; Hugh, 23, 26, 34,
  65, 79, 97, 101, 110, 120; John,
  97
DURHAM, Daniel, 12, 18, 57
DURY, Hannah, 12, 81
DURY'S PURCHASE, 12

DYER, Edward, 125; John, 16

-E-

EAGLE, ---, 3; Lydia, 3; Solomon, 3,
  123; William, 3
EARECKSON, Johnson, 40, 119
EARICKSON, Johnson, 61, 92
EARLE, M., 120
EBTHARP, Elizabeth, 132; Thomas,
  100, 132
EDENFIELD, John, 124
EDENTON, 28, 69, 73, 77
EDGE, Andrew, 31
EDINGFIELD, John, 97, 121;
  Persis, 121, 124
EDINGTON, 133
EDMISTON, Francis, 24
EDMONDSON, Elizabeth, 1;
  Francis, 1, 89, 135, 136; John, 1,
  89, 98, 113; Solomon, 45, 89;
  Thomas, 11, 98, 113
EDMUNDS, John, 25
EDWARD, John, 64
EDWARDS, John, 64, 65, 89;
  Thomas, 65
EGBERT, James, 50
EGGMEN, Bartholomew, 121, 122;
  Christopher, 122; Cornelius, 122
ELBERT, Henry, 26, 99, 100
ELIZABETH'S LOTT, 66
ELLIOTT, Elizabeth, 91
EMERSON, ---, 51, 80, 81, 84, 125;
  John, 41; Jonathan, 51, 58, 59,
  80, 81, 84, 112, 116, 125, 126;
  Ruth, 116; Solomon, 126;
  Vincent, 84, 122
EMLEN, George, 32, 76
EMMERSON, Govey, 10; Jonathan,
  9
EMORY, Charles, 122; Thomas, 71
ENOCH'S LANE, 14
EVANS, Curtis, 44, 113, 124;
  Edward, 137; Elizabeth, 126;
  Henry, 126; Martin, 99; Rebecca,
  82, 83, 137

EVELL, John, 65
EVENS, Majar, 110; Major, 110
EXCHANGE, THE, 67, 86, 94

-F-
FAIR HILL, 63
FAIRFIELD, 17, 18, 39, 64, 66, 79, 82, 122, 129
FALCONER, John, 82, 122, 82
FANCY'S ADDITION, 100
FARIES, John, 63
FARMSELLSWORTH, 67
FARQUARSON, John, 132
FARQUHARSON, John, 133, 134
FARSET, Smith, 16
FARSON, Henry, 19, 93, 127, 128, 129; Heny, 19; William, 93, 114
FAST LANDING, 115
FEARSET, Smith, 16
FIFTY ACRES, 67
FINNEY, ---, 74; David, 8, 73, 74
FINSTHWAIT, Jonathan, 5
FISHER, ---, 16, 99; Adam, 42, 126; Edward, 41, 58, 79, 97; Fenwick, 9, 15, 30, 99, 125; Finwick, 19, 25, 30, 56, 74, 112; John, 125, 126; Mary, 19, 99; Miers, 6, 16, 44; Molleston, 42; Samuel, 44; Squire, 15
FISHER'S DELIGHT, 42
FITZ JARROLD, Eleazer, 129, 130; James, 129; Sarah, 129, 130
FITZGARRALD, Robert, 22
FITZGARRIL, James, 47
FITZJARREL, Robert, 25
FITZRANDOLPH, Edward, 54
FITZSIMMONDS, Elenor, 68; Sassy, 68; Shokely, 68; Thomas, 68
FITZSIMMONS, ---, 94; Mary, 94; Thomas, 68, 94
FIZRANDOLPH, Edward, 44; Mary, 44
FLEMING, ---, 4, 119; Alexander, 110; Archibald, 119; Elizabeth, 119; George, 3, 4, 49; Joseph, 119; Margaret, 3; Mary, 36; Nathan, 15; Robert, 3, 4, 36; William, 4, 110
FLYING JIBB, 11
FOOTMAN, Peter, 14, 53; Richard, 53
FORCUM, Hannah, 1; Reynatur, 1
FORSITH, Elizabeth, 126, 127; Nathaniel, 126
FOSTER, John, 38
FOTHERGILL, John, 28, 77, 78, 93, 105, 117, 118
FOULK, Judah, 53
FOX HALL, 128
FRAZER, John, 91
FRAZIER, Elizabeth, 23; John, 42
FREELAND, John, 106
FREEMAN, Ann, 138; John, 45, 56; Moses, 45, 60; Penelope, 20, 74; Thomas, 23; William, 138
FRENCH, ---, 96; Catherine, 92, 133, 134; John, 11, 48; Katharine, 29; Katherine, 92, 96; Mary, 92; Robert, 29, 54, 74, 92, 133, 134; Thomas, 92, 96; William, 123
FULLERTON, Ann, 19; Catharine, 19; John, 19, 43; Mary, 19; Thomas, 19; William, 19
FUNHAS, John, 18
FURBEE, Caleb, 39, 57, 90
FURBY, Caleb, 9
FURCHAS, John, 51, 57, 58
FURCHASE, ---, 63, 65; Frances, 18; John, 18, 63, 65, 71
FURCHASE'S OUTLET, 18

-G-
GAINSBOROUGH, 47
GALLOWAY, Ann, 40; Peter, 27, 102; Samuel, 40
GAOL LOT, 88
GARDEN, James, 4

GARDNER, Francis, 10; James, 8, 54, 104, 114, 126; Mary, 114; Theos., 14
GASKIN, Ann, 46
GEORGE, John, 75
GEORGE THE THIRD, 9
GERALD, Robert, 97
GIBBS, ---, 66; Aneas, 80; David, 80; Edward, 13, 66, 67; Elizabeth, 67; Eneas, 67
GIBSON, John, 126
GILDER, Reuben, 122
GILDERSLEVE, John, 134
GILDERT, Reuben, 10
GILFORD, 109
GILLESPIE, George, 57
GLENN, ---, 7; John, 7
GLOVER, ---, 7; John, 7, 8, 14, 28, 61, 69; Mary, 8; Richard, 7, 8, 14, 61
GODDEIN, N---, 78
GODDIN, Ezekiel, 41, 42; Nathan, 105
GODSIN, Kemmel, 79
GODWIN, Kemuel, 91
GOFORTH, ---, 102, 108; Celia, 68; George, 68, 101, 107, 108; Zachariah, 102, 126
GOLDEN GROVE, 74
GOOD LUCK, 34, 48, 104
GOODEN, Elizabeth, 104; Samuel, 104
GOODIN, Nathan, 105
GOODING, Daniel, 79
GOODWIN, Elizabeth, 126; Samuel, 126
GORDEN, Mary, 93
GORDIN, Nathaniel, 79
GORDON, ---, 45, 96, 102; Coe, 47, 113; Cox, 32, 136; David, 101; Elizabeth, 25; Griffith, 25, 32, 97; Hanah, 48; Hannah, 24, 25; James, 45, 56, 62, 92; John, 24, 25, 32, 92, 95, 96, 110, 113; Joshua, 22, 93; Letitia, 32; Robert, 38; Ruth, 102; Sarah, 32; Thomas, 127
GORREL, James, 68
GORRELL, James, 106
GRASSY RIDGE, 64
GRAVESEND, 14. 24, 25, 30, 49, 74, 76, 102, 114, 118, 120, 125
GRAY, John, 87, 89, 97, 118; William, 11, 89
GRAYDON, John, 56
GREAT GENEVA, 11, 47
GREAT PIPE ELM, 22, 31, 32, 65, 70, 71, 72, 87
GREAT TINHEADS CORTE, 133
GREAT TYNHEAD CORTE, 28
GREAT TYNHEADS CORTE, 133
GREEN, ---, 114, 137; Cuthburt, 103; Hannah, 65; James, 13, 14, 25, 30, 43, 125; Marcy, 30; Martha, 137; Mary, 14, 25, 30, 65, 99; Thomas, 13, 14, 25, 30, 31, 76, 80, 99, 106, 108, 114, 125, 131; William, 64, 65, 125
GREENLEE, Robert, 70
GREENLY, Michael, 64
GREENWICH, 23, 104, 125, 126
GREENWOOD, Joseph, 92; Sarah, 92
GREERS, John, 136
GREY, William, 130
GRIER, John, 1; Mary, 1, 2
GRIFFETH, ---, 55, 56; Elizabeth, 40; Martha, 55, 56; Samuel, 55, 56
GRIFFIN, Elizabeth, 64; Isaac, 64, 125; Martha, 55, 63; Mary, 64, 125; Matthew, 28, 49, 125; Samuel, 17, 64, 125; William, 49, 50
GRIFFITH, ---, 39, 40, 55; Samuel, 39, 40, 55, 61, 79, 125; William, 79
GRIGG, ---, 121; Joshua, 121
GRONENDYKE, Peter, 40
GROUNDIKE, Peter, 67

GROVE, Silvanus, 28, 77, 78, 105, 117, 118
GROVE, THE, 109, 139, 140
GROVES, Thomas, 57
GRUBBY RIDGE, 44
GUILFORDS, 23
GULLET, George, 24, 26; John, 26
GULLETT, John, 93, 95

-H-
HAGAN, Jacob, 28, 77, 78, 105, 117, 118
HALE, Thomas, 6
HALL, ---, 53, 74, 91; David, 70, 74, 76; Easter, 68; Easther, 68; Elizabeth, 53; Ellioner, 53; Ester, 68; Esther, 68; Hannah, 53; Jerusha, 42, 91; John, 12, 25, 48, 53; Letitia, 53; Lucy, 12, 18; Mary, 74; Moses, 68; Robert, 42, 53, 91; Thomas, 40, 80; William, 12, 18, 60, 110; Winlock, 18, 57
HAM, John, 33, 106, 128; Moses, 19
HAMILTON, Alexander, 16, 110, 119; James, 9, 111, 119, 139; Robert, 61
HAMMETT, John, 57
HAND, Samuel, 115
HANDY, William, 123, 124
HANG MAN'S NECK, 109
HANSON, ---, 121, 131; Samuel, 10, 20, 27, 70, 87, 120, 121, 134; Sarah, 70; Thomas, 6, 9, 10, 20, 24, 27, 46, 47, 112, 121; Timothy, 131
HANZER, ---, 34; Cornelius, 34; Nehemiah, 34; William, 23, 34
HARDIN, ---, 74, 119; Ann, 34; Edmond, 118; John, 74, 76
HARFORD, Charles, 28
HARGROVE, ---, 119
HARMASON, John, 44; Sarah, 44
HARPER, ---, 84; Mark, 54; Samuel, 71; Thomas, 92; William, 117, 123

HARRING, ---, 118
HARRINGTON, James, 138; Samuel, 114; Sarah, 114
HARRIS, Francis, 106, 107, 136; William, 7
HART, Aaron, 70; Hannah, 87; John, 22, 72; Nathan, 115, 116; Sarah, 22
HARTSHORN, Rebecah, 114
HARWOOD, Elizabeth, 62; Susannah, 94, 95; Thomas, 62, 94
HASLET, John, 74
HASTING, Isaac, 99
HASTINGS, Isaac, 100
HATFIELD, James, 110; John, 92; Sarah, 26; Thomas, 26, 87, 113; William, 92
HATHORN, Ebenezer, 86
HATHORNE, Ebenezer, 93, 95; Mary, 93; William, 92, 93, 95
HATTFIELD, James, 122
HAWKIN, John, 1
HAWKINS, Arnold, 94, 95; John, 94; Thomas, 65
HAWTHORN, Ebenezer, 71
HAY POINT, 97
HAYFIELD, 138
HAYSON, James, 104
HAZARD, 7, 8, 14, 61
HAZEL, ---, 134; Barthia, 127, 128; Benjamin, 134; Isaac, 20, 127, 128, 130
HAZELTON, Miriam, 25; William, 25
HAZLET, ---, 100; Matthew, 100, 101
HEATHARD, Thomas, 25, 75
HEATHER, Thomas, 82
HEATHORD, Thomas, 49
HEIGHE, James, 114
HENDERSON, Andrew, 80; Mager, 48
HENDRICKSON, Grace, 43
HENRY, William, 8
HERMAN, Ephr., 28

HERON, William, 28, 77, 78, 105, 117, 118
HERRING, ---, 37; Curtis, 37, 118; Elizabeth, 37; George, 37, 118; James, 37, 118; Mary, 37, 118
HERRING'S CHOICE, 15
HEWS, Samuel, 122
HIATT, James, 2
HICKEY, Thomas, 54, 78
HICKS, William, 9
HIGHAMS ---, 139
HIGHE, James, 118
HILFORD, David, 3, 4, 15, 88, 91
HILL, ---, 37; Arthur, 15; John, 15; Joseph, 37, 99, 104; Richard, 47; Thomas, 37
HILLIARD, John, 98, 103
HILLIARD'S ADVENTURE, 139, 140
HILLLYARD, John, 41, 94
HILLYARD, Charles, 10, 20, 53, 94; Elizabeth, 53; John, 1, 23, 68; Joseph, 132
HIND, Luke, 77, 78, 105, 118
HINDS, George, 67; Luke, 28
HINES, Elizabeth, 107, 116, 136; Frederick, 136; John, 39; Mary, 136
HINESLEY, Amos, 26
HIRONS, Elizabeth, 124; Mary, 121, 124; Robert, 124; Simon, 11, 121, 124
HODGE, William, 100
HODGES, William, 100
HODGSON, ---, 51; Priscilla, 51; Robert, 6, 41, 51, 62, 86, 89; Roert, 59
HOFF, Rachel, 14; Richard, 14
HOLLIDAY, ---, 114; Joseph, 99; Richard, 30; Robert, 19, 76, 125
HOLSTON, John, 98
HOME TRACT, 17, 18
HOOKFIELD, 68
HOPMAN, Charles, 62
HOUR GLASS, 67

HOUSMAN, John, 15, 90, 101, 107
HOW, Richard, 28, 77, 78, 105, 118; Thomas, 28, 77, 78, 105, 117, 118; William, 105
HOWARD, Allen, 26; Armwell, 11
HOWEL, ---, 8; David, 7, 8, 61; James, 6, 7, 8, 41, 61; Joseph, 7, 8, 61, 81; Joshua, 117; Thomas, 7, 8, 61; William, 63, 64
HOWELL, James, 44, 80; Joshua, 28, 77, 105; Samuel, 101
HOWELL'S LOTT, 7, 45, 46, 135
HOWGIN, William, 93, 104
HUBBARD, John, 26
HUDGSON, Robert, 86
HUDSON, ---, 80, 83; Absalom, 24, 26; Alxander, 89; Arnald, 80; Arnold, 83; Elizabeth, 45, 46, 48, 49; Henry, 59, 60; Margaret, 23; Moses, 134; Penelope, 134; Rachel, 24, 26, 27; Sarah, 59, 60; Thomas, 64; William, 16, 45, 48, 49
HUGG, Patrick, 4, 61, 119
HUGHES, Edward, 50
HUGHS, Thomas, 138
HUNN, Caleb, 131; David, 131; John, 38, 131; Mary, 131; Nathaniel, 16
HUNTER, ---, 4
HUNTING QUARTER, 73, 138
HUSSEY, Lydia, 15
HUSTON, Alexander, 4, 5, 19, 43; Ann, 4, 5, 19, 43
HUTCHINGS, James, 71, 103
HUTCHINGSON, Matthew, 118
HUTCHINS, James, 60
HUTSON, Moses, 134
HYAM, Thomas, 77, 105
HYRAM, Thomas, 117

-I-

IMPROVEMENT, THE, 4, 88
INCREASE, (The) 21, 42, 71

IRONS, John, 14, 97; Owen, 20, 74;
Penelope, 20; Thomas, 5, 56, 74;
Timothy, 44, 130, 131; Titus, 20;
William, 130
ISAAC WEBB'S BRANCH, 123

-J-

JACKSON, Elizabeth, 136; Ezekiel,
136; John, 57; Moses, 36, 135,
136; Richard, 136; S---, 134
JACOB, William, 123
JAKENS, John, 68
JAMES, Daniel, 57
JAMES'S PARK, 3, 109
JAMISON, ---, 111; Alexander, 56,
111; Andrew, 19, 31, 56, 124;
Catharine, 131, 132; Joshua, 31;
Mary, 56; Thomas, 31, 76, 131
JANNEY, Abel, 123
JARRARD, James, 98, 116, 117;
Matthew, 98, 116, 117; William,
98; Willson, 98, 116, 117
JEFFREY, Simon, 78
JENKIN, Timothy, 2
JENKINS, Jabez, 53; Mary Ann,
122; Rebecca, 53; Timothy, 10,
29, 42, 101, 121, 124
JESTER, ---, 34, 71; Delilah, 137;
Francis, 2, 15, 34, 48, 71, 93, 95,
104; Jehu, 34; Rebecah, 86;
Rebeckah, 86; Richard, 86, 95;
William, 86, 95, 137
JESTERS PLAINE, 137
JOHN THOMPSONS PATENT, 61
JOHNS, Richard, 23; Samuel, 117
JOHN'S PURCHASE, 24
JOHNSON, Charles, 115; Daniel,
115; David, 115; John, 16, 64;
Lewis, 1, 36; Purnal, 137; Robert,
31
JOLLEY'S NECK, 34
JONES, ---, 10; Benjamin, 60, 97,
103; Daniel, 87; Enoch, 17, 134,
135; Evan, 33, 63; Hannah, 83,
94; Isaac, 83; Issac, 14; Jacob, 2,
123; James, 94, 103, 108; John,
13, 15, 107; Moses, 10; Nicholas,
103; Pierce, 82, 113; Robert, 39;
Thomas, 94; William, 63, 129
JONES'S LOTT, 100
JORDAN, Thomas, 102; William,
11, 13, 14, 15, 24, 25, 102
JORDDON, Aaron, 93
JOSEPH MOORE'S GUTT, 123
JOSIMS, ---, 125
JOY, John, 1, 56, 74, 111

-K-

KATON, 4
KEARNEY, Philip, 7
KEARNY, Edmund, 93
KEARSEY, Archibald, 26
KEATON, John, 84
KEETH, Thomas, 12
KEITH, Thomas, 23, 62, 63
KELLY, Katharine, 139; Mary, 4;
Rebekah, 17, 18; Thomas, 17, 18
KENNADY, David, 99
KENNEDY, David, 43, 131
KILLAM, Catharine, 19, 43; Isaac,
43
KILLEN, ---, 36, 79, 81; Adam, 108;
Anne, 108; Catharine, 19; Henry,
15, 48, 49, 71, 107, 108, 109;
Isaac, 19; John, 16, 107, 108;
Mark, 15, 107, 108, 109, 137;
Martthew, 107; Robert, 15, 49,
58, 107, 108, 109, 110, 119;
Roger, 81; Susannah, 49, 107,
108; Will, 19, 40, 52; William, 15,
16, 17, 18, 20, 26, 28, 32, 36, 37,
38, 39, 42, 47, 49, 59, 60, 66, 67,
68, 75, 76, 79, 81, 83, 84, 88, 93,
95, 97, 108, 111, 116, 118, 124,
126, 127, 138
KILLING, William, 2
KIMMEY, Charles, 24, 26, 40, 45,
61; Mary, 24, 26, 27, 40; Solomon,
138; William, 138
KIMMY, Charles, 4

KING, ---, 21, 22, 91, 124; Andrew, 42; Ann, 90, 42, 44, 90, 124; Anne, 21, 22, 91, 92, 123; Isaac, 21, 22, 42, 58, 67, 90, 91; James, 21, 42, 71; Martha, 67; Miriam, 71; Peter, 43, 66, 67, 71, 123, 124; Valentine, 91, 92
KINGSALE, 115
KINGSTON UPON HULL, 29, 39, 133
KINNARD, Daniel, 100
KIRKLEY, William, 6, 8, 51, 61
KNOCK, Ezekiel, 119
KNOCKS, Robert, 110
KNOX, Robert, 4, 110, 119

-L-

LACEY, ---, 18; James, 17, 18; Mary, 17; Rebekah, 17
LAMBDEN, George, 125
LAMBDIN, Elizabeth, 12; George, 12, 136
LAMDIN, George, 26, 69
LANGAREL, ---, 86; George, 95; Margaret, 95; William, 95
LARDNER, Lynford, 9
LEADENHAM, John, 2
LEATHERBURY, Perry, 103
LEE, Joseph, 93, 95; Mary, 93, 95
LEVI, Sampson, 89
LEVICK, Clayton, 5, 120; Hannah, 120; John, 5; Richard, 87; William, 139
LEVY, Sampson, 92
LEWEY-COLLY, John, 22
LEWIS, ---, 79; Daniel, 87; David, 49, 79; Elizabeth, 46; Evan, 94; Hannah, 87; James, 12, 19, 23; Joel, 94; John, 74; Joseph, 135; Margaret, 87; Mary, 75; Richard, 75; Ruth, 135; Sampson, 45; Sarah, 87; Stephen, 6, 32; Thomas, 8; William, 46
LISBON, 32, 33, 96, 97
LISBONE, 92

LISBORN, 96
LISBURN, 25
LISTER, Joseph, 71; William, 73
LITTLE NECK, 108
LITTLE PIPE ELM, 28, 69, 73, 77, 133
LITTLE TOWER HILL, 128
LITTLE TYNHEAD CORTE, 133
LLOYD, Abraham, 28; Caleb, 28; Edward, 28
LOCKERMAN, Ned, 110
LOCKWOOD, Armisell, 62; Armwell, 65; Richard, 5, 9, 95, 111, 112, 115; Sarah, 111
LOFTIS, John, 9
LOGAN, Charles, 44; James, 47; William, 9, 111
LONDON, 5, 121
LONG, John, 71; Timothy, 68, 116
LONG ACRE, 36, 77, 81, 105
LONG BRANCH, 83
LONG CHAISE, 100
LONG DAY, 130
LONG GREEN, 10, 95
LONG MEAD, 71
LONG POINT, 97
LONG REACH, 23, 32, 54, 104, 125, 126, 127
LONGFORD, 56, 105
LONGINA, 70
LOOCKERMAN, ---, 2, 46, 63, 80; Nicholas, 29, 67, 79; Vincent, 2, 3, 34, 42, 46, 67, 79, 80, 111, 115, 116, 125, 136
LOWBER, Catharine, 19; Catherine, 6; Isaac, 45, 46, 48, 71, 92, 107, 108, 113, 116; Mary, 116; Peter, 6, 19, 107
LUCAS, ---, 23; Susannah, 67; Thomas, 23, 122
LUCKE, David, 126
LUFF, ---, 123; Caleb, 21, 32, 39, 71, 96, 123; Nathaniel, 14, 39, 123
LUKENS, John, 111
LURTEY, Elizabeth, 1; Mary, 1

LYCAN, Jacob, 93
LYNCH, Edmond, 103; Edmund, 100, 101; Nicholas, 101; William, 100
LYON, Charles, 29, 30

-M-

MC BRIDE, Morris, 74, 100
MC CALL, Archibald, 53; George, 8, 18, 24, 27, 35, 45, 46, 49, 52, 60, 61, 66, 68, 75, 79, 101, 123, 127, 128, 129, 131; Mark, 6, 7, 8, 11, 14, 20, 21, 27, 29, 30, 31, 34, 36, 40, 42, 46, 49, 51, 56, 57, 59, 60, 61, 62, 66, 67, 69, 71, 75, 76, 78, 79, 87, 89, 91, 92, 96, 98, 99, 100, 101, 103, 104, 105, 107, 108, 109, 111, 117, 118, 119, 121, 123, 124, 125, 126, 127, 132; Samuel, 1, 5, 6, 8, 18, 20, 21, 22, 24, 26, 27, 31, 32, 34, 35, 36, 37, 38, 40, 42, 46, 47, 48, 54, 56, 57, 59, 60, 61, 62, 63, 66, 67, 69, 71, 73, 74, 75, 76, 77, 79, 80, 81, 87, 89, 91, 93, 96, 99, 101, 102, 103, 104, 105, 106, 107, 108, 109, 110, 111, 113, 114, 118, 121, 123, 124, 127, 129, 130, 132, 111; Sarah, 20, 27, 38, 47, 60, 61, 67, 68, 71, 80, 114, 119, 123, 127
MC CLEN, ---, 123
MC DONALD, ---, 36, 81; Alexander, 36, 77, 81; James, 36
MC DONNALD, Bryan, 46; Jeremiah, 46; Joseph, 46; Thomas, 46; William, 46
MC DONOUGH, John, 102
MC GERMANT, Robert, 5
MC ILLROY, Edward, 78, 83
MC ILLVOY, Edward, 78
MC KEAN, Thomas, 14, 29, 30; William, 50
MC KEE, John, 13
MC KEMMEY, Edward, 123
MC KINNEY, John, 27

MC KNATT, James, 110; John, 27
MC KNATT'S RANGE, 27
MC LAIN, John, 100, 101
MC LAIN'S ADDITION, 100
MC LANE, Allen, 14, 131
MC LEANE, Allen, 56, 74, 76, 91, 95, 99
MC MIN, Willim, 56
MC MULLAN, James, 11, 137; John, 46; Mary, 46; Robert, 46
MC MULLEN, James, 134, 135
MC MULLIN, James, 125
MC NATT, Anne, 24, 26; Benjamin, 95; Elizabeth, 5, 26; James, 49; John, 5, 27; Richard, 2, 27, 62, 65, 80, 88, 137, 138; William, 5, 24, 26
MC SPARRAN, ---, 17; Archibald, 11, 17
MC SPARRANT, Archibald, 17
MC SPARREN, ---, 33; Archibald, 33
MC WAIT, Richard, 110
MC WILLIAM, Richard, 89
MC WILLIAMS, Richard, 70
MC YARMANT, Robert, 107, 108
MC YARMENT, Robert, 105, 106, 108
MC YARNNENT, Robert, 33
MCALL, Sarah, 47
MCMULLAN, Robert, 46
MAGAW, Samuel, 2, 17, 139; Sarah, 17
MAIDSTONE, 99
MANLOVE, ---, 4, 16, 41, 65, 101, 106; Asa, 106; Boaz, 137; Ebenezer, 139; Elizabeth, 95; George, 63, 65, 76, 96, 134; John, 82; Jonathan, 7, 16; Kesiah, 41; Margaret, 41; Mark, 41, 67, 83, 84, 122; Mary, 76; Matthew, 7, 16, 23, 76, 83, 96, 99, 104, 122, 123, 125; Nathan, 7, 89; Samuel, 34; Treadwell, 80; Violet, 83, 84; William, 4, 41, 45, 94, 95, 101, 134

MANLOVE BERRY, 39
MANLOVE'S BERRY, 56
MANN, Samuel, 23, 89, 109
MANNER OF FRIETH, 28
MANNERING, Richard, 26;
    William, 75
MANNY, ---, 59; Frances, 59
MANOR OF FRIETH, 64, 102, 125
MANSON, Mary, 8, 14; William, 8
MANY, Francis, 59
MARCHANT, William, 56
MARIM, Charles, 22, 31, 32, 69, 70,
    72, 73, 77; John, 31, 69, 70, 72,
    73, 77; Ruhannah, 73
MARIN, Elener, 4
MARREL, Isaac, 95
MARRET, Mark, 104
MARRETT, Mark, 48
MARRINER, William, 111
MARRIT, ---, 26; Anne, 26;
    Elizabeth, 26; Isaac, 26; Joseph,
    27; Mary, 26; Rachel, 26; Sarah,
    26
MARRIT'S ADVENTURE, 26
MARRITT, Isaac, 26
MARSH, Thomas, 100, 101
MARSHAHOPE, 95, 104
MARSHALL, David, 93
MARSHY HOPE, 68, 110
MARTIN, George, 33, 74; John, 14,
    86
MASON, ---, 18; Isaac, 18, 55, 58,
    129; Joseph, 4, 17, 18, 129; Luke,
    104; Mary, 17, 18
MASTEN, William, 57
MASTERS, William, 29, 30
MASTIN, ---, 66; Hezekiah, 10;
    John, 95; Matthias, 10; William,
    10, 66
MAXFIELD, Ann, 29; John, 29;
    Nimrod, 15
MAXWELL, ---, 11; Ann, 133, 134;
    David, 44, 138; James, 102, 138;
    John, 133, 134; Nimrod, 11, 88;
    98, 113; Peter, 1; Robert, 44, 102,
    138; Sarah, 98, 113; Susanna, 44
MAXWELL'S ADVENTURE, 44,
    138
MAY, Petr, 34
MEAD'S ADDITION, 71
MEKINN, Pene O., 125
MELLECHOP, George, 52
MELVIN, Edward, 123
MERCHANT, William, 45
MEREDITH, Elizabeth, 64; Joseph,
    56; Joshua, 20, 26; Josiah, 64;
    Philis, 49; Robert, 7; Samuel, 7;
    Wheeler, 87; William, 23
MEREFIELD, Edward, 31
MEREITH, Elizabeth, 125; Joseph,
    125
MERITT, Isaac, 26
MERONY, Elizabeth, 38
MERRIT, Isaac, 24; William, 60
MERRIT'S ADVENTURE, 24
MERYDITH, William, 90, 103
MIDDLETOWN, 21, 22, 71, 103
MIFFLIN, ---, 57; Joseph, 32;
    Warner, 9, 34, 47, 57, 68
MILCHAM, Walter, 3
MILEHAM, Ann, 68; Walter, 66, 68
MILES, David, 17
MILL LAND, 107
MILL NECK, 19, 43
MILLER, Adam, 99; Chilion, 99;
    Conrad, 99; John, 99; Robert, 108
MILNER, Rachel, 127; Thomas, 127
MINER, Peter, 68
MINER'S FOLLY, 68
MINORS, Robert, 96
MITCHAM, Anne, 68
MOLLESTON, Henry, 45, 48, 88;
    Jonathan, 14, 45, 108; William,
    14, 48
MONTGOMERY, Dorcas, 133, 134;
    Robert, 84; Thomas, 84
MOON, James, 66
MOOR, ---, 6; John, 37; Joseph, 6;
    Thomas, 6, 35

MOORE, ---, 26; David, 120;
  Edward, 25, 26; Henry, 56; Jacob,
  112; James, 79, 94, 97, 100, 101,
  104, 107, 108, 109, 131; John, 98,
  99, 103; Joseph, 110, 124, 125;
  Letitia, 100, 101; Thomas, 35
MOORE'S PURCHASE, 100, 101
MORGAN, George, 5; Jacob, 44, 66,
  67; Jonathan, 22, 52;
  Marmaduke, 95; Martha, 66, 67;
  Marthew, 66; Thomas, 129;
  William, 98, 113
MORRIS, Absalom, 98; Absolom,
  117; Elijah, 10, 95; Eliphaz, 80;
  James, 99, 128; John, 42, 109,
  113; Joseph, 95; Martha, 97;
  Mary, 10; Samuel, 2, 24, 28, 76,
  114; Sarah, 109, 113; Thomas,
  56, 74; William, 12, 62, 64, 65,
  81, 97, 106
MORTON, James, 68; William, 45
MOTT, ---, 2; Elizabeth, 2, 10;
  Richard, 2, 31; Richbell, 2, 10
MOUNT PLEASANT, 96, 115
MULLET, Penelope, 134; William,
  134
MULLIN, ---, 71; James, 70;
  Margaret, 70; William, 70, 71
MUNCH, Levy, 101
MUNCY, ---, 73; Francis, 102; Levi,
  73; Thomas, 29, 51
MURDUCH, John, 63
MURPHEY, Comfort, 52; John, 52;
  Thomas, 97
MURPHY, Hannah, 94; Samuel, 94;
  Susannah, 94; Thomas, 94, 108;
  William, 94

-N-

N---, Joseph, 120
NANCY, Elizabeth, 132
NEAL, Jonathan, 104
NEALL, ---, 75; Jonathan, 49, 75
NEEDHAM, Anna, 25; Benjamin,
  139; Daniel, 53; E., 99; Edmund,
  25; Ezekiel, 25, 75, 104, 120, 127;
  Jonathan, 120, 139
NEGRO, Doller, 7; Frank, 7; George
  7; Grace, 7; Jude, 7; Moll, 7; Nan,
  7; Poll, 7; Pompey, 7
NEILL, Hugh, 93
NEW, Robert, 117
NEWCOMB, Baptist, 21, 42
NEWELL, ---, 64; John, 47, 118;
  Rachel, 64; Thomas, 64
NEWMAN, ---, 22; John, 22
NEWNAM, ---, 108; Daniel, 120;
  Daniel Wright, 41
NEWPORT, Jesse, 79
NICHOLAS, ---, 39, 55, 56; Samuel,
  39, 45, 55, 136
NICKERSON, George, 70, 72;
  Hannah, 70; John, 22, 28, 31, 68,
  69, 70, 71, 72, 73, 77, 133;
  Joshua, 69, 72, 73; Mary, 69, 70,
  72, 73, 77; Sarah, 70
NICOLLS, ---, 79; Joseph, 79
NICOLS, Zachariah, 2
NIELSOS, Elizabeth, 12
NIXON, Nicholas, 46; Thomas, 1,
  16, 36, 68, 74, 76, 107, 108, 118,
  121, 123, 126
NOBLE, Richard, 28, 57
NOCK, Ezekial, 113; Ezekiel, 109,
  110, 112, 113; J., 113; Sarah, 109;
  Thomas, 109, 110, 112, 113
NORRIS, Isaac, 47
NORTH, Thomas, 34
NORTHAMPTON, 110
NOWELL, George, 39
NOXON, Thomas, 80
NUMBERS, John, 100, 101, 132
NUNEZ, Daniel, 137
NUTTER, James, 52

-O-

O' NEALL, Bryan, 75
OFFLEY, Michael, 24, 28, 49, 50;
  Rachel, 114
OGLE, Thomas, 12

OLDFIELD, John, 6, 87
OLDFIELD'S RANGE, 35, 87
OLIVER, Joseph, 82, 87, 88; Levi, 88
OUSBY, 25, 49
OWEN, William, 54
OWEN'S FOLLY, 106
OWSBEY, 75

-P-

PAINTER, George, 3, 7, 23, 30, 39, 43, 50, 56, 90, 102
PAIRMAN'S CHOICE, 111
PAIRMAN'S PLAINS, 111
PALMATREE, Allan, 1; John, 1; Lettice, 1; Robert, 1
PALMETRY, Allen, 94; Eleoner, 94; Elizabeth, 94; Roberrt, 94; Robert, 94, 95; Robrt, 94
PARADEE, Hannah, 123; Margaret, 87; Stephen, 70, 72, 87
PARKE, Ann, 53; John, 118; Thomas, 23, 53, 83, 97, 124
PARKER, John, 137
PARKISON, Thomas, 42
PARRY, Rowland, 24, 28; Thomas, 63, 115, 116, 139, 140
PARSON, Joseph, 63, 65
PARSONS, ---, 82; Joseph, 81, 82, 122; Margaret, 122
PARTNERSHIP, THE, 8, 17, 61, 132
PATHALIA PLAINS, 36, 106
PATHELIA PLAINS, 81
PATON, Elizabeth, 95
PATTEN, John, 10, 20
PATTERSON, John, 61
PATTISON, John, 17, 64, 124, 125; William, 64
PEA HILL, 138
PEAK, Alec, 106; Alice, 36
PEARMAIN'S CHOICE, 56
PEARSE, William, 45, 46, 76, 135

PEGG, ---, 4, 61, 62; Rachel, 4, 61, 119; William, 4, 40, 45, 56, 61, 119
PELOPONNE, 107
PELOPONNESEES, 109
PEMBERTON, John, 66; Sarah, 31, 70, 72, 87
PEMBERTON'S SAVANNAH, 66
PENN, John, 9, 52, 58, 70, 89, 90, 91, 112; Richard, 9, 111; Thomas, 9
PENNELL, ---, 75; John, 52, 74
PENNROSE, Thomas, 126
PERMAINE PRICE, 124
PERRY, Thomas, 115; William, 133
PETERKIN, David, 58; John, 51, 57, 58; Sarah, 51, 57, 58; Thomas, 21, 22, 39, 44, 94
PETERS, Richard, 9, 111
PETERSON, Andrew, 124
PHILIPS, Mary, 39
PICKRELL, Ann, 57; William, 57
PIDGION, Joseph, 41
PINER, Edward, 94
PIPE ELM, 87
PIPER, ---, 67; Susannah, 13
PLAINS OF JERICHO, 36
PLAINS, THE, 57
PLEASANT, 5
PLEASANTON, ---, 63, 64; Jonathan, 63, 64
PLEASONTINE, Amey, 47; John, 48; Jonathan, 47, 48; Mary, 48
PLEASONTON, Amey, 48; Daniel, 70; David, 22, 72, 73; Deborah, 123; Jonathan, 64; Ruhamay, 48
PLUMBSTEAD, Mary, 53; William, 53
POINT LOOKOUT, 83
POLLAR, William, 136
POLLARD, William, 116, 137
POOLE, John, 50
POPE, ---, 114; Charles, 137
PORTER, Robert, 28; William, 34
PORTER'S LODGE, 28, 120, 121

POTTER, Enoch, 14
POWEL, James, 12; Joseph, 40;
    Lucy, 12; Martha, 54; Nicholas,
    12; William, 54
POWELL, James, 18; John, 89, 90;
    Joseph, 29, 130; Lucy, 18;
    Martha, 130; Nicholas, 34, 122;
    William, 81, 89, 90, 130
PRATT, ---, 23; George, 113
PRIMROSE, William, 88
PRIOR, Joseph, 65
PROCTOR, Thomas, 99, 100
PROPRIETORSHIP, 118
PRYOR, John, 17, 42, 43, 47, 62, 68;
    Joseph, 8, 68, 71, 80, 88
PUGH, ---, 50; Mary, 114; Roger, 28,
    50, 79; Sarah, 15; William, 28,
    50, 79
PUGH'S LOTT, 79
PURDEN, James, 89

-Q-
QUINCY, Edmond, 133; Edmund,
    133, 134
QUINNALLY, Mary, 52; Richard,
    52

-R-
RASH, ---, 1; Henry, 45, 46, 135;
    James, 1, 36; John, 1, 45, 46, 56,
    135; Joseph, 1, 29; Mary, 45, 46;
    Samuel, 45, 46, 135
RASIN, ---, 54; Anne, 54; Benjamin,
    39, 45, 54, 55; Phillip, 123;
    Rachel, 54, 55
RATLEDGE, Anne, 5, 6; Moses, 5
RATLIDGE, Anne, 24, 26, 27;
    Moses, 24, 26
RATTLEDGE, John, 77
RAWLEY, James, 71, 86
RAWLINGS, Anthony, 3, 4, 45;
    John, 105
RAWLING'S LOTT, 3
RAWLINS, John, 118
RAWLINS LOTT, 118

RAYMOND, ---, 132; Angelica, 128;
    Elizabeth, 132; James, 33, 45, 90,
    111, 128, 132; John, 132; Presley,
    128
READ, George, 16, 44; John, 65
REDDICK, Catharine, 19; John, 19;
    Robert, 19
REDMAN, John, 25
REED, ---, 23; Ann, 23; James, 23,
    89; John, 1, 2, 9, 12, 26, 31, 118
REES, David, 19; Edward, 124;
    Hester, 19; John, 12, 19;
    Jonathan, 44, 103, 111, 130, 131;
    Martha, 137; Priscilla, 111;
    Prisila, 103; Robert, 20, 90, 127,
    128, 130; William, 14, 20, 49,
    102, 114, 125, 127, 128, 129, 130,
    131, 137
REESE, William, 15
REGISTER, John, 46
REGISTER'S RANGE, 46
RESERVE, THE, 6, 47, 52
REVEL, ---, 51; Amelia, 51, 57, 58;
    John, 50, 51, 57, 58
REVELL, John, 63
REYNALDS, Richard, 13; Thomas,
    78
REYNOLD, Henry, 17, 18; John,
    110
REYNOLDS, ---, 82; Alexander, 11;
    Ephraim, 81, 82; Henry, 82;
    Robert, 52; Thomas, 77, 105, 117
RHOADS, William, 13
RHODE, William, 67
RHODES, ---, 62, 85; John, 98, 102,
    117, 122, 136; William, 9, 18, 20,
    25, 33, 37, 56, 62, 65, 66, 85, 89,
    91, 95, 108, 112
RHODE'S FOREST, 46
RICCARDS, Philip, 27
RICHARDSON, Mary, 5
RICHMAN'S WORTH, 57
RICHMORE, 21, 22, 42

RIDGELY, ---, 2; Charles, 1, 2, 6, 9, 23, 31, 36, 37, 47, 52, 60, 73, 74, 81, 88, 112, 119, 122, 125, 139
RIGHT, Mary, 115
RINGGOLD, ---, 41; Thomas, 120
ROADS, John, 123
ROAD'S FORES, 122
ROBART'S CHANCE, 74
ROBEMAN, John, 104
ROBERT, William, 129
ROBERTS, Hugh, 105, 106
ROBERT'S CHANCE, 1, 94
ROBINSON, ---, 41, 108; Charles, 128; Daniel, 41, 48, 57, 75, 108, 134; George, 31, 72, 87; Hannah, 31, 70, 72, 87; James, 96; John, 45, 48, 126, 128; Jonathan, 48; Jordan, 19; Jordon, 128; Laurance, 70; Lawrence, 72, 73; Patience, 41; Samuel, 134; Sarah, 72, 87
ROBINSON'S ARM, 3
RODNEY, ---, 32, 70; Caesar, 6, 14, 16, 22, 32, 44, 46, 47, 52, 61, 70, 74, 76, 81, 93, 107, 108, 112, 118, 140; Daniel, 46; Lydia, 70, 71, 72; Margaret, 39; Thomas, 16, 32, 43, 93, 99, 112, 129; William, 2, 6, 7, 8, 65, 69, 70, 71, 72, 73, 77, 87, 97
ROGERS, Catherine, 47; Joseph, 6, 47, 52
ROLPH, William, 100
ROSS, Samuel, 37, 118; Thomas, 13, 14, 30
ROW, David, 129; Susannah, 129
ROWE, Elizabeth, 106; James, 107
ROWLAND, David, 91; Robert, 109, 113
RUSH, Jacob, 44, 63; Mary, 116
RUSSEL, John, 13, 14, 103
RUSSELL, ---, 111; Elizabeth, 59, 60; John, 111; Joseph, 66; Thomas, 67; William, 59, 60
RUSSUM, Elizabeth, 63, 65; Peter, 63, 65; Thomas, 63

RUTHERFORD, Alexander, 78

-S-
ST. COLLAM, 84
ST. COLLUM, 24, 84
SAINT COLLUMN, 109
SAINT COLUMN, 108
SAP, John, 69, 135
SAVIN, William, 110, 123
SAWMILL RANGE, 35, 82, 83, 88, 137
SAWYER, Richard, 37
SAXTON, ---, 98, 113; Andrew, 97, 98, 113; George, 23, 57, 89, 106, 107, 109, 129
SCANDLIN, William, 23
SCANDRETT, John, 28
SCANTLIN, William, 11
SCHOOL HOUSE TRACT, 87
SCHOOLHOUSE LOTT, 5
SCIPTOP, 23
SCOTEN, James, 44
SCOTTEN, James, 3, 100; John, 3
SCOTTON, James, 109
SEAMAN, ---, 3
SEAMANS, ---, 2; Elizabeth, 2, 10; Rachel, 10; Solomon, 2, 9, 10
SEATON, 67
SEENA, Bryan, 130
SEENEY, Brian, 61; Bryan, 8
SENEY, ---, 101; Owen, 101
SEVERSON, Elizabeth, 94, 95; James, 74, 94; John, 75
SHANKMIRE, Peter, 107, 116, 136
SHANNAN, ---, 103; Daniel, 103
SHANNON, ---, 111; Ann, 29, 133, 134; Catherine, 133, 134; Daniel, 111; John, 29, 133, 134; Katharine, 29; Mary, 29, 133, 134
SHARP, Thomas, 132
SHAW, Ephraim, 71; Thomas, 43
SHAWN, Elizabeth, 14; Joseph, 14
SHERIFF, Thomas, 48, 59, 60, 129
SHIPPEN, Edward, 9, 112
SHIRLEY, Richard, 25

SHOEMAKER, David, 76; S., 83;
  Samuel, 28, 77, 105, 117
SHOEMAKERS HALL, 52
SHOULDER OF MUTTON, 87
SHREWSBERRY, 131
SHREWSBURY, 38
SHURMER, Benjamin, 70, 123;
  Margaret, 70
SHURMER'S SURVEY IN THE
  MANNER, 49
SICAMORE PLAINS, 101
SIMONS, Mary, 19, 43; Stephen, 19,
  43
SIMPSON, ---, 16; John, 16
SIMPSON'S CHOICE, 38, 131
SIPPLE, Alice, 122; Anne, 56;
  Caleb, 88, 96; Christopher, 45,
  56, 118, 122; Elijah, 5, 25, 45, 59,
  89; Elizabeth, 122; Garrat, 129,
  131; Garret, 3, 20, 38; John, 25,
  68, 84, 122; Jonathan, 5, 25, 45,
  56, 59, 60, 78, 79, 89; Mary, 96,
  122; Ruth, 25; Sarah, 96;
  Waitman, 21, 22, 25, 29, 41, 49,
  68, 75, 100; William, 11
SIPPLE'S LOTT, 129
SKIDMORE, Deborah, 43; Edward,
  43; Elizabeth, 38; Mary, 38;
  Samuel, 38, 88; Thomas, 38, 43,
  57, 88
SKILLINGTON, ---, 99; Thomas, 14,
  15, 23, 27, 51, 68, 74, 76, 99, 102
SKIPTON, 2, 17, 139
SKYPTON, 23
SLIPE, THE, 37
SMALL TINHEADS CORTE, 133
SMALL TYNHEADS CORTE, 138,
  33
SMALLEY, John, 5
SMALLY, John, 6
SMITH, ---, 63; Abram, 16; Daniel,
  20, 36, 81, 92, 130; Hannah, 83;
  James, 103; John, 20, 48, 83, 89,
  97, 103, 112, 127; Joseph, 114;
  Mark, 85; Mary, 92; Richard, 9,
  19, 20, 37, 44, 85, 107, 108, 111,
  112, 128; Robert, 16, 52, 83;
  Samuel, 20, 130; Sarah, 97;
  Tamsey, 20, 21, 130; Thomas, 83,
  84, 92, 97, 106; William, 63, 103
SMITHER, Nathaniel, 120
SMITHERS, John, 11, 46, 65, 106,
  107, 109, 120; Nath., 30;
  Nathaniel, 65
SMOTHERS, ---, 79; Patience, 79
SMTH, Robert, 83
SMYRNA, 123
SMYTH, James, 3; Richard, 3
SNOW, ---, 37; Anthony, 94; Rachel,
  94, 95; Silas, 37, 71, 92, 109, 111,
  125, 132
SOWARD, George, 68; Thomas, 79
SPALDEN, John, 15
SPARKS, Caleb, 94
SPENCE, Betty, 2; James, 2
SPENCER, Joshua, 102, 103
SPICY GROVE, 100
SPRINGFIELD, 65, 107
SPRUANCE, John, 102
STAFFORD, Richard, 28
STANDBURY, Nathan, 110
STANDLEY, Joseph, 48, 104; Mary,
  104
STANTON, John, 107; Stephen, 15
STARLIGHT, 80
STARLING, James, 63
START, Benjamin, 60
STATEN, John, 133; Widow, 48
STEEL, James, 20, 56, 128;
  Rebecca, 140; Widow, 140
STEELMAN, Matthias, 68
STERELE, William, 82
STERLING, James, 82, 94
STEUART, John, 116
STEUERT, Daniel, 110
STEVEN, William, 116
STEVENS, ---, 8; Daniel, 48;
  Elizabeth, 1; George, 22, 66;
  Henry, 52, 53, 57, 78, 105; James,

7, 8, 14, 54, 61, 72; Letitia, 48;
   Mary, 1; William, 1
STEVENSON, George, 25, 59, 78,
   107, 138
STEWARD, Thomas, 93
STEWART, Thomas, 128
STILL, James, 132
STOCKFIELD, 94
STOREY, Penelope, 134; Peter, 134
STOUR, Emmanuel, 33
STOURT, Iml., 115
STOUT, ---, 53; Emmanuel, 33, 122;
   Immanuel, 115, 116; Jacob, 9, 14,
   45, 85, 86, 110, 112; Peter, 34, 53,
   108; Rebecca, 53
STRADLEY, Abraham, 37; Absolom,
   118
STREEP, Auther, 127; Jane, 127;
   Rachel, 127; Robert, 127; Uriah,
   127; William, 127
STREET, William, 127
STRETTELL, ---, 120; Amos, 119,
   120, 121; John, 120
STUART, Aaron, 49; Moses, 23
STURGIS, Stokely, 53
STUTTELL, John, 120
SUITER, Hugh, 128
SUMMER, Thomas, 116
SUMMERS, ---, 39; John, 39; Mary,
   39; Thomas, 39; William, 80
SUTTON, John, 121
SWETMAN, Richard, 28
SYKES, Agnes, 139; James, 9, 17,
   28, 29, 31, 60, 61, 85, 112, 133,
   134, 139; Mary, 28, 29, 133, 134

-T-

TANNER, Christian, 67; David, 67;
   Katharine, 67
TANTAN COURROW, 7, 8
TANTANBOURROW, 61
TANTEN BURROW, 6
TANTROY, Abraham, 111
TANYARD LOTT, THE, 19

TAPHAM, ---, 80; Christopher, 80,
   81
TAPPAHANNAH, THE, 26, 68, 100
TARRING, ---, 110; William, 110,
   111
TAYLOR, Adam, 104; James, 108
TAYLOR'S HALL, 4
TESESTOR, Francis, 138
THARP, ---, 129; Sarah, 71; William,
   3, 94, 123, 129
THISELWOOD, James, 15
THISSELWOOD, James, 110
THOMAS, Daniel, 52; James, 52;
   Jonah, 124; Thomas, 29; William,
   5, 41
THOMPSON, ---, 7; David, 49;
   Ezekiel, 1, 2, 135; John, 7, 8, 15;
   William, 109, 122
THOMSON, Peter, 28, 29, 30
THOROFARE, 50
THORP, Samuel, 122
THOUSAND ACRE TRACT, THE,
   12, 18
TILDEN, Thomas, 81
TILGHMAN, Ann, 40; Edward, 10,
   20, 40; Elizabeth, 10, 20, 40;
   James, 9, 112; Matthew, 100;
   Richard, 16, 40; William, 40, 52
TILTON, James, 70, 75, 93, 119;
   John, 14; Joseph, 14; Nehemiah,
   128; Thomas, 9, 12, 13, 33, 83,
   99, 112, 139, 140
TIMBER FORK, 100
TINHEAD COURT, 69
TOMLIN, Nathaniel, 66
TOMLINSON, ---, 92; Richard, 90,
   91, 92
TORBERT, Peter, 87, 103
TORBET, Peter, 68
TOWN POINT, 39
TOWNSEND, James, 31, 102, 137;
   Littleton, 55; Solomon, 3
TOY, Rachel, 62
TRAIL, James, 53

TRAIN, Bathsheba, 46, 47; Esther, 46, 47; Hamilton, 46, 47; James, 46, 47; Mary, 46, 47; Roger, 46, 47; Sarah, 46, 47
TRAVILLERS DELIGHT, 128
TRINACRIA, 59, 89
TRIPPET, Govey, 21, 22, 42, 75, 90; Rachal, 75; Rachel, 75; William, 11, 23
TRIPPIT, Gove, 89; Govey, 49; Rachel, 49
TROY, 97
TRUAX, Benjamin, 1
TUCKER, ---, 12; Caleb, 95; John, 12, 18, 54; Margaret, 12, 54
TUMBLIN, ---, 94; Cecelia, 66, 67; Covil, 94; Isaac, 94; Jacob, 94; John, 66; Joseph, 15; Nathaniel, 94
TUMLIN, Covil, 44; John, 13
TURNER, ---, 120; George, 110; John, 16; Joseph, 9, 111, 119, 120, 121; Robert, 126
TYNHEAD CORTE, 133

-U-
UNDERWOOD, Joshua, 138; Mary, 138; Richard, 27
UNDERWOOD'S FOREST, 119, 138

-V-
VAN DYKE, James, 29, 133, 134
VANBURCOLO, Peter, 120; Sarah, 120
VANDERFORD, Hollingsworth, 106; Thomas, 68
VANDIKE, Nicholas, 132
VANDYKE, James, 40, 74, 114, 125; Nicholas, 13, 14, 43
VANHOY, Abraham, 104, 121
VANNOY, Abraham, 10
VANOY, Abraham, 2
VANWINKLE, Mary, 25; Simon, 137
VERNUM, Daniel, 131

VINING, ---, 6, 31; Benjamin, 123; John, 6, 10, 31, 47, 52, 60, 74, 76, 85, 99, 119, 125, 137; Nicholas, 37; Phebe, 15, 16, 31, 60
VIRDIN, Absalom, 80; John, 55, 56; Sarah, 80; William, 89, 90
VOSHAL, Elizabeth, 136; John, 136
VOSHALL, ---, 56; Elizabeth, 75; James, 56; Mary Anne, 56; Maryanne, 56; Obediah, 75
VOSHELL, Elizabeth, 49; James, 74; John, 111; Obediah, 49
VOXHALL, Elizabeth, 75; Obediah, 75

-W-
WADFORD, 57
WALKER, J., 119; John, 28, 99; William, 57
WALLACE, Elizabeth, 13; James, 13, 14; Katharine, 126; Matthew, 101; Robert, 126; Rubin, 80, 113; Solomon, 85, 92; Thomas, 6; William, 2, 8, 23, 125, 126
WALTERS, Ruben, 98; Samuel, 100
WAPPIN, 128
WARE, David, 32; John, 32, 96; Mary, 32; Rodney, 32; William, 32
WARNER, Joseph, 44
WARREN, Benjamin, 19, 25, 43; Elizabeth, 19, 43; John, 43; Mary, 43; Samuel, 43; Zipporah, 43
WARRINGTON, ---, 79
WATER, James, 129
WATSON, ---, 5, 25; Francis, 25, 26; William, 4, 25
WATTSON, Purnal, 88
WEAR, John, 25
WEB, Isaac, 6
WEBB, ---, 101; Caleb, 6, 101; Isaac, 8, 47, 54, 104, 127
WEDMAN, 8
WEDMORE, 6, 8, 51, 61, 101
WELL, Mary, 69

WELLS, ---, 88; Benjamin, 34;
    Henry, 15, 29, 69, 88, 101, 138;
    James, 7, 50, 52, 54, 78, 84, 88,
    111, 131, 132; Mary, 69; Sarah,
    29; William, 24
WEST, ---, 134; Samuel, 134
WETHERED, John, 132, 133, 134;
    Mary, 132, 133, 134
WHARTON, Isaiah, 54, 70, 71;
    Joseph, 44; Walker, 63; Walter,
    64
WHEATFIELD, 17, 18
WHEATLEY, Alexander, 138
WHEELAR, Joshua, 91
WHEELER, Joshua, 82
WHEELOR, ---, 79; John, 41;
    Kesiah, 41; Winlock, 79
WHEELTON, John, 38; Mary, 38
WHITACRE, ---, 66; Hannah, 25;
    Henry, 35; Isaac, 66
WHITAKER, ---, 25; Henry, 35;
    Moses, 35
WHITE, ---, 6; Isabell, 86, 87;
    James, 4, 33, 73, 82, 102; John, 6,
    43, 76, 86, 87, 124; Richard, 37,
    118; Robert, 73; Thomas, 112,
    118; Tryphena, 35; William, 6,
    35, 87
WHITE HALL, 40
WHITE OAK SURVEY, 10, 20
WHITE OAK SWAMP, 120
WHITEHEAD, George, 28; John, 28
WHITELEY, Arther, 41
WHITELY, Abraham Bing, 116;
    Alexander, 116
WHITEWELL'S CHANCE, 14
WHITEWELL'S DELIGHT, 19
WHITLEY, Alexander, 68
WHITTINGTON, ---, 41; Thomas, 41
WHITWELL'S CHANCE, 132
WHITWELLS DELIGHT, 43
WHORTLEBERRY RIDGE, 44
WIKOFF, Peter, 106
WILD, Richard, 13; Robert, 14;
    Thomas, 43

WILDS, Robert, 13
WILLCOCKS, John, 3; Robert, 3
WILLIAM, James, 37
WILLIAMS, Ann, 55; Anne, 55;
    Aron, 58; Charles, 41; Ezekiel,
    81, 82; James, 35, 37, 69, 88;
    John, 35, 36, 39, 69, 124; Mary,
    36, 69, 81, 88; Penelope, 51, 57;
    Rachel, 39; Reynear, 51, 55, 57,
    58, 102; Richard, 42; Thomas, 36,
    81
WILLIAM'S CHOICE, 63, 75
WILLINGBROOK, 5, 53
WILLIS, John, 128; Joshua, 137
WILLOBY, Elizabeth, 118; Job, 118
WILLOUGHBY, ---, 118; Elizabeth,
    37; Job, 37, 69, 135; Samuel, 37
WILLOWBY, Elizabeth, 118
WILLSON, David, 37; John, 3, 45,
    65, 66, 110; Jonathan, 51; Robert,
    23; Samuel, 23; Simon, 49; Simon
    W., 22, 34, 103, 122; Thomas, 66;
    William, 22
WILLSON'S CHOICE, 53
WILSON, Abel, 87; Hosea, 121, 124;
    Mathew, 87; Nancy, 19; Simon
    W., 68
WINSMORE, ---, 32; Robert, 48;
    William, 22, 32, 65, 72, 87
WITHERED, John, 133; Mary, 133
WOLSTON, John, 113
WOOD, Elias, 118, 119; John, 19,
    42, 99, 119; Joseph, 8
WOODERSON, Ann, 44, 138
WOOTER, Jacob, 34
WOOTERS, Anne, 26; Jacob, 26
WORKNOTTS, Alexander, 102
WORKWELL, Allexander, 76
WORTON, Isaiah, 123
WRIGHT, Daniel, 108; N. S., 26
WYATT, Sarah, 3; Thomas, 3
WYNCOOP, Abraham, 5; Benjamin,
    6

WYNKOOP, Abraham, 15, 16, 18;
  Benjamin, 15, 16, 18, 27, 31, 47,
  52, 60, 74, 125; Mary, 15, 16
WYNN, Benjamin, 121, 124;
  Elizabeth, 121, 124
WYSE, Christopher, 34

-Y-
YORK, 2, 10
YOUNG, Robert, 85

-Z-
ZACHARY, Daniel, 28, 78, 105, 117,
  118; David, 77
ZACKARY, Daniel, 28, 77, 105

www.ingramcontent.com/pod-product-compliance
Lightning Source LLC
Chambersburg PA
CBHW051103160426
43193CB00010B/1292